Higher Education in an Era of Digital Competition: Choices and Challenges

by Donald E. Hanna and Associates

Atwood Publishing
Madison, WI

Higher Education in an Era of Digital Competition:
Choices and Challenges
by Donald E. Hanna and Associates

© 2000
Atwood Publishing
2710 Atwood Ave.
Madison, WI 53704

Printed in the United States of America.
9 8 7 6 5 4 3

Cover art by Mark Roeder.
Cover design by Tamara L. Dever, TLC Graphics.

Library of Congress Cataloging-in-Publication Data
Hanna, Donald E., 1947-
    Higher education in an era of digital competition: choices and chal-
lenges/by Donald E. Hanna and associates.
    P. Cm.
Includes bibliographical references and index.
ISBN 1-891859-32-3
1. Education, Higher—Effect of technological innovation on—United States.
2. Universities and colleges—United States—Data processing. 3. Educational
change—United States. I. Title.
LB2395.7 .H25 1999
378'.00285—dc21   99-047611

Acknowledgments

It is always other people who make any accomplishment worth noting possible. I start with my family and most especially, my wife, Karna, whose continuous encouragement and flexibility made this book doable, and I end with my collaborators and chapter contributors, who were a delight to work with and a source of continuous input and knowledge. In between are the many colleagues who have contributed so much to my thinking and perspectives about higher education and the challenges ahead, including most especially Professor Alan Knox of the University of Wisconsin-Madison, who was constantly available to me for review and feedback, and Linda Babler and her associates at Atwood Publishing for their support and diligence from beginning to end. I also wish to thank those who read the book and offered specific suggestions and comments in advance of publication, including: Sally Johnstone, Janis Hall, Parker Palmer, Bob Threlkeld, Steve Crow, and the many graduate students at the University of Wisconsin-Madison who have influenced my thinking and the selection of topics for the book.

Donald E. Hanna
1999

Table of Contents

Preface

By Donald E. Hanna

This book is being published at the dawn of a new millennium. The symbolic passage from one era to another invites speculation about the future and reflection about the past and its meaning for the future. *Higher Education in an Era of Digital Competition: Choices and Challenges* focuses upon critical knowledge and perspectives that will guide us in building a new system of higher education.

The authors begin with a fundamental belief that higher education can use new technologies as a positive shaping force in creating a responsiveness to all people and their increasing need for education and learning throughout a lifetime. Yet this is not, per se, a book about technology. Rather, the book provides a framework for viewing technology, especially the new digital technologies, as an agent of positive change within universities. The authors' goal is to assist the reader in developing a more complete understanding of how teaching and learning, knowledge generation and preservation, organizational design and evaluation, and leadership can all function together within a changing and increasingly competitive external environment to produce a new responsiveness and diversity within higher education. While the context of *Choices and Challenges* focuses upon four-year colleges and universities more than on community colleges, much of the book's content is applicable to all of higher education.

The book is organized around five basic ideas or themes that shape the selection and content of its chapters. These themes are:

1. the emergence of a global learning society;
2. changing the patterns of learning to respond to changing individual, organizational, and societal needs;
3. the dynamic new possibilities and challenges of learning via advanced technologies;
4. transformational change in higher education on a global scale and views of the leadership our institutions require;
5. the importance of ethics and equity of access as elements that must drive decision making and leadership at an organizational level.

Each of the book's chapters is connected to one of these themes, although the chapters are ordered in such a way as to mix the development of each theme throughout the book.

The Emergence of a Global Learning Society

McLuhan's concept of the *global village* is about to come to life for every person on the planet.

This global communications capability has already had an enormous impact upon the international economy, empowering small farmers and small business owners in the smallest and most remote villages in the world by connecting them to global markets. This connection, which is in its infancy, and the resulting globalization of the economy will have a dramatic effect upon the demand for continuous learning worldwide in the years to come. The result will be a global learning society. Naisbitt (1994) points out, "The bigger the world economy, the more powerful its smallest players become." With electronic communication available via global digital satellite and fiber optics, we will see a day in the not too distant future when it will be possible to communicate interactively at a very personal and at an organizational level completely independent of location, geography, political boundaries, and time and technical barriers. More important, this interaction and the resulting exchange of ideas, goods, and services will be fundamental to personal and societal well-being.

How quickly is change occurring? Nicholas Negroponte, founding director of the Media Laboratory at MIT, states:

> When it comes to technological and regulatory changes, as well as new services, things are moving faster than even I can believe — there is obviously no speed limit on the electronic highway. It's like driving on the autobahn at 160 kph. Just as I realize the speed I'm going, zzzwoom, a Mercedes passes, then another, and another. Such is life in the fast lane of the infobahn (Negroponte 1995, 75).

However, the development of this powerful capability of technology to transcend distance, time, and geography, best described by Chris Dede in chapter 3, "Advanced Technologies and Distributed Learning in Higher Education," does not mean that societies and especially universities can or will organize themselves to take advantage of these new opportunities. There is much to be learned about what works and what doesn't when we use technologies as an assistive learning device. We also have much to explore about education and learning that takes place across cultures.

Changing the Patterns of Learning

A second theme of this book is that *our approaches to creating positive environments for learning must change* to engage learners more directly with the world at hand. Teaching and learning strategies must meet learners where they are and build from the knowledge and understanding they bring to the learning situation. This challenge exists in both face-to-face classrooms and technology-assisted classrooms. For many colleges and universities, changing the learning environment to achieve this goal will be the major challenge of the next decade and beyond. Campuses will expand beyond being learning environments that operate on the empty vessel theory of knowledge acquisition, in which the goal is to fill the student's mind with as much content as he or she can assimilate within a given time frame. As John Dewey (1964, 5) put it eloquently sixty-five years ago:

...[T]he *initiative* in growth comes from the needs and powers of the pupil [sic]. The first step in the interaction that results in growth comes from the reaching out of the tentacles of the individual, from an effort, at first blind, to procure the materials that his [sic] potentialities demand in order that they may come into action and find satisfaction.

In the same work, Dewey stresses that skills are a means to an end, not the end themselves:

... As the material of genuine development is that of human contacts and associations, so the end, the value that is the criterion and directing guide of educational work, is social. The acquisition of skills is not an end in itself. They are things to be put to use, and that use is their contribution to a common and shared life (ibid. 10).

In chapter 2, "Emerging Approaches to Learning in Collegiate Classrooms," Donald Hanna explores possibilities for creating learning environments that engage the learner in social and authentic learning, beginning with the mental framework and needs of the learner rather than the content-driven definitions defined by traditional, lecture-based strategies that are prevalent in university classrooms.

In chapter 12, "Integrated Technology Systems Design: A Model for Aligning Pedagogical Quality with Learning Technology," Kathy Schmidt and Don Olcott present an integrated model for designing instructional environments utilizing a systematic approach to incorporating learning technologies. They describe how learning technologies can be organized effectively to contribute to building a positive classroom environment for students learning at a distance. They also recommend the choice of technology as the last step in designing positive learning environments, not the first as so often happens in higher education today.

In chapter 13, "Learning and the Web: Reflections on Assessment," Gary Brown reinforces this concept of learning being a social activity as much as an intellectual activity, and urges that our strategy for assessing learning reflect the goals we establish for the learning exercise. If we establish goals for assessment that measure learning as a recall exercise, it will be of little surprise when students focus upon "getting the right answer" as opposed to understanding the process of "getting to a right answer." Brown powerfully points out that we should not be surprised to get back what we intend to measure. If we want "deep learning," the kind that learners incorporate into who they are, then we must devise ways of helping students to integrate their learning into their social definitions of themselves.

Learning Challenges of Advanced Technologies

A third theme of this book is that we are *entering uncharted territory when we leave the venue of the physical classroom* as a home for creating active and engaged learning and the book as a primary communication device. We have thousands of years of experience with physicality as our primary means of defining ourselves, our relationships with others, and our preferred mode of learning from each other. We have hundreds of years of experience with print as a primary means of conveying and passing on a circumscribed body of knowledge. By contrast, learning at a distance involves new skills, new uses of our senses, new communication strategies, and new learning technologies that challenge our capabilities even further.

Without question, the possibilities for new learning technologies are significant, as Dede demonstrates in chapter 3, "Advanced Technologies and Distributed Learning in Higher Education." But Dede also cautions that our solid historical, biological, and cultural linkages with physical place and our neophyte experiences with the impact of virtuality as a new communal space for learning should cause us to carefully and strategically consider the choices we make about learning. What we know about the virtual world is limited. Experimentation is warranted and documentation is needed. The creation of virtual social space requires a new framework for furthering democratic and participatory learning and possibly even new social languages and protocols. As Dede carefully points out, higher education has quickly made the transition to "distance scholarship," in which faculty members exchange and improve their ideas electronically, a practice that is preceding a dramatic remapping of scholarly processes. However, the transition to electronic scholarship and learning in the classroom has not been rapid, and most faculty members have not embraced it. One important reason is that faculty will not successfully integrate learning technologies into the classroom until they change their basic assumptions about the characteristics of well-designed teaching and learning environments.

Transformational Change and Leadership in Higher Education

A fourth key element of this book is the theme of *organizational change in higher education*. There is a critical need for bold leaders who can help shape the changes that are transforming our colleges and universities — changes resulting from new pressures that are increasing outside of the academy. Learning throughout life is a requirement in today's global economy and multicultural world, and the world needs colleges and universities that will respond to this need.

While universities have existed for centuries and have adapted successfully to changing conditions, the rate of change for most of our history has been dramatically less than that which our society is experiencing today. Previously, organizational changes consisted primarily of adding more programs, more capacity, and more levels. The underlying organizational assumptions of the university — physical place and convocation — articulated by James Hall (1995, 1) were not challenged during this entire period.

For nearly a millennium, the organizing concept of the university could best be described by the word convocation. Beset in its earliest manifestation by an often barbaric and intrusive world, and fearful that, in a moment's time, the knowledge and wisdom passed down from generation to generation, recorded painstakingly in precious, hand-lettered parchment manuscripts, could be suddenly and irrationally erased from the human record, the university has always organized for defense. Small pockets of scholars, huddled together within moated, cloistered, or even fortified walls, blossomed, over time, into a fortuitous "calling together" of the finest minds; the most precocious students; the distinguished collections of monographs, texts, serials, and artifacts that came to be libraries or bibliothecas; and the study spaces, commons, laboratories, and lecture halls that both scholars and students cohabited.

With this history as background (and as an indication of the power of a shared history and background), it is little wonder that the challenge of organizational change for universities is so significant. John Kimberly (1987) suggests that when an organization is established important decisions are made that tend to define the organization over a very long period of time, especially in an environment of stability of purpose and form. John Hannan and Michael Freeman (1989) suggest that "organizations develop lives of their own, with actions at least partly disconnected from organizational goals, from the demands of relevant environments, and often from the intention of organizational leaders." They further suggest that uncertain, volatile environments will support diverse organizational forms. It is little surprise, then, that in a dramatically changing environment like the one we are currently experiencing, new forms of universities would emerge. Furthermore, we should not be shocked to discover that the task and challenge of leadership and of developing new paths for the future of both traditional and new universities would be daunting. This rapidly developing "biodiversity" of higher education is a major element of change. It is occurring more rapidly in some environments than in others, but it is a global phenomenon nonetheless.

In chapters 1 and 14, Hanna outlines major characteristics of the changing U.S. environment and global patterns and discusses the many challenges of organizational change. In chapter 7, Janet Poley frames important questions, options, and strategies for leaders of higher education at all levels across emerging organizational models.

In chapters 4, 5, and 6, Hanna elaborates on the need for traditional colleges and universities to adapt themselves in response to the global phenomenon of lifetime learning that is necessary for people to live full and productive lives. He further details how traditional campuses are changing and how new organizational models are developing to address this need.

Fundamental change in universities involves not just a shift in norms, structures, processes, and goals, but also an essential alteration of views, perspectives, and understanding about what a university is and does. In chapter 11, "Redefining Faculty Policies and Practices for the Knowledge Age," Olcott and Schmidt explore the many changes, opportunities, and challenges ahead for college and university faculty members as they encounter new opportunities and new expectations.

In chapter 8, "Who Owns Knowledge in a Networked World?", John Tallman addresses the changing technologies of the Internet and the World Wide Web. His analysis carefully outlines current societal and legal understandings and concepts regarding the preservation and transmission of knowledge. He also portrays how these concepts of creating, preserving, and exchanging or transmitting knowledge are being challenged in an electronically connected world.

Peter Drucker has stated that the development of the World Wide Web is as powerful in its impact as was the development of the printing press some 500 years ago. He further indicates that "it took more than 200 years (1440 to the late 1600s) for the printed book to create the modern school. It won't take nearly as long for the big change [in which the university as a whole is transformed]" (Lenzner and Johnson 1997, 126-127). We know the impact the printing press had on the sharing of knowledge and upon the speed with which knowledge creation and discovery accelerated over the past two or three centuries. The printing press transformed the idea of knowledge from an orally shared and interpreted genre to one that was fixed, enabling for the first time the possibility that knowledge apart from the act of communication had economic value and currency. In short, the printing press enabled the creation of books and journals, and these two avenues have become the lingua franca of university scholarship, in turn creating a system of legal protection of intellectual property in the form of various artistic and creative expressions.

What will be the impact of new technologies that enable radical new forms of sharing and accessing information, and how will these new technologies change our consideration of the economic value of ideas? How are electronic concepts being incorporated into current legal interpretations of copyright law, and what do people in knowledge enterprises such as universities need to know about these changes as they plan for this new future?

Ethics, Equity, and Personal Values: Leadership for a New Age

The final theme of this book is *the critical importance and interrelationship of ethics, leadership, and equity* in shaping how learning technologies in higher education will be employed in response to the rapidly growing world demand for knowledge and education. In chapter 10, "Global Access to Learning: Gender, Poverty, and Race," Janet Poley positions the questions of equity and the matter of who benefits (and who is left behind) from learning technologies in a global context. It is not a pretty picture in its global composite, with worldwide knowledge discovery and application accelerating fastest among those already in privileged economic circumstances. But even in knowledge-rich environments some are being left behind, a trend that, if projected far into the future, would be frightening in its consequences. Poley's discussion is thought provoking and challenging to those in leadership positions in higher education, who often listen to constituencies who have the greatest access to them as well as the most political power.

Dede (chapter 3) also outlines both a positive and potentially dark side of new learning technologies and suggests that decisions currently being made in largely uncharted territory will set a policy framework and direction long into the future. In the same vein, Olcott (chapter 9) analyzes technology and ethical issues as they relate to higher education access in a world increasingly dependent upon knowledge. He proposes an ethical framework and values structure for the academy leadership and its decision making related to the use of learning technologies and the role these technologies play in ensuring broad-based access for all.

This current period of time around the millennium is a significant transitional point in the history of our world, largely because of the connective capabilities of emerging digital technologies that we have only begun to experience and test. These new capabilities enable learning and education to be within the reach of every person on the planet, no matter their location or their economic circumstances. This is the vision that is exciting to the authors and the editor of this book as we close out a five-hundred-year history of industrial economic development and begin a new knowledge-based economy with learning as its central core, and with the role of universities very much a central question and challenge for the future.

We are no longer living in a postmodern world. New digital technologies signal the beginning of a new, more dynamic and interactive world, with many different risks and new challenges, just as Guttenberg's invention of the printing press signaled the beginning of the modern world. Peter Drucker puts it this way in his call for leadership and action to expand our access to knowledge and our access to learning beyond that provided by traditional universities of the modern period:

> Nothing "post" is permanent or even long-lived. Ours is a transition period. What the future society will look like, let alone whether it will indeed be the "knowledge society" some of us dare hope for, depends on how the developed countries respond to the challenges of this transition period, the post-capitalist period — their intellectual leaders, their business leaders, their political leaders, but above all each of us in our own work and life. Yet surely this is a time to "make the future" — precisely because everything is in flux (Drucker 1993, 16).

The opportunity to make a difference is here for those who care about lifelong learning, about equity of access, and about opening the academy to new light, new processes, and new ideas. These are the learning challenges of the next century.

References

Dewey, John. [1934] 1964. Need for a philosophy of education. In *John Dewey on education*, edited by R. D. Archambault. New York: Random House.

Drucker, Peter Ferdinand. 1993. *Post-capitalist society*. New York: HarperBusiness.

Hall, James W. 1995. The revolution in electronic technology and the modern university: The convergence of means. *Educom Review* 30(4).

Hannan, Michael T., and John Freeman. 1989. *Organizational ecology*. Cambridge: Harvard University Press.

Kimberly, John R. 1987. The study of organization: Toward a biographical perspective. In *Handbook of Organizational Behavior*, edited by Jay W. Lorsch. Englewood Cliffs, NJ: Prentice-Hall.

Lenzner, Robert, and Stephen S. Johnson. 1997. Seeing things as they really are: An interview with Peter Drucker. *Forbes Magazine*, 10 March: 126-127.

Naisbitt, John. 1994. *Global paradox: The bigger the world economy, the more powerful its smallest players*. New York: William Morrow.

Negroponte, Nicholas. 1995. *Being digital*. New York: Knopf.

Chapter 1

Higher Education in an Era of Digital Competition: Global Consequences

By Donald E. Hanna

Introduction

Major organizational changes and new developments in higher education are being accelerated by dynamic advances in global digital communications and increasingly sophisticated learning technologies. These technical advances are an additional driving force for change in traditionally organized universities in the twenty-first century. Emerging competitors to traditional colleges and universities see opportunities in: 1) increasing costs of university tuition; 2) growing demand for learning; 3) demand for content that can be applied in work settings; and 4) new technologies. These new organizations are competing directly with traditional universities and with each other, and through this competition they are beginning to cause significant change in traditional universities.

Barriers to accessing higher education learning opportunities are being reduced globally because of improved learning technologies. As with all organizations seeking to utilize new technologies effectively, universities need to examine their products, their processes, and their organizational assumptions in order to be positioned both for leadership and survival in the future. Such thorough examination of challenges, opportunities, and organizational options inevitably leads to changes in institutional vision, policy, and fundamental approaches and assumptions. What is needed now in many universities is: 1) a vision of learning for the future; 2) an analysis of organizational options that can move the university as a whole toward a positive vision; and 3) a map of challenges that universities will face in the future, with or without a plan in hand. This book, through its focus on learning, organizational options, and challenges, offers valuable perspectives and possible new directions for leaders, faculty, students, and others concerned with the future of higher education in an era of digital competition.

The focus of this book is on four-year universities rather than community colleges, although many of the challenges and choices discussed for four-year universities are also applicable to two-year colleges.

Characteristics of Traditional Colleges and Universities

Conceptually, higher education can be viewed as an open system with advanced learning as its core purpose. For more than a century, the system of higher education institutions in the United States has developed in an environment that has been stable in terms of its expectations, even though these expectations have become increasingly complex economically, politically, and socially. Throughout the industrial era, universities have focused their teaching activities primarily upon meeting the educational needs of youth preparing for a lifetime of work. Today it is clear that the future will involve a lifetime of learning so that people may work and live productive, satisfying lives.

The more than three thousand traditional higher education institutions in the United States are diverse in mission, size, curricula, selectivity, faculty expertise and background, level of offerings, and location. And new types of institutions, such as land grant universities and community colleges, have emerged with the changing times over the last century, consistent with the idea that a system with greater organizational diversity is better able to deal with increasing complexity in the society.

However, most universities established before 1970 share a number of characteristics that serve to define them. Because these characteristics are widely accepted and understood, they offer a point of departure for further discussion throughout this book. The basic characteristics that help to define traditional universities and colleges, as noted in Hanna (1998), are the following: 1) a residential student body; 2) a recognized geographic service area from which the majority of students are drawn. (This service area can be a local community, a region, a state, or, in the case of a few elite institutions, a nation.); 3) full-time faculty members who organize curricula and degrees, teach in face-to-face settings, engage in scholarship, often conduct public service, and share in institutional governance; 4) a central library and physical plant; 5) nonprofit financial status; 6) evaluation strategies of organizational effectiveness based upon measurement of inputs to instruction, such as funding, library holdings, facilities, faculty/student ratios, faculty qualifications, and student qualifications (see table 1.1 for a more complete analysis).

Fundamental assumptions and major characteristics of traditional universities and colleges emerged during the nineteenth century and evolved in the United States along four distinct paths and threads:

1. the generally small, liberal arts colleges, following a tradition begun in New England;

2. the graduate research university, adapted from Germany;

3. the uniquely American land grant university that sought to broaden access to universities and to combine the practical sciences and arts;

4. two-year, community-based, open-admissions colleges offering technical preparation for a variety of careers and basic academic courses necessary for transfer to baccalaureate institutions.

Each of these paths and threads was a unique response to the societal need for:

- better application of knowledge to the real-world problems of agriculture and industry;

- increased access to higher education;

- discovery of scientific and applied knowledge that could advance industrial and agricultural productivity;

- accessible education and acculturation of an increasingly diverse community of urban and rural learners.

The basic assumptions and characteristics of each of these forms of universities and colleges were refined during the twentieth century. In general, these assumptions have not been seriously challenged during this century. More specific characteristics and assumptions of these institutions are noted in table 1.1.

Strategies for evaluating universities in the United States generally are concerned with measuring inputs to the instructional process. Inputs such as those noted in table 1.1 (the institution's philosophy and mission, funding, curricula, faculty experience, student quality, facilities, and governance structure), taken together, are believed to be effective indices for measuring organizational effectiveness and anticipated student learning, more so than single measures of student learning based upon final examinations that are common practice in European universities. Perhaps of greater importance, these factors help to define the status of the degree awarded, and therefore the value of the degree in the marketplace.

As the decade of the '90s draws to a close, many national higher education organizations have noted the emerging promise (and threat) of new learning technologies applied to traditional residential universities. These organizations have developed conferences and study groups on learning technologies, on teaching and learning with technology, on the purpose and functions of universities, and on the impact of universities on the economy. These activities are a signal that major changes in universities are under way.

Table 1.1
**Characteristics and Assumptions of Traditional Institutions
of Higher Education**

Input Measurement	Characteristics and Assumptions
Philosophy	Students come to campus
Mission	Defined by level of instruction — offering graduate-level programs often implies increased quality, as does student and faculty selectivity
Funding	Measured by money spent per full-time student equivalent (FTE)
Curricula	Relatively stable and comprehensive curricula
Instruction	Primarily face-to-face lecture, teacher-centered formats prevalent at undergraduate level. Instruction is measured by clock hours of seat-time (Carnegie units of credit) and evaluation of student content acquisition; seminars at graduate level
Faculty	Number of full-time faculty; faculty preparation and credentials, research productivity, and external grants imply increased instructional quality
Students	Greater selectivity at admission suggests higher-quality programs — very little measurement of change in overall learning from entry to exit
Library	More volumes in library, with greater depth of disciplinary holdings, implies greater quality (although with advances in electronic sharing of resources this assumption is beginning to be challenged)
Learning Technology	Generally used to supplement or enhance lecture format; tiered, high-technology lecture halls are one example
Physical Facilities	Central physical plant includes residence halls, student union(s), health facilities, classrooms, and campus environment, which together are believed to add to the quality of the education received

Input Measurement	Characteristics and Assumptions
Productivity Outcomes	Productivity is measured in student credit-hours and degrees. Student credit-hours are measures of classroom seat-time and content acquisition; degrees are measures of completion of pre-approved courses
Governance	Independent board of trustees — independence from political or business environment is a goal
Accreditation	Institutional by region; individual programs or disciplines are also accredited by professional accreditation associations

Why Universities Will Change

Pressure for change in universities is coming not only in the form of increasing competition from new organizational forms of higher education specifically oriented to serving adults, but also from legislators who expect public universities to deliver what the public wants, and from students themselves, who indicate in study after study their need to continue their education (Dillman et al. 1995). In a national survey of what the adult public wants from higher education, Dillman et al. (1995) reported that 94 percent of adults between the ages of eighteen and twenty-nine indicated that additional training or education was definitely or probably important for them to be successful in their work. Surprisingly, 58 percent of adults sixty-five years and older reported the same assessment (see table 1.2).

Dillman et al. (1995) came to three very important conclusions from their analysis of these data:

1. Higher demand for lifelong education and training means that colleges and universities have many more potential customers than in the past.

2. Distance education methods offer one means of meeting the demand for lifelong learning.

3. Colleges and universities must change how they do business to meet the needs of lifelong learners.

A boom in part-time student and external-degree enrollments; growth in community-college enrollments; growth in
continuing-education enrollments (usually at the margin of traditional institutions); and, most of all, growth in nonformal education being pursued independently by adults in their own time,
place, and format — all are examples of this fundamental educational change in consumer demand. It is a change that no higher
education institution can afford to ignore.

Why is Change in Higher Education So Difficult?

The literature of organizational change is replete with examples
of organizations that have matured in one environment and suddenly are faced with survival in an environment that has changed
rapidly due to technology, competition, product (program) innovation, and organizational malaise. For example, traditional
colleges and universities now confront the emergence of new
competitors for both traditional-age and adult students. Universities that have been established to teach at a distance using
print-based materials are suddenly faced with the global emergence of the Internet and the World Wide Web. These universities must make necessary adjustments or face becoming less
productive and relevant to the needs of society.

The environment for higher education has become much
more dynamic and even more complex with the recent development of new digital technologies. With the market for higher education becoming more diverse, the probability of an increasing
number of organizational forms is assured. All theories of organizational adaptation and change support the idea that multiple
organizational structures are valued more when the future is uncertain and turbulent. Stable and certain environments generate
low levels of organizational diversity, as organizations feel little
pressure to adapt or change.

Kimberly (1987, 1988) suggests that when an organization is
established, four important decisions are made, related to domain, governance, core values (often embedded in expertise), and
organizational design. These decisions are made within a particu-

Table 1.2
Importance of Additional Training or Education

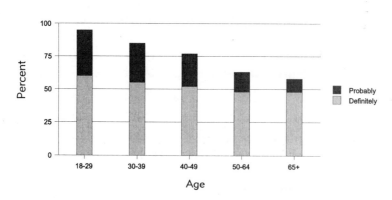

Source: What the Public Wants from Higher Education, SESRC Washington State University, 1995. Used with permission.

lar set of circumstances, challenges, and opportunities existing at the time of organization. These decisions determine the kinds of products or programs that will be offered, the particular markets that will be served, the types of people who will be recruited, the structure for accountability, and the functioning of the internal organization. They also determine the future course of the organization by defining the range of feasible alternatives, shaping the internal culture, and defining the organization's identity.

Decisions about core values and governance greatly influence the culture of the organization, and decisions about domain and organizational design shape the organization's identity. Stinchcombe (1965) asserts that groups or cohorts of similar organizations, such as a particular type of university, are imprinted with the social, cultural, and technical features that are common in the environment at the time of founding, and that it is very difficult to adapt these characteristics to change. Given this framework, it is not surprising that major forms and types of universities that have developed to date have significant staying power and are resistant to organizational transformation, especially since the environment has been relatively stable.

Hannan and Freeman (1989) indicate that organizations founded to accomplish particular purposes within a stable environment that is conducive to the organization's survival develop formalized roles, rules, and procedures over time for enforcing their rules. These organizations also consume substantial resources in simply maintaining their structures. An excellent example of this phenomenon, but by no means the only one, is the well-developed faculty governance process in universities.

Organizational politics also enter into the equation of adaptation and competition, especially in times of resource contraction or decline, as has been the experience of higher education in the 1980s and '90s. According to Hannan and Freeman (1998, 5), "Organizations develop lives of their own, with action at least partly disconnected from organizational goals, from the demands of relevant environments, and often from the intentions of organizational leaders."

As the environment changes and this disconnection grows, the pressure for the organization to change intensifies. This gap between demands of the external environment and the internal organizational realities creates internal and external awareness of the need for change, and leads to the development of efforts to initiate change processes that will improve organizational capacity to adapt to a changing environment. Organizational theory emphasizes the encouragement of new organizational forms when environmental conditions and competitive relations change. In extreme cases, organizational theory advocates the organization's replacement through organizational decline and death. This is the classic outcome predicted by Jack Welch (cited in Davis and Botkin 1994, 109), the CEO of General Electric, in discussing the decline and demise of organizations: "When the rate of change outside exceeds the rate of change inside, the end is in sight."

Stinchcombe (1965) indicates that new organizations are created when people find or learn about better ways of doing things that are not easily done within existing social arrangements, and when they believe that the new organization will continue to be effective enough to pay for the trouble of building it and for the resources invested in it. This suggests that the new and emerging organizational models outlined in chapters 4, 5, and 6 of this book are likely to continue to grow in importance, assuming ongoing new growth in demand for learning worldwide, which seems assured.

But the emergence of new demand and new organizational forms of higher education also places significant pressure on existing traditional universities to adapt and to undergo fundamental changes in order to compete — or, in some cases, survive. Mintzberg (1979) suggests that a move from a stable but complex environment to a dynamic one requires adjustments to organizational forms that reduce bureaucracy and increase responsiveness in traditional organizations. Many universities are engaged in strategic change processes, quality improvement activities, and environmental scans intended to produce awareness of the need for such change. Fundamental change involves not just a shift in norms, structures, processes, and goals, but also an essential alteration of views, perspectives, and understanding of the organization. The success of these change processes depends both on the organization's ability to undergo a significant shift in values, vision, and direction and on the ability of stakeholders to understand and accept a new conceptualization of the organization. The initiators of this transformation often are the leaders of the organization who articulate the need for, and the intended nature of, the impending change.

Change in universities is often inhibited by organizational inertia rather than resistance to change by leaders, faculty members, or students. Reorganization and transformation are expensive, difficult, and energy consuming, especially in organizations with well-developed internal maintenance structures. As a result, Kimberly (1998, 168) suggests that, for fundamental change to occur, the energy and perspective required to transform an organization in fundamental ways must come from outside its own culture: "Those who have become a part of the culture and the identity of the organization are those least able to precipitate major changes."

Baldridge, Deal, and Ingols (1983) support Kimberly's general organizational theory, arguing that to understand opportunities for change in universities, one must understand that the external environment is by far the most powerful source of internal change. They join Cohen and March (1974) in describing the typical academic structure within the modern university as an "organized anarchy" in which almost any idea can be justified and can also be attacked as illegitimate, making internally driven change difficult. Decision making is diffused, and overall organizational leadership is problematic, causing one regent at a leading public university in the Midwest to charge that getting a university to change is like trying to move a battleship at rest with one's bare hands (Weinstein 1993).

Toffler (1985, 14) suggests that developed organizations change significantly only when three conditions are met: "First, there must be enormous external pressures. Second, there must be people inside who are strongly dissatisfied with the existing order. And third, there must be a coherent alternative embodied in a plan, a model, or a vision." The first of these conditions, external pressure, certainly describes higher education as a system, especially when viewed in relation to radical changes in communications technologies and the world economy. The second condition for change, insiders who are strongly dissatisfied with the existing order, is being driven both by changes imposed by the external environment — changes in sources of funding, the need to be more responsive to changing educational needs, and many other changes discussed earlier in this chapter — and internal factors, including increasing diversity, changing patterns of teaching and learning, and a recognition of the importance of learning as a lifetime activity. The intensity of this internal debate and controversy regarding the nature of changes to be made are reflective of an administration-versus-faculty divide that must be bridged if real and lasting organizational change is to occur in the majority of institutions.

The third condition for change outlined by Toffler, a coherent model or plan for change, requires a thorough examination and analysis of alternative visions for responding to this uncertain and volatile environment. It also necessitates an exploration of key issues, concepts, and processes that are central to the development of a coherent plan. This book is intended to sketch a landscape of such a vision for change in our models of higher education — a vision that is supportive of reorganizing and reconstructing our view of positive learning environments in higher education, of how we incorporate learning technologies into our environment, of possible new organizational models for the future, and of leadership options and strategies necessary to achieve a successful transition to these new organizational models.

External Pressures for Changing Our System of Higher Education

A consumer revolution in learning has been under way throughout the world over the past thirty years. Adults entering the workforce and progressing through several careers are forcing major, dynamic changes in our system of higher education. The change is global, but it is most pronounced in countries well along in the transition from an industrial economy to one based upon information and knowledge. While learning through formal schooling has been the dominant feature of educational systems throughout most of the past century, adults are encountering changing knowledge requirements that have forced them to learn to even stay in the workforce, let alone get ahead in life. In what is rapidly becoming "big business," and a major force in our economy, this shift in the needs of the labor force and in the adult population in general is already having dramatic effects upon all of higher education.

U.S. expenditures on K-12, postsecondary, and workplace education account for almost $700 billion, or more than nine percent of the U.S. Gross National Product (Ghazi and Irani 1997). More than $300 billion is spent on K-12 education alone, and the U.S. spends more for each K-12 student and for each university student than any industrialized country other than Switzerland (Ghazi and Irani 1997; U.S. Department of Education et al. 1996). Despite these expenditures, however, the critical need for new skills in the workplace and for greater accountability for what is learned, along with the poor performance of students on tests, have resulted in increased attention to alternative approaches to education (Andrew Mellon Foundation 1998; Johnson and Rush 1995; Privateer 1999; Mendels 1999; Primary Research Group 1997a; Stuart 1998).

A study by the National Center for Education Statistics found that almost sixty million adults were engaged in continuing education courses in 1995. More than 68 percent were engaged in work-related training, and only 24 percent were enrolled in degree programs. Of those enrolled in degree programs, fewer than one-third were enrolled in full-time programs, with the remaining two-thirds enrolled in career-oriented or part-time programs (Ghazi and Irani 1997; U.S. Department of Education 1996).

Most U.S. colleges and universities have built their comparative advantages around their specific geography and location. Institutions with a limited geographic perspective are not well equipped to adjust to a new environment where ease of access, appropriateness of format, and level of learner competencies achieved will be among the more important measures of consumer attractiveness. In particular, regional, location-bound public universities may find it difficult to break into a marketplace where geographic proximity is becoming less important to students and the number of alternative providers is on the increase.

Two-career families are now the norm in America. As a result, the trend toward workplace learning, described earlier, affects many more people than was the case only thirty years ago. Sixty-five percent of all U.S. households are now two-income or single-parent families. Accompanying the emergence of two-career families is a reduction in the amount of available time for learning, with increasing pressure to learn in the most effective manner possible. People are also better educated than ever before, and their education has resulted in better outcomes in the workplace. In 1996, the average college-educated worker was paid 77 percent more than an employee with only a high school diploma. The college-educated worker was paid only 28 percent more in 1980 (Bureau of Labor Statistics 1998b; Ghazi and Irani 1997; Stuart 1998).

Technology is changing so quickly that the technical knowledge acquired by engineers who graduate from universities quickly becomes obsolete. A university degree in any field of study is no longer the endpoint of learning, but simply a stepping stone to learning that must continue throughout one's career. And technology affects everyone's careers, not just those people who are technically trained. To be competitive in the job market, an individual must be conversant with the most recent tools, and these tools are increasingly technology- and computer-based.

The requirement for education is becoming readily apparent to those who are choosing between entering the workforce and pursuing higher education. In just two years, from 1995 to 1997, the percentage of high school graduates immediately continuing on in higher education in the United States rose five full percentage points (from 62 percent to 67 percent) after remaining steady for several years preceding 1995 (Bureau of Labor Statistics 1998a).

A fast-paced economy has also forced people to change careers more than ever before. Americans can now expect, on average, to change careers at least six times during their lifetime (Smith 1986; Sperling and Tucker 1997). With each career change the individual must meet the requirement to gain new knowledge in order to be productive. At the same time, the change in perspective and environment gives the individual new opportunities for learning.

The changing demographics of the American population are also affecting the need for learning. People are living longer, and the age of retirement is projected to increase. This longer work span, coupled with a rapidly changing knowledge base, creates new demand for relearning what was once known, unlearning what is no longer true, and paying attention to new knowledge that is essential to job performance. Clearly, individuals must develop skills in learning to learn, not just to acquire knowledge, but to know intuitively how to learn in many different settings with many different purposes and goals.

Changing demographics and improved communications are creating demand for learning about the diversity of languages and cultures throughout the world. Language ability and facility are becoming essential to citizenship and to commerce, and this change demands both learning and practice. The prospect of the global student, suggested by Parker Rossman in 1992, is now within the realm of possibility, although to date there are no well-developed examples of institutions that have as their core mission a global reach. However, numerous universities are targeting specific programs toward a global marketplace, especially in the field of business and economics.

Businesses are investing heavily in new information technologies to bolster productivity. A recent analysis by the Bureau of Economic Analysis and the Bureau of Labor Statistics shows that average investment in technology per employee doubled from May 1991 to September 1996 (Ghazi and Irani 1997).

The nature of the overall workforce is changing dramatically as well. In 1950, most workers (60 percent) were unskilled. In 2000, most (65 percent) will be skilled, with only 15 percent of them being unskilled (Ghazi and Irani 1997). The Bureau of Labor Statistics projects that most new jobs in the first decade of the new century will require managerial, technical, and professional skills. As recently as the 1950s, 20 percent of the workforce were professional, 20 percent were skilled, and 60 percent were unskilled. In dramatic contrast, by 1997, while professionals continued to encompass about 20 percent of the workforce, fewer than 20 percent were unskilled workers while more than 60 percent were skilled workers (Murane and Levy 1997). Individuals in these jobs require continuous learning and upgrading of skills, and they take greater advantage of employer-supported educational opportunities than do other segments of the workforce (Sperling and Tucker 1997).

Communication changes are also putting pressure on learners to engage in continuous and regular learning. We are confronted daily by a barrage of information conveyed to us electronically. In the past, when we didn't know what we didn't know, it was easy to ignore the need to learn because we weren't confronted with our own ignorance on a daily basis. Now we have multiple channels covering news on a national and worldwide basis, and events that were once remote have become directly related to our daily lives.

New skills and abilities are being emphasized in the workplace. Teamwork, problem solving, critical analysis, and creativity in group settings are becoming requirements for success in many work environments. Traditional schools have not emphasized these skills, which require learning and practice to develop. As a result, employers are demanding that workers acquire these skills in the workplace and are creating and supporting strategies and educational programs to build a more productive workforce (Champy 1995; Perelman 1993; Tapscott and Caston 1993). The public, through employers, businesses, and parents, is also applying pressure on elementary and secondary schools to develop these skills. In addition, the return on an individual's investment of time in educational programs is also significant, as noted in table 1.3, adding to the pressure on institutions to provide increased access.

Globalization in both commerce and communication has also created new demand for learning. Understanding relationships, being able to think across boundaries, and linking a myriad of perspectives and facts together are all becoming more essential as the world becomes smaller. As the world shrinks, small business grows, the world economy becomes bigger and more open, and small and middle-sized companies dominate (Naisbitt 1994). The effect of these major developments, combined with the revolution of the World Wide Web, is that more and more people are operating commercial ventures that cross international and linguistic boundaries, creating entirely new conventions, structures, and requirements for learning at all levels of the organization.

With this growing emphasis on and importance of learning for commerce and citizenship, employers and employees alike are searching for new approaches to providing learning opportunities, examining what those opportunities include, how they are measured, and how they are funded. This new demand for learning will ensure that new or changed institutions are organized to make learning available anytime, anyplace, at an affordable cost, with results that can be measured in an objective manner and with the credibility that serves both employers and employees.

Technology and, especially, the World Wide Web have been important drivers of change. Among young people there has been a dramatic increase in learning through personal computers and, more recently, the Web. As recently as 1990, personal computers were found in fewer than 10 percent of U.S. homes. By 1995, they were in 36 percent of all homes, and by 1997 this figure

Table 1.3.
Average Annual Income for Various Levels of Education

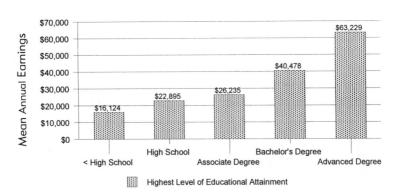

Source: Stuart, Lisa. 1998. 21st Century Jobs. Washington, DC: U.S. Department of Labor. Used with permission.

had increased to 46 percent. According to Donald Tapscott (1998, 1-2): "For the first time in history, children are more comfortable, knowledgeable, and literate than their parents about an innovation central to society."

Because learners are learning in diverse ways and are often doing so independently of existing formal institutions, the demand for alternative certification of knowledge is also accelerating. Employers must be able to assess what people know, what skills they have, and what work they can perform. Employees must be able to present certifiable and reliable evidence of their skills and knowledge. Traditional institutions have focused on elaborate measures of seat-time, accumulation of credits, and individual knowledge acquisition. They are not well equipped or inclined to develop the capability to certify skills and competencies, and they have been slow to recognize the validity of this emerging need.

Traditional nonprofit universities and colleges seek to capture the growing adult learning market. Such institutions have dominated youth-oriented higher education for a century, and some of the more aggressive and comprehensive universities have a long history of offering significant programs for adults, usually operated at the margin of the institution. Most traditional universities have only in the past decade begun to view their graduates as potential repeat customers, the way a typical business might, through extending their traditional university academic programs in such a way as to make these programs available anytime, anyplace, any pace.

People are intuitively aware of the trends outlined here, and they are taking greater responsibility for pursuing their own learning. And more and more of their learning is being done outside the confines of traditional institutions. While demand for higher education offered in traditional classrooms to eighteen to twenty-two-year-olds in face-to-face settings has grown over the past thirty years, this growth is being overshadowed by other forms of learning.

The Politics of Internal Dissatisfaction in Higher Education

Universities are responding to these global trends toward increased access and flexibility. A 1995 study by the National Center for Education Statistics found that one-third of higher education institutions offered distance education courses in the fall of 1995. Another one-quarter planned to offer such courses in the next three years, and 42 percent did not offer and did not plan to offer distance education courses in the next three years (Primary Research Group 1997b).

Only two years later, in a study of forty-four universities with distance education programs, 95.3 percent of the campuses with an established distance education program planned to expand the program. Among reasons for expansion, meeting greater demand, staying competitive, and serving new markets were the three most frequently cited motivations. At the same time, 40 percent of distance education programs in this same study reported operating at a loss (Primary Research Group 1997b).

Institutions are recognizing that the adult learning marketplace is increasingly competitive and full of opportunity, both for existing institutions and for new ones. Recognition that the marketplace is growing and that new technologies dramatically improve access to learning resources is both enabling and driving change within the academy. New technologies offer the potential of linking learners and teachers in new ways. Like most rapidly developing markets where practices are not yet proven, many organizations are feeling their way, sometimes making enormous but risky investments and sometimes hedging their bets by minimizing risks.

Some changes are controversial and provide fertile ground for substantial dissatisfaction among faculty, students, administrators, and staff, in part because the changes are highly threatening to the status quo. Faculty voices within higher education have emerged to articulate this threat. Noble (1999) states unequivocally that higher education is being commercialized and that instruction is becoming a commodity to be automated, the net result being that faculty will no longer be needed.

Because education, again, is not what all this is about; it's about making money. In short, the new technology of education, like the automation of other industries, robs faculty of their knowledge and skills, their control over their working lives, the product of their labor, and, ultimately, their means of livelihood.

In Noble's analogy, universities are becoming the equivalent of health maintenance organizations, which have already radically altered the delivery of health care. This suggests that university faculty members are about to suffer the same loss of control experienced by physicians. Noble suggests that this change is being driven by a combination of technology businesses, university administrators, and technozealots who simply like to play with technology. According to Noble:

> With the avid encouragement of their private sector and
> university patrons, they [the technozealots] forge ahead,
> without support for their pedagogical claims about the
> alleged enhancement of education, without any real evidence of productivity improvement, and without any effective demand from either students or teachers.

Noble's perspective is one likely to be attractive to many faculty members who are protective of the status, security, and collegial (at least in the ideal) environment within the modern university. An indication of this potential development is the incorporation of many of Noble's ideas into a 1998 letter to Washington State's governor, Gary Locke, signed by hundreds of faculty members of the University of Washington (University of Washington Faculty Members 1998). The letter decries the damage likely to be done to the academy by Western Governors University's unbundling of services and programs that have been traditionally provided by modern universities (discussed in chapter 6). These responses provide some indication of how difficult it will be to initiate and propel internally initiated responses to change, despite the relatively positive assessment regarding faculty leadership articulated by Olcott and Schmidt in chapter 11.

In a more humorous but darker vein, expressing similar misgivings about the future, Langdon Winner summarizes comments made by Christine Maitland, coordinator of higher education for the National Education Association, who sketched several fantasies of campuses of the future in her presentation at a recent conference:

> One of them, McCollege, yellow arches and all, would offer a complete line of drive-through, fast-consumption educational products, including "The Big Degree." A special attraction of "Wired U" would be occasional performances by "The Three Tenures," the last three tenured professors on the planet. On the walls of her projected E.M.O. — Education Maintenance Organization — were signs reading: "Truth is the best commodity," "Scholarship means dollarship," and "Money in the bank is the best tenure."

Whether they realize it or not (according to Maitland) college teachers are now involved in a fierce struggle over the control of the curriculum. The increasing use of technology in higher education raises persistent questions about what the curriculum will include and who decides. "It is the faculty that are the best judges of the content and quality of courses in their discipline," she insisted. With a "knowledge explosion" under way in all areas of learning, the idea that software developers can simply package lectures and lessons and pump them through digital pipes year after year is an illusion. Such knowledge would have a limited shelf-life. Hence, the best strategy is to allow those active in various fields of learning to oversee changes in the substance of courses (Winner 1998).

Talbott (1998), in a thoughtful essay entitled "Who's Killing Higher Education? Or Is It Suicide?", frames the issue differently. He asserts that universities in the main are simply employing emerging technologies to continue providing programs and courses in the same old way, and that technologies are not promoting change but simply extending the product of an organization — a product that is no longer in order given changes that have taken place in our economy and society. He indicates that:

- A growing consensus holds that new information technologies foretell the end of higher education as we have known it. I suspect this is true. Its truth, however, is not that the technologies are positively revolutionizing education. Rather, what we are watching is more like the end — the final perfection and dead-end extreme — of the old regime's shortcomings.

- For a long while now we have slowly been reconceiving education as the transfer of information from one database or brain to another. Access to information is the universal slogan, and by "information" we demonstrate with countless phrases every day that we mean something routinely transferable between containers.

While in one sense these arguments are highly political and worlds apart, what they have in common is the plea for universities to be forward thinking and to plan the path ahead carefully.

A Vision for the Future

Organizational patterns of universities are being affected by the development of new learning technologies and by an increase in demand for learning, primarily from adults who must learn continuously to stay current in the workforce. Increasingly, the marketplace for learning by adults is defined as lifelong education and training that keeps people current in their professional lives and stimulated in their personal quests. Higher education can no longer be defined solely as preparation for a career or for life with a focus on the eighteen- to twenty-two-year-old student, as has been the case for most of the twentieth century.

To be effective in this era of digital competition, leaders of all institutions and programs need first to recognize the powerful external forces at work — especially the new demands for lifelong learning, new competitors, and the development of new learning technologies, all outlined in this chapter. They must also identify and understand issues that are important to meeting these competitive challenges.

In the case of traditional universities, leaders need to be cognizant of the powerful forces resisting change, and understand the academic and administrative culture of their organizational environments. What is needed is not simply organizational change, but the development of features and characteristics that will position the organization for the future.

Once resistances to change are recognized, leaders must develop a strong rationale and framework for organizational change and for addressing important new choices and challenges that organizational change will present. Critical organizational choices and challenges for universities that are addressed in the remaining chapters of this book include:

- developing patterns of learning that engage learners and that yield effective learning experiences in both physical and virtual contexts, and preparing for the utilization of advanced learning technologies of the future;

- recognizing and promoting changing understanding of knowledge creation, knowledge exchange, and knowledge ownership, thus strengthening an understanding of new challenges and possibilities for the university;

- enabling organizational structures and decision-making patterns that are responsive to emerging educational needs of people and organizations;

- developing new leadership strategies to meet new organizational challenges for leaders, faculty, and students.

REFERENCES

Andrew Mellon Foundation. 1998. *Initiative on the cost-effective uses of technology in teaching* [Web site]. Andrew Mellon Foundation, 28 December. Available from < http://www.mellon.org/cutt.html >.

Baldridge, J. Victor, Terrence E. Deal, and Cynthia Ingols. 1983. *The dynamics of organizational change in education.* Berkeley: McCutchan Publishing Corp.

Bergquist, William H. 1992. *The four cultures of the academy: insights and strategies for improving leadership in collegiate organizations.* San Francisco: Jossey-Bass, Publishers.

Bureau of Labor Statistics. 1998a. *College enrollment and work activity of 1997 high school graduates.* Washington, DC: Bureau of Labor Statistics.

Bureau of Labor Statistics. 1998b. *Employment and total job openings, 1996-2006, and 1996 median weekly earnings by education and training category.* Washington, DC: Bureau of Labor Statistics.

Champy, James. 1995. *Reengineering management: The mandate for new leadership.* New York: HarperBusiness.

Cohen, M.D., and James G. March. 1974. *Leadership and ambiguity: The American college presidency.* New York: McGraw-Hill.

Dillman, Don A., James C. Christenson, Priscilla Salant, and Paul D. Warner. 1995. *What the public wants from higher education: Workforce implications from a 1995 national survey.* Pullman, WA: Washington State University.

Ghazi, Kian, and Isabelle Irani. 1997. *Emerging Trends in the $670 billion education market.* New York: Lehman Brothers.

Hanna, Donald E. 1998. Higher education in an era of digital competition: Emerging organizational models. *Journal of Asynchronous Learning* 2(1).

Hannan, Michael T., and John Freeman. 1989. *Organizational ecology.* Cambridge: Harvard University Press.

Johnson, Sandra L., and Sean C. Rush, eds. 1995. *Reinventing the university: Managing and financing institutions of higher education.* New York: John Wiley & Sons.

Kimberly, John R. 1987. The study of organization: toward a biographical perspective. In *Handbook of organizational behavior,* edited by Jay W. Lorsch. Englewood Cliffs, NJ: Prentice-Hall.

Kimberly, John R. 1988. Reframing and organizational change. In *Paradoxes and transformation: Toward a theory of change in organization and management*, edited by Robert E. Quinn and Kim S. Cameron. Cambridge, MA: Ballinger Publishing Company.

Mendels, Pamela. 1999. Can new technologies revitalize old teaching methods? [Web site]. *The New York Times*, 24 March. Available from < http://www.nytimes.com/library/tech/99/03/cyber/education /24education.html >.

Mintzberg, Henry. 1979. The structuring of organizations: A synthesis of the research. In *Theory of Management Policy Series*, edited by Henry Mintzberg. Englewood Cliffs, NJ: Prentice-Hall.

Murane, Richard J., and Frank Levy. 1997. *Teaching the new basic skills principles for educating children to thrive in a changing economy.* New York: Free Press.

Naisbitt, John. 1994. *Global paradox: The bigger the world economy, the more powerful its smallest players.* New York: William Morrow.

Noble, David. 1999. *Digital diploma mills* [Website]. Available from < http://www.firstmonday.dk/issues/issue3_1/noble/index.html >.

Perelman, Lewis J. 1993. *School's out: A radical new formula for the revitalization of America's educational system.* New York: Avon Books.

Primary Research Group Inc. 1997a. *Restructuring higher education: Cost containment and productivity enhancement efforts of North American colleges and universities.* New York: Primary Research Group.

Primary Research Group. 1997b. *The survey of distance learning programs in higher education.* New York: Primary Research Group.

Privateer, Paul Michael. 1999. Academic technology and the future of higher education: Strategic paths taken and not taken. *The Journal of Higher Education* 70(1): 60-79.

Rossman, Parker. 1992. *The emerging worldwide electronic university: Information age global higher education, contributions to the study of education,* no. 57. Westport, CT: Greenwood Press.

Smith, Peter. 1986. *Your hidden credentials.* Washington, DC: Acropolis Books.

Sperling, John G., and Robert W. Tucker. 1997. *For-profit higher education: Developing a world-class workforce.* New Brunswick, NJ: Transaction Publishers.

Stinchcombe, Arthur L. 1965. Social structure and organizations. In *Handbook of Organizations,* edited by James G. March. Chicago: Rand McNally.

Stuart, Lisa. 1998. *21st century skills for 21st century jobs.* Washington, DC: U.S. Department of Labor.

Talbott, Steve. 1998. Who's killing higher education? Or is it suicide? *Net Future,* 15 October.

Tapscott, Don. 1998. *Growing up digital: The rise of the net generation.* New York: McGraw-Hill.

Tapscott, Don, and Art Caston. 1993. *Paradigm shift: The new promise of information technology.* New York: McGraw-Hill.

Toffler, Alvin. 1985. *The adaptive corporation.* New York: McGraw-Hill.

U.S. Department of Education, National Center for Education Statistics. 1996. *National household education survey 1995.* Washington, DC: U.S. Government Printing Office.

U.S. Department of Education, National Center for Education Statistics, Nancy Matheson, Laura Hersh Salganik, Richard P. Phelps, Marianne Perie, Alsalam Nabeel, and Thomas Smith, M. 1996. *Education indicators: An international perspective.* Washington, DC: U.S. Government Printing Office.

University of Washington Faculty Members. 1998. *Open letter To Governor Gary Locke and the 2020 Commission on the future of higher education* [Website]. University of Washington chapter, American Association of University Professors. Available from < http://weber.u.washington. edu/~uwaaup/let.html > .

Weinstein, Laurence A. 1993. *Moving a battleship with your bare hands: Governing a university system.* Madison, WI: Magna Publications.

Welch, Jack. Cited in Davis and Botkin. 1994. In *The monster under the bed: How business is mastering the opportunity of knowledge for profit,* edited by S.M. Davis and J.W. Botkin. New York: Simon & Schuster.

Winner, Langdon. 1999. Report from the digital diploma mills conference [Website]. Chatham Center for Advanced Study. Available from < http://www.oreilly.com/people/staff/stevet/netfuture/ 1998/Jun0298_72.html#3 > .

Chapter 2

Emerging Approaches to Learning in Collegiate Classrooms

By Donald E. Hanna

... Knowing is literally something which we do. — John Dewey

The justification for a university is that it preserves the connection between knowledge and the zest of life, by uniting the young and the old in the imaginative consideration of learning ... At least, this is the function which it should perform for society. A university which fails in this respect has no reason for existence. — Alfred North Whitehead

Student learning frequently occupies a secondary position in internal assessments of higher education, which are often focused upon establishing institutional accountability using measures such as faculty teaching loads, cost containment, revenue generation, program assessment, and research outcomes and productivity (Privateer 1999; Andrew Mellon Foundation 1998; Mendels 1999; Primary Research Group 1997). However, widespread concern about the skills and proficiencies of university graduates has caused an external reassessment of the entire educational process (Boyer 1990; Light 1990; Michaelsen, Jones, and Watson 1993; Primary Research Group 1997; Privateer 1999). Understanding emerging approaches for creating more effective learning environments in an interconnected world is central to addressing the future challenges facing universities and colleges.

The Role of Technology and the Work Environment

Approaches to and theories of learning and teaching have evolved in concert with the development of technologies and demands from the work environment for different knowledge and skill sets from those previously required by a highly structured, compartmentalized, and ordered industrial economy. Knowledge that people need to live and work in today's society is increasingly interdisciplinary, problem focused, and process based rather than linear, routine, and well defined. Proficiencies required include the ability to work in teams, excellent presentation skills, critical thinking processes, and the capacity to use a variety of technologies and software (Gardiner 1994). More than ever before people will need to develop an internal process for learning that will enable them to be continuous learners.

Therefore, the first requirement for, but also a major challenge to, our educational system and to our institutions is to enable students to have the experiences necessary to develop knowledge and skills appropriate for living and working in a rapidly changing, technology-based society. The second fundamental requirement is to enable students to develop the habits and attitudes that will enable them to be lifetime learners.

Meeting these two challenging requirements means transforming our educational system from one in which students learn specified content in order to prepare for a lifetime of work to one in which students learn to learn throughout their lifetimes in order live productive lives (Smith 1990). Critical to this change is the systematic creation of new models for learning environments — models that support the development of active, engaged learners (Bonwell and Eison 1991; Gardiner 1994).

In the engaged-learner classroom, the teacher provides the environmental framework and context but is also a learner and co-investigator with the students. The teacher is not the primary source of all information relevant to the content of the course, nor even the primary interpreter or integrator of such knowledge and information. That role becomes the learner's. The teacher's role becomes one of modeling effective learning behaviors, coaching and guiding, and mediating among possible classroom activities and pursuits within the framework of overall course content.

The concept of engaged learning builds upon the work of diverse thinkers such as John Dewey (1916) and Lev Vygotsky (1962), both of whom argued strongly that learning occurs most effectively when it is connected to the personal experience and knowledge base of the learner, and when it is situated in a social context in which the learner leads the "construction" of his or her own knowledge through interaction with others and with guidance from the teacher. This "constructivist" learning environment is based upon six core principles identified by Lambert et. al. (1995, 17-18):

1. Knowledge and beliefs are formed within the learner.

2. Learners personally imbue experiences with meaning.

3. Learning activities should enable learners to gain access to their experiences, knowledge, and beliefs.

4. Learning is a social activity that is enhanced by shared inquiry.

5. Reflection and metacognition are essential aspects of constructing knowledge and meaning.

6. The outcomes of the learning process are varied and often unpredictable.

Winn (1997) asserts that learning occurs when "students generate knowledge from within, not when they receive information from outside." Thus, learning must necessarily actively involve and engage the learner, beginning with the knowledge that the learner carries into the classroom environment. According to Winn, understanding arises as the learners work to reconcile what they already know and believe with information they are encountering for the first time or with old information on which they are gaining a fresh perspective. It is this struggle to construct knowledge within an existing framework — one that is, within limits, personal and idiosyncratic — that results in learner enthusiasm, involvement, and engagement.

Jones et al. (1994) outline indicators of environments that induce and support engaged learners and provide examples of student abilities that are supported in such an environment. According to Jones et al., engaged learners are actively responsible for defining their own learning goals:

> Successful engaged learners are responsible for their own learning. These students are self-regulated and able to define their own learning goals and evaluate their own achievement. They are also energized by their learning; their joy of learning leads to a lifelong passion for solving problems, understanding, and taking the next step in their thinking. These learners are strategic in that they know how to learn and are able to transfer knowledge to solve problems creatively. Engaged learning also involves being collaborative, that is, valuing and having the skills to work with others.

Indicators of learning environments that encourage active learning include evidence of tasks that are challenging, authentic, and multidisciplinary. Learning activities and tasks often relate the knowledge being learned to real and practical problems and issues that are relevant to the learner's experience. Tasks are frequently presented in the form of projects, and they usually involve some sort of collaboration with others as well as using resources within the learner's own environment, community, organizational setting, and personal surroundings. Inquiry and research, whether individually generated or conducted as a part of a group, is also a core activity in knowledge building in these classrooms. Learners become explorers and integrators of knowledge. They are encouraged to share the knowledge they have developed with others and to build their understandings and insights into the content of the classroom. They do this not only for the benefit of other learners, but also for themselves because the process of sharing involves increased reflection and integration of the knowledge they have acquired.

This active, engaged, collaborative approach to learning can be analyzed from a theoretical perspective through the lens of social interdependence theory, which suggests that learning outcomes can be predicted by the assumptions regarding learning that precede the learning activity. Johnson and Johnson (1998) assert that there are essentially three possible underlying assumptions regarding the organization of any learning activity. Assumption one is that the learner's activities and contributions are largely cooperative with those of others. The second possible assumption is that the learners are largely competitive, in that one person's "success" may diminish the measurable success of all other class members (as in grading on a curve). The third possible assumption is that individual learners have no effect on each other, as might be the case for learners studying a subject independently from an organized class or through a correspondence course. Social interdependence theory, Johnson and Johnson suggest, predicts the following possible outcomes depending upon the assumptions established at the beginning of the learning activity (see table 2.1).

Note that Johnson and Johnson do not suggest that every individualistic learning activity results in those outcomes listed in table 2.1. They do, however, suggest an overall recognition of learning as a social activity that builds healthy perspectives in contrast to a view of learning as a competitive or isolating activity that reinforces more negative patterns of behavior.

Johnson and Johnson (1998) also note two elements that greatly enhance the learning outcomes of class members in cooperative learning settings: trust and controversy. Trust among learners must be present before controversy yields a positive result, however. In an overall comparative analysis of learning outcomes that involved meta-analysis of more than 375 similar studies of social interdependence theory conducted between 1898 and 1989, Johnson and Johnson found that the average person cooperating performed at about two-thirds of a standard deviation above the average person learning within a competitive or individualistic situation (effect size = 0.64). Although quality of the studies varied, this meta-analysis of research suggests con-

Table 2.1.
Social Interdependence Theory

Process	Cooperative	Competitive	Individualistic
Interdependence	Positive	Negative	None
Interaction Pattern	Promotive	Oppositional	None
Outcome 1	High Effort to Achieve	Low Effort to Achieve	Low Effort to Achieve
Outcome 2	Positive Relationships	Negative Relationships	No Relationships
Outcome 3	Psychological Health	Psychological Illness	Psychological Pathology

Source: Johnson and Johnson 1998. Used with permission.

firmation of the value of a social, collaborative, interactive approach to learning.

Clearly such an approach is inconsistent with the lecture mode of teaching that dominates universities today. And equally, it is inconsistent with much of what is currently labeled as distance education, which is often no more than the singular experience of an individual learner acting in isolation from other learners and is often even largely independent of the instructor.[1] The challenge for colleges and universities is not to cling to a model such as the lecture, which frequently disengages students from each other, their own feelings and experiences, and immediate applications of content. Nor is the challenge to latch onto a trend of totally independent learning via the Web, whose opponents claim it will be the 'death knell of the faculty.' What uni-

[1]   Brown (1998) states: "Yet this last point suggests an interesting challenge and perhaps outlines the most crucial next step. Washington State University has been using the Flashlight CSI to generate solid evidence suggesting that the most effective uses of technologies occur when relationships between learners and technologies encourage, at least in part, activities and experiences that rely on meetings with facilitators and collaborations with peers. This evidence runs contrary to many advocates of models of education that envision remote learners working efficiently, independently, and entirely in their own time and at their own pace."

versities must do in the twenty-first century is build a new learning environment, one that intentionally and systematically:

- connects learners with each other and with mentors and teachers;
- connects this learning with experience;
- takes advantage of a wealth of accessible information and knowledge available through new technologies.

The intent of creating such an environment, whether through an individual course or a degree program or an entire institution, is to enable engaged learners to pursue their quest for knowledge. The effect is to create learning environments that must be centered around the learner rather than the teacher, or even worse, the institution, in several important ways.

The challenge for colleges and universities is to model this approach in existing traditional classrooms, and, important to people who need to learn throughout a lifetime, to explore how technology can be used to engage and support learners in multiple contexts, cultures, and schedules.

Learning Environments for the Future

Many teachers are actively creating new learning environments that respond to these challenges. Chickering and Gamson (1991) and Chickering and Ehrmann (1996) define seven principles of good teaching practice as a framework for organizing these new learning environments. Positive learning environments:

1. encourage student-faculty contact;
2. encourage cooperation among students;
3. encourage active learning;
4. give prompt feedback;
5. emphasize time on task;
6. communicate high expectations;
7. respect diverse talents and ways of learning.

Multiple theoretical frameworks — especially those organized within the previously discussed constructivist theoretical framework — have emerged to describe environments that foster these characteristics. Terms such as collaborative learning, cooperative learning, problem-based learning, communities of practice, and learning communities are coming into the common lexicon of the classroom. Other terms, such as interactive learning, team learning, discourse communities, and case teaching, are also frequently used. While each term carries with it subtle differences in approach, all of these categories of learning environments share a common purpose relative to the classroom: they imply the purposeful creation of an active, engaged learning environment.

As Parker Palmer (1998, 90) has eloquently and simply described such a space, with a clear goal in mind for teachers, "To teach is to create a space in which the community of truth is practiced." According to Palmer, such a teaching and learning space, which engages learner and teacher collaboratively and communicatively, should:

- be bounded and open;
- be hospitable and charged;
- invite the voice of the individual and the voice of the group;
- honor the "little" stories of the students and the "big" stories of the disciplines and tradition;
- support solitude and surround it with the resources of community;
- welcome both silence and speech.

The remainder of this chapter examines in greater detail several major constructivist approaches to creating active and engaging learning environments.

Collaborative and Cooperative Learning

Collaborative and cooperative learning share a number of basic assumptions about learning (Matthews et al. 1997):

1. Learning in an active mode is more effective than passively receiving information; the teacher is a facilitator, coach, or midwife rather than a "sage on the stage."

2. Teaching and learning are shared experiences between teacher and students.

3. Balancing lecture and small-group activities is an important part of a teacher's role.

4. Participating in small-group activities develops higher-order thinking skills and enhances individual abilities to use knowledge.

5. Accepting responsibility for learning as an individual and as a member of a group enhances intellectual development.

6. Articulating his or her ideas in a small-group setting enhances the student's ability to reflect on his or her own assumptions and thought processes.

7. Developing social and team skills through the give and take of consensus building is a fundamental part of a liberal education.

8. Belonging to a small, supportive academic community increases student success and retention.

9. Appreciating (or at least acknowledging the value of) diversity is essential for the survival of a multicultural democracy.

According to Panitz and Panitz (1998), collaborative learning is a personal philosophy, not just a classroom technique. It suggests a way of dealing with people that respects and highlights individual group members' abilities and contributions. Authority and responsibility among group members are shared, and all are equally responsible for the group's actions.

Underlying collaborative learning is the belief that students learn best in social interactions based upon consensus building and cooperation rather than competition, which pits each learner against all other learners:

> Collaborative learning is related to social construction in that it assumes learning occurs among persons rather than between a person and things. Some teachers who have adopted social constructionist assumptions have found that they understand better what they are trying to do and, understanding better, have a better chance of doing it well (Bruffee 1986, 787).

The role of the teacher in creating a positive and orderly learning environment is different than in traditional, lecture-dominated modes of instruction. According to Flannery (1994, 22):

> Collaborative learning requires an authoritative instructional presence if it is to be successful. However, the role of the teacher in exercising such authority is substantially different from his or her role when using didactic teaching strategies. For collaborative learning, instructors must set up the process and facilitate its operation. ... Once groups are operating, the instructor may also need to draw on his or her knowledge of the discipline to guide group inquiry. However, this knowledge needs to be used as a basis for posing investigatory or generative questions, not for supplying the "correct" answers to students' inquiries.

In summary, collaborative learning relies heavily upon the input, direction, and shaping of content by learners. It is this feature that perhaps most distinguishes it from cooperative learning instructional approaches, which assumes a more assertive and directive role for the teacher.

Cooperative learning is often defined as students working together in groups to achieve joint learning, while being *organized and monitored by a teacher* (Johnson, Johnson, and Holubec 1992). Myers (1991) illustrates this subtle but fundamental difference in the role of the teacher and the relative emphasis on the product compared with the process, pointing out that the definition of "collaboration," derived from its Latin root, focuses on the process of working together; the root word for "cooperation" emphasizes the product of such work. Cooperative learning emanates from the philosophical writings of John Dewey, stressing the social nature of learning and the work on group dynamics by Kurt Lewin. Collaborative learning has British roots, based on the work of English teachers exploring ways to help students respond to literature by taking a more active role in their own learning. The cooperative learning tradition tends to use quantitative methods that look at achievement: i.e., the product of learning. The collaborative tradition takes a more qualitative approach, analyzing student talk in response to a piece of literature or a primary source in history.

To summarize these subtle differences in greater detail, collaborative and cooperative learning are dissimilar to a degree in the following ways (Matthews et al. 1997):

- the style, function, and degree of involvement of the teacher;

- the issue of authority and power relationships between teacher and students;

- the extent to which students need to be trained to work together in groups;

- the way knowledge is assimilated or constructed;

- the purpose of groups to emphasize different outcomes, such as the mastery of facts, the development of judgment, and/or the construction of knowledge;

- the importance of different aspects of personal, social, and/or cognitive growth among students; and a variety of additional implementation concerns, including, for example, group formation and task construction;

- the degree of individual and/or group accountability necessary to ensure equitable distribution of work and accurate grading.

To elaborate on these differences, collaborative learning is generally less dependent upon authority, more likely to enable group decision making independent of the instructor, and more flexible in accommodating the interests and preferences of students.

Despite these differences, cooperative learning and collaborative learning are clearly closer together in theoretical foundation and execution than either is with the more content-driven, lecture-based approach. An analysis of similarities between collaborative and cooperative learning and comparisons with a more traditional lecture format are displayed in table 2.2.

Despite these differences, cooperative and collaborative learning provide systematic models for approaching the classroom though the lens of the learner.

Problem-Based Learning

Problem-based learning is a form of cooperative learning that organizes group learning around a structured problem created by the instructor. It shares many fundamental assumptions with both collaborative and cooperative learning, including the idea that learning is a constructive process and that social and contextual factors influence learning (Gijselaers 1996).

Problem-based learning is usually very structured, and it often involves group learning and discussion activities designed to yield a "correct" solution or answer to the problem. As such, while problem-based learning involves teamwork, cooperation, and collaboration, its structure always implies a prominent role for the teacher both in developing the problem and in assessing the performance of the teams or groups addressing the problem. According to Wilkerson (1995), high-quality problem-based learning environments are led by teachers who:

- balance student direction with assistance;
- contribute knowledge and experience;
- create a pleasant learning environment;
- stimulate critical evaluation of ideas.

Table 2.2.
Comparative Framework for Collaborative, Cooperative,
and Lecture Formats for Learning

Collaborative Learning ➤ Cooperative Learning ➤	Traditional Lecture-Formats
Learner-centered ➤ ➤ ➤	teacher-centered
intrinsic learner motivation ➤ ➤ ➤	extrinsic learner motivation
knowledge construction ➤ ➤ ➤	knowledge transmission
loose, trusting students to do ➤ ➤ ➤	structured, do it right, social engineering

Adapted with permission from *Collaborative Versus Cooperative Learning* (Panitz 1995)

The teacher closely monitors, but does not interfere with, student efforts to address a problem. He or she is readily available to act as a consultant when assistance is requested.

Defining the problem appropriately and effectively is critical for learning to occur (Stinson and Milter 1996). Useful problems are those that cross disciplinary boundaries, are authentic and found in professional practice, and are contemporary in nature. Given this definition, it should be no surprise to find that problem-based learning is often employed in professional fields such as medicine, business, and law; however, it is increasingly employed as well in a range of disciplines to help students think creatively beyond the boundaries of the classroom.

The overall intent of problem-based learning is to produce students who will:

- engage a challenge (problem, complex task, situation) with initiative and enthusiasm;
- reason effectively, accurately and creatively from an integrated, flexible, usable knowledge base;
- monitor and assess their own adequacy to achieve a desirable outcome given a challenge;

- address their own perceived inadequacies in knowledge and skills efficiently and effectively;
- collaborate effectively as a member of a team working to achieve a common goal.

Problem-based learning is clearly constructivist in theoretical origin in that it requires learners to play a role in deciding what will be learned. It also demands a different role for instructors than the one they have in traditional, lecture-style classrooms. However, its reliance on problems organized and selected by the instructor places it somewhat apart from more student-initiated collaborative and team approaches to learning.

Learning Communities

Learning communities are intentionally created environments for learning that bridge courses, programs, academic departments, or living facilities to create a joint quest for learning among members and participants. Through the intentional creation of a safe psychological climate or a space for learning, learners with different backgrounds, ethnicities, religions, or other characteristics are able to learn from each other intensively and cooperatively. Learning communities can help to integrate fragmented curricula, build social and team skills, reduce boredom and attrition rates from courses and institutions, and validate the worth of each as a person and learner (Gardiner 1994).

Learning communities are generally developed at a curriculum level and are unique in that they cross over traditional academic boundaries such as courses, departments, and faculty members. As a result, learning communities emphasize the value of differences, and they are frequently less structured and more informal opportunities for sharing ideas and perspectives rather than the formal systematic learning opportunities.

Communities of Practice

Creating *communities of practice* is an increasingly common approach to developing positive learning environments, especially for professionals who need to keep up with current ideas, knowledge, and applications in a field or discipline. This approach views learning as an act of membership in a community of common interests. Beginning with an understanding of the structure of communities and how to create learning opportunities within communities, communities of practice are based on the following assumptions (On Purpose Associates 1998), all of which are derived from constructivist learning theory:

- Learning is social in nature. People organize their learning around the social communities to which they belong. Therefore, schools are only powerful learning environments for students whose social communities coincide with that school.

- Knowledge is integrated in the life of communities that share values, beliefs, languages, and ways of doing things — called communities of practice. Real knowledge is integrated in the doing, social relations, and expertise of these communities.

Communities of practice are increasingly created and utilized by professional associations and others interested in fostering access to new knowledge emerging from practice. Within a community of practice, the processes of learning and membership are intertwined. It is presumed that one joins a community of practice in order to learn, and it is that goal that sustains the learner's membership in the community. It is the goal of the community of practice as a whole to anticipate and respond to learner needs. Knowledge is integrated with practice. Knowing in a community of practice involves the interaction between doing and knowing, and learning is the result of doing. As the Chinese proverb states, "I hear, and I forget; I see, and I remember; I do, and I understand."

Within communities of practice all are learners, and all have the opportunity and the ability to contribute to the knowledge of the community and to the learning of its members. Because learning is connected with action, the consequences of successful learning are immediate, real, and powerful. And because people are social and are involved in communities of practice broadly conceived, technology offers many possibilities for connecting more effectively the communities of practice that people are already involved with. It also offers the opportunity to build new learning communities of practice across distances.

What Do We Know from Research?

Collaborative, cooperative, and team-based learning are often viewed as appropriate for small seminars in the social sciences and humanities, in which "there are no right answers" to the problems and issues being discussed. But these approaches are often assumed to be inappropriate for larger classes or for classes in science and technology-oriented subjects. However, more than seventy comparative research studies on cooperative learning, conducted primarily since 1970, show that, across all subjects, cooperative learning generally produces better learning results, both immediate and longer term, than do competitive or individual approaches (Johnson and Johnson 1993). Johnson and Johnson (1993) also found that these results "held for verbal tasks (such as reading, writing, and orally presenting), mathematical tasks, and procedural tasks (such as swimming, golf, and tennis)."

> Cooperative learning promotes greater motivation to learn, more frequent use of cognitive processes such as reconceptualization, higher-level reasoning, metacognition, cognitive elaboration, and networking, and greater long-term maintenance of the skills learned.

They also found that greater levels of trust and better personal relationships among learners were developed, even among students from different ethnic, cultural, language, social class, ability, and gender groups. According to Johnson and Johnson, the benefits of utilizing cooperative learning approaches are many[2], the most significant being that the use of collaborative

---

[2] According to Johnson and Johnson (1993), cooperative learning groups also provide a setting in which students can (a) construct and extend conceptual understanding of what is being learned through explanations and discussion; (b) use shared mental models learned in flexible ways to solve problems jointly; (c) receive interpersonal feedback as to how well the procedures are performed; (d) receive social support and encouragement to take risks in increasing one's competencies; (e) be held accountable by peers to practice and practice until the procedures and skills being taught are overlearned; (f) acquire attitudes (such as continuous improvement) needed to refine the procedures learned; (g) establish a shared identity with other group members; and (h) observe the most outstanding group members as behavioral models to be emulated.

groups promotes the simultaneous learning of both academic and teamwork skills. In addition, Michaelson et al. (1982) found that a major benefit of developing learning teams and collaborative learning strategies is that these strategies can actually be used to offset many of the disadvantages of large classes. Moreover, Kurfiss (1988) found that developing and using learning teams or collaborative learning is an excellent means of building students' higher-level cognitive skills in large classes.

Individual learners vary in their preferred mode of learning, and teachers at all levels must take this variation into account. Nevertheless, collaborative, interactive environments demonstrate many positive outcomes that simply do not present themselves in more isolated and individual learning situations.

The Role of Technology in Creating Collaborative Environments

With no more than twenty-five years of experience in the use of technology to create collaborative learning environments (Woolley 1994), we are only beginning to explore how technology can build more effective collaborative learning environments. Recent developments with computer conferencing software linked to the Web environment are especially promising in their possibilities (Gilbert 1995). To restate the task before us in relation to learning technologies, the challenge is not simply to incorporate learning technologies into current instructional approaches, but rather to change our fundamental views about effective teaching and learning and to use technology to do so, as Schmidt and Olcott elaborate upon in chapter 12. Privateer (1999, 64) frames this challenge very well:

> One suggestion for carving out a different strategic path is to think of instructional technologies as tools for re-engineering and reinventing curriculum. By making us rethink the relationship between new pedagogical forms (e.g., learning as collaborative, application-driven instances of constructivist, impasse, discovery, or problem-based cognitive theories) and new ways of justifying their costs, instructional technologies can play a vital role in creating a new mythology for higher education.

In essence, how can computer- and telecommunication-mediated instruction assist colleges and universities in reinventing themselves as "virtual" and "real" places in which students can transcend outmoded ways of gathering information to become new kinds of learners, driven by the desire to use their intelligence to solve problems?

According to Privateer (1999, 68), to be truly a revolutionary force in higher education, academic technologies should:

- be deployed in new kinds of academic environments driven by a real understanding of change;

- reflect an understanding of the underlying catalysts for this change;

- be driven by an understanding of how new digital technologies require radically new and different notions of pedagogy.

Hanna and Conceição-Runlee (1999) describe a course built around collaborative and team learning that utilizes computer conferencing to create multiple opportunities for collaboration. According to Hanna and Conceição-Runlee, a major challenge for the future is whether or not technology can truly compensate for the significant advantages of face-to-face environments for collaboration, which many believe to be necessary to overcome feelings of separation and to build trust — a condition widely recognized as necessary for establishing the environment required for collaborative learning.

In a time of rapid change, when technology offers many more capabilities for accessing information than ever before, it seems ironic that perhaps the greatest challenge for technology is one of enabling people to communicate with each other as if they were physically present with one another.

Teamwork in Virtual Environments

The discussion of constructivist learning environments in this chapter is predicated on the assumption that individuals learn best not only through designing their own learning experiences within the context of an organized learning experience, but also in situations that involve others in pursuit of a common goal. This collaborative learning context is often created in virtual environments through collaborative team-based activities and team-based learning (Hanna and Conceição-Runlee 1999). According to Hanna and Conceição-Runlee, the goals of team-based learning include:

- integrating personal values, beliefs, and attitudes into course experiences in a manner that enables authentic, engaged learning;

- building leadership, facilitation, and problem-solving skills necessary to contribute positively and productively to organizational life;

- applying content in real and imaginative ways to problems or issues that learners may find personally interesting or challenging.

While these goals are common to both physical and virtual environments, some special and critical challenges emerge for team-based learning in virtual environments, including the following (Hanna and Conceição-Runlee 1999):

- variations in student interest and readiness to use technology;

- variations in student interest and readiness to work in teams;

- creating trust and collegiality in virtual, communication-rich environments;

- building trust among team members at the onset of the course;

- maintaining collaborative work groups throughout the course.

Summary

A major challenge for universities in the knowledge age is to transform instruction from a teacher-centered, discipline-based approach in which information is disseminated to one that is student-centered, collaborative, and interdisciplinary. This change is required for students to gain the skills necessary to live and work in a rapidly changing economy.

Among the skills that are developed in collaborative environments (Bosworth 1994) are interpersonal skills; group building/management skills; inquiry skills; conflict prevention, management, and resolution skills; presentation skills.

These benefits accompany the positive effect of social interaction in promoting individual learning of content within collaborative environments (Johnson and Johnson 1989; Light 1990).

Such a transition toward collaborative or cooperative learning will be difficult for faculty to accomplish and for institutions to support adequately. Faculty reluctance to adopt collaborative learning as an instructional approach is reflected in the following very real concerns (Gunawardena 1992; Panitz and Panitz 1998):

- loss of control in the classroom;
- lack of self-confidence among teachers;
- fear of the loss of content coverage;
- lack of prepared materials for use in class;
- teachers' egos;
- lack of familiarity with alternative assessment techniques;
- concern with teacher evaluation and personal advancement;
- students' resistance to collaborative learning techniques;
- lack of familiarity with collaborative learning techniques;
- lack of teacher training in collaborative teaching methods;
- lack of familiarity with alternative student assessment techniques.

The nature of these fears suggests that much time and energy and substantial resources will be required to accomplish the transition described in this chapter. The role of new learning technologies, widely thought of by many as simply tools for distributing information and knowledge more effectively and efficiently rather than as organizational and communications pathways to achieve greater cooperation and collaboration among learners and teachers, will also need to be reconsidered (Privateer 1999). As Bruffee (1993, 186) states:

> ...[A]ppropriate use of any educational technology requires giving up foundational assumptions and integrating technology with social relationships. Television and microcomputation can fulfill their educational promise only if we exploit their potential as mediators of intellectually constructive, educationally productive social relations: collaborative learning.

It is this promise that recent developments with the World Wide Web and in advanced communications capabilities which will allow colleges and universities that are willing to take the risk to embrace learning technologies in their efforts to transform themselves.

REFERENCES

Andrew Mellon Foundation. 1998. *Initiative on the cost-effectiveness of technology in teaching* [Website]. Andrew Mellon Foundation, 28 December. Available from < http://www.mellon.org/cutt.html >.

Bonwell, Charles, C., and James A. Eison. 1991. *Active learning: Creating excitement in the classroom.* Washington, DC: George Washington University, School of Education and Human Development.

Bosworth, Kris. 1994. Developing collaborative skills in college students. In *Collaborative Learning: Underlying Processes and Effective Techniques,* edited by Kris Bosworth and Sharon J. Hamilton. San Francisco, CA: Jossey-Bass, Publishers.

Boyer, Ernest L. 1990. *Scholarship reconsidered: Priorities of the professoriate.* Princeton, NJ: Carnegie Foundation for the Advancement of Teaching.

Brown, Gary. 1998. *Flashlight at Washington State University* [Website]. Available at < http://www.ctl.wsu.edu/resources/publications/flcases.htm >.

Bruffee, Kenneth A. 1986. Social construction, language, and the authority of knowledge. *College English* 48(8): 773-790.

Bruffee, Kenneth A. 1993. *Collaborative learning: Higher education, interdependence, and the authority of knowledge.* Baltimore: Johns Hopkins University Press.

Chickering, Arthur W., and Stephen Ehrmann. 1996. Implementing the seven principles: Technology as lever. *AAHE Bulletin* (October): 3-6.

Chickering, Arthur W., and Zelda F. Gamson. 1991. *Applying the seven principles for good practice in undergraduate education.* San Francisco: Jossey-Bass, Publishers.

Dewey, John. 1916. *Democracy and education: An introduction to the philosophy of education.* New York: Macmillan.

Flannery, James L. 1994. Teacher as co-conspirator: Knowledge and authority in collaborative learning. In *Collaborative learning: Underlying processes and effective techniques,* edited by Kris Bosworth and Sharon J. Hamilton. San Francisco: Jossey-Bass, Publishers.

Gardiner, Lion F. 1994. *Redesigning higher education: Producing dramatic gains in student learning.* Washington, DC: Association for the Study of Higher Education, ERIC Clearinghouse on Higher Education.

Gijselaers, Wim H. 1996. Connecting problem-based practices with educational theory. In *Bringing problem-based learning to higher education: Theory and practice*, edited by LuAnn Wilkerson and Wim H. Gijselaers. San Francisco: Jossey-Bass, Publishers.

Gilbert, Steven W. 1995. Teaching, learning and technology. *Change* 27(2): 20-27.

Gunawardena, Charlotte N. 1992. Changing faculty roles for audiographics and online teaching. *The American Journal of Distance Education* 6(3): 59-71.

Hanna, Donald E., and Simone Conceição-Runlee. 1999. Building learning teams through computer-mediated conferencing. *Journal of Family Sciences,* forthcoming issue.

Johnson, David W., and Roger T. Johnson. 1989. *Cooperation and competition: Theory and research.* Edina, MN: Interaction Book Company.

Johnson, David W., and Roger T. Johnson. 1993. *What we know about cooperative learning at the college level* [Website]. Instructional Innovation Network. Available from < http://bestpractice.net/ccl/models/what weknow.html >.

Johnson, David W., and Roger T. Johnson. 1998. *Cooperative learning and social interdependence theory: Social psychological applications to social issues* [Website]. University of Minnesota. Available from < http://www.clcrc.com/pages/SIT.html >.

Johnson, David W., Roger T. Johnson, and Edythe Holubec. 1992. *Advanced cooperative learning.* 2nd ed. Edina, MN: Interaction Book Company.

Johnson, David W., Roger T. Johnson, and Edythe Holubec. 1993. *Circles of learning: Cooperation in the classroom.* 4th ed. Edina, MN: Interaction Book Company.

Jones, Beau Fly, and Educational Resources Information Center. 1994. *Designing learning and technology for educational reform.* Oak Brook, IL [Washington, DC]: North Central Regional Educational Laboratory: U.S. Department of Education Office of Educational Research and Improvement Educational Resources Information Center.

Kurfiss, J. G. 1988. *Critical thinking: Theory, research, practice, and possibilities.* Washington, DC: The George Washington University, School of Education and Human Development.

Lambert, Linda, et al. 1995. *The constructivist leader.* New York: Teachers College Press.

Light, R.J. 1990. The Harvard assessment seminars: Explorations with students and faculty about teaching, learning, and student life. Cambridge, MA: Harvard University, Graduate School of Education.

Matthews, Roberta S., James L. Cooper, Neil Davidson, and Peter Hawkes. 1997. *Building bridges between cooperative and collaborative learning* [Website]. Instructional Innovation Network, 25 September

1997 [cited 7 April 1999]. Available from < http://bestpractice.net/ccl/ models/building.html >.

Mendels, Pamela. 1999. Can new technologies revitalize old teaching methods? [Web site]. *The New York Times,* 24 March. Available from < http://www.nytimes.com/library/tech/99/03/cyber/education/ 24education.html >.

Michaelsen, L. K., C. F. Jones, and W. E. Watson. 1993. Beyond groups and cooperation: Building high performance learning teams. In *To improve the academy: Resources for faculty, instructional and organizational development,* edited by D. L. Wright and J. P. Lunde. Stillwater, OK: New Forums Press Co.

Michaelsen, L. K., W. E. Watson, J. P. Cragin, and L. D. Fink. 1982. Team learning: A potential solution to the problems of large classes. *Exchange: The Organizational Behavior Teaching Journal* 7(1): 13-22.

Myers, John. 1991. Co-operative or collaborative learning? Towards a constructive controversy. *Cooperative Learning* 11(4): 19-20.

On Purpose Associates. 1998. *Communities of practice* [Website]. Funderstanding. Available from < http://www.funderstanding.com/ learning_theory_how9.html >.

Palmer, Parker. 1998. *The courage to teach: Exploring the inner landscape of a teacher's life.* San Francisco: Jossey-Bass, Publishers.

Panitz, Theodore. 1995. *Collaborative versus cooperative learning* [Website]. Available from < http://ericae.net/k12assess/ colcoo.htm >.

Panitz, Theodore, and Patricia Panitz. 1998. Encouraging the use of collaborative education in higher education. In *University teaching: International perspectives,* edited by James J. F. Forest. New York: Garland Publishing, Inc.

Primary Research Group. 1997. *Restructuring higher education: Cost containment and productivity enhancement efforts of North American colleges and universities.* New York: Primary Research Group.

Privateer, Paul Michael. 1999. Academic technology and the future of higher education: Strategic paths taken and not taken. *The Journal of Higher Education* 70(1): 60-79.

Smith, Robert McCaughan. 1990. *Learning to learn across the life span.* San Francisco: Jossey-Bass, Publishers.

Stinson, John E., and Richard G. Milter. 1996. Problem-based learning in business education: Curriculum design and implementation issues. In *Bringing problem-based learning to higher education: Theory and practice,* edited by LuAnn Wilkerson and Wim H. Gijselaers. San Francisco: Jossey-Bass, Publishers.

Vygotsky, Lev. 1962. *Thought and Language.* Cambridge, MA: MIT Press.

Whitehead, Alfred North. 1959. *The aims of education and other essays.* New York: Macmillan.

Wilkerson, LuAnn. 1995. Identification of skills for the problem-based tutor: Student and faculty perspectives. *Instructional Science* 23(4): 303-315.

Winn, William. 1997. *Learning in hyperspace* [Website]. University of Maryland University College. Available from < http://www.umuc. edu/ide/potentialweb97/winn.html >.

Woolley, David R. 1994. *PLATO: The emergence of online community* [Website]. Available from < http://thinkofit.com/plato/ dwplato.htm >.

Chapter 3

Advanced Technologies and Distributed Learning in Higher Education

By Chris Dede

This chapter depicts visions of how sophisticated information technologies may influence the nature of higher education over the next few decades. Its purpose is not to present predictions of an inevitable future, but instead to stimulate reflection upon how we can collectively evolve colleges and universities by creatively moving beyond almost unconscious assumptions we hold about teaching, learning, and schooling. The rapid advance of information technology is driving shifts in every other form of societal institution, in ways that often are unplanned and sometimes unfortunate. Hopefully, the academy can do better in influencing its own fate through deliberate choice and collaborative action to achieve the full educational potential of advanced computers and telecommunications.

Emerging Interactive Media

The development of the Internet is fostering the creation and proliferation of emerging interactive media, such as the World Wide Web and shared virtual environments. A medium is, in part, a channel for conveying content; as the Internet increasingly pervades society, university instructors can readily reach extensive, remote resources and audiences on demand, just in time. Just as important, however, a medium is a representational container enabling new types of messages (e.g., sometimes a picture is worth a thousand words). Since expression and communication are based on representations such as language and imagery, the process of learning is enhanced by broadening the types of instructional messages students and faculty can exchange (Dede 1996).

Below is a list of devices, media, and virtual contexts enabled by sophisticated information technologies, along with the author's estimates of a conservative time frame for their technological and economic feasibility (table 3.1). Even though no financial or technical barriers exist, note that many current capabilities are not yet widely used instructionally. University scholarship rapidly employs new knowledge-sharing media, but pedagogical and assessment practices in higher education are slow to alter their methods and approaches.

Later in this chapter, images of future learning situations will illustrate how these capabilities might be applied at various levels of schooling, shaping the students who enter higher education and altering the nature of colleges and universities.

The important issue for university instruction is not the availability and affordability of sophisticated computers and telecommunications, but the ways these devices enable powerful learning situations that aid students in extracting meaning out of complexity. New forms of representation (e.g., interactive models that utilize visualization and other means of making abstractions tangible and sensory) make possible a broader, more powerful repertoire of pedagogical strategies. Also, emerging interactive media empower novel types of learning experiences; for example, interpersonal interactions across networks can lead to the formation of virtual communities. As described in chapter 2, the innovative kinds of pedagogy enabled by these novel media make it possible to evolve university instruction beyond synchronous, group, presentation-centered forms of education, and beyond conventional "teaching by telling" and "learning by listening."

Below, "distributed learning" is discussed as a new form of interaction enabled by advanced information technologies and as a conceptual framework that could guide the evolution of higher

Table 3.1
Time Frame and Feasibility for Technology Acquisition

Functionality	Uses	Time Frame
Hypermedia (nonlinear traversal of multimedia information)	Interlinking of diverse subject matter; easier conceptual exploration; multiple simultaneous representations for learning	Current
Cognitive audit trails (automatic recording of user actions)	Support for finding patterns of suboptimal performance	Current
Computer-supported cooperative work (design, problem solving, decision support)	Facilitation of team task performance	Current
Intelligent tutors and coaches for restricted domains	Models of embedded expertise for greater individualization	Current
Optical-disc systems with multiple read/write and mixed media capabilities	Support of large databases; cheap secondary storage; shared distributed virtual environments	Current
Standardization of computer and telecommunications protocols	Easy connectivity, compatibility; lower costs	Current
User-specific, limited vocabulary voice recognition	Restricted natural language input	Current
High-quality voice synthesis	Auditor natural language output	Current
Sophisticated authoring and user interface management systems	Easier development of applications; reduced time for novices to master a program	Current
Widespread, high-bandwidth, fiberoptic networks	Massive real-time data exchange	3-5 years

Table 3.1

Time Frame and Feasibility for Technology Acquisition

Functionality	Uses	Time Frame
Fusion of computers, telecommunications	Easy interconnection; universal "information appliances"	3-5 years
Information "utilities" (synthesis of media, databases, and communications)	Access to integrated sources of data and tools for assimilation	3-5 years
Microworlds (limited alternate realities with user control over rules)	Experience in applying theoretical information in practical situations	3-5 years
Semi-intelligent computational agents embedded in applications	Support for user-defined independent actions	5-7 years
Advanced manipulatory input devices (e.g., gesture gloves with tactile feedback)	Mimetic learning that builds on real-world experience	5-7 years
Artificial realities (immersive, multisensory virtual worlds)	Intensely motivating simulation and virtual experience	7-10 years
"Information appliance" performance equivalent to current supercomputers	Sufficient power for simultaneous advanced functionalities	7-10 years
Consciousness sensors (input of user biofeedback into computer)	Monitoring of mood, state of mind	7-10 years
Artifacts with embedded semi-intelligence and wireless interconnections	Inclusion of smart devices in real-world settings	2010+

education. To illustrate the many possible variants of distributed learning, vignettes (images of plausible futures) are depicted exemplifying how the application of this framework might reshape teaching, learning, and the organization of educational institutions.

The objective of these vignettes is not to detail blueprints of an unalterable future, but instead to show the range of possibilities enabled by emerging interactive media, and the consequences — desirable or undesirable — that may flow from their application in pre-college and higher education settings. Such visions suggest decisions that academicians should make today to explore the potential of these technologies while minimizing unintended and negative outcomes of their use.

Distributed Learning

Distributed learning provides the conceptual framework that underlies the visions of higher education's future presented in this chapter. Distributed learning consists of educational activities orchestrated via information technology across classrooms, workplaces, homes, and community settings. It is based on a mixture of presentational and "constructivist" (guided inquiry, collaborative learning, and mentoring) pedagogies. Recent advances in "groupware" and experiential simulation enable guided, collaborative, inquiry-based learning even though students are in different locations and often are not online at the same time. With the aid of "tele-mentors," students can create, share, and master knowledge about authentic, real-world problems. Through a mixture of emerging instructional media, learners and educators can engage in synchronous or asynchronous interaction: face to face, in disembodied fashion, or as "avatars" expressing alternate forms of individual identity. Instruction and learning can occur across space, across time, and across multiple interactive media.

Below is a vignette that illustrates the types of distributed learning that elementary school students might routinely experience before they attend high school and college — if our society were to extensively implement current information technologies for educational purposes (Dede 1998).

"Take a deep breath," Maria told her mother, "then blow it out into the balloon." Deftly, as soon as her mother finished, Maria used a plastic clamp to pinch the neck of the special balloon, then measured its circumference.

"All done, Mama!" she said, writing down the number in her notebook. Her mother sneezed, then sank back on the couch with a smile of approval. Even though her sinuses ached — and that deep breath had not helped — she enjoyed helping Maria with her daily homework. After all, participating in the allergy study project not only involved her child more deeply in school, but also subsidized the Web-TV box that provided the family access to sports and entertainment Web sites.

Maria was navigating to the appropriate site, then logging her mother's lung-capacity figure into the national database. Her little brother watched, fascinated by the colored visualizations displaying the complex ecological, meteorological, and pollution factors that predicted today's likely allergic responses in Maria's region.

Maria's teacher, Ms. Grosvenor, was also sighing a deep breath at that moment, but not into a balloon. While eating a Ho-Ho for breakfast, she was using her home computer to access a different part of the allergy study Web site, a section with guidance for teachers about how to cover today's classroom lesson on regional flora. Her preservice education a decade ago had provided some background in ecology, but — now that fifth-grade students were mastering material she had not learned until the end of high school — Ms. Grosvenor frequently used the Web site to update her knowledge about allergenic plants. Sometimes the sophisticated, multi-level model scientists and doctors were developing, made possible by micro-regional data supplied by learners all across the country, made her head ache for reasons other than sinuses! On the other hand, at least the students were quite involved in this set of science activities. Discussions in the "Teachers' Forum" of the Web site reaffirmed her own feeling that most teachers would rather have the small hassle of keeping up with new ideas than the constant struggle of trying to motivate students to learn boring lessons.

At the same time, in her elementary school's computer lab Consuela was threading her way through a complex maze. Of course, the maze was not in the lab but in the "Narnia" MUVE (a text-based, Multi-User Virtual Environment developed around the stories by C.S. Lewis). Her classmates and fellow adventurers Joe and Fernando were "with" her, utilizing their Web-TV connections at their homes, as was her mentor, a small bear named Oliver (in reality, a high school senior interested in mythology who assumed the role of a Pooh-like "avatar" in the virtual world of the MUVE).

Mr. Curtis, the school principal, watched bemused from the doorway. How different things were in 2009, he thought — students scattered across grade levels and dispersed across the city, yet all together in a shared, fantasy-based learning environment a full hour before school even starts! (The school building opens at the crack of dawn to enable lab-based Web use by learners like Consuela, whose family has no access at home.)

"The extra effort is worth it," thought Mr. Curtis. Seven years into the technology initiative, student motivation was high (increased attendance, learners involved outside of school hours), and parents were impressed by the complex material and sophisticated skills their children were mastering. Even standardized test scores — which measured only a fraction of what was really happening — were rising. Most important, young girls such as Consuela were more involved with school. Because of their culture, Hispanic girls had been very reluctant to approach adult authority figures, like teachers, but the MUVE had altered that by providing a "costume party" environment in which, wearing the "mask" of technology, children's and teachers' avatars could mingle without cultural constraints.

"I wonder what this generation will be like in high school — or college!" mused Mr. Curtis.

This vignette depicts how some students who are silent and passive in classroom settings may "find their voice" in an interactive medium. Even the best instructor, expert in facilitating discussion, knows that a substantial percentage of students will "lurk" in face-to-face interactions in groups. These learners are awake and listening, but they do not become actively involved unless forced to do so — and then they relapse into silent observation. Such students may be shy, prefer time to reflect before answering, or feel at a disadvantage because of gender, race, physical appearance, disabilities, or a lack of linguistic fluency. That face-to-face learning may be "half a loaf" for some participants although it helps to explain why many residential college students have chosen to take advantage of their campus's distance education offerings, much to the surprise of the faculty, who see face-to-face teaching as the best possible medium. Beyond the simplistic visual/auditory/kinesthetic/symbolic categorization of learning styles, much research is needed to understand the opportunities that emerging interactive media offer students who are disenfranchised by face-to-face interaction (Dede 1999a).

The previous vignette depicting elementary pupils engaged in distributed learning invites a question: in the next decade, what types of educational technologies might some secondary students experience before college (Dede 1995a)? The following scenario illustrates a possible pre-college student experience:

> In a rural area about sixty miles from the city, Karen, a high school student, sits down at her information appliance (a notepad device with the power of today's supercomputers), currently configured as an electronics diagnosis/repair training device. When sign-in is complete, the device acknowledges her readiness to begin Lesson 12: "Teamed Correction of Malfunctioning Communications Sensor." Her "knowbot" (a machine-based agent) establishes a telecommunications link to Phil, her partner in the exercise, who is sitting at a similar device in his suburban home thirty miles away.
>
> "Why did I have the bad luck to get paired with this clown?" she thinks, noting the vacant expression on his

face in the video window. "He probably spent last night partying instead of preparing for the lesson."

A favorite saying of the faculty member to whom she is apprenticed flits through her mind: "The effectiveness of computer-supported cooperative work can be severely limited by the team's weakest member."

"Let's begin," Karen says decisively. "I'll put on the DataArm (a manipulatory device that incorporates force-feedback to its user) to find and remove the faulty component. You use the hypertext database to locate the appropriate repair procedure."

Without giving Phil time to reply, she puts on her head-mounted display, brings up an AR (artificial reality) depicting the interior of a TransStar communications groundstation receiver, and begins strapping on the DataArm. The reality engine's meshing of computer graphics and video images presents a near-perfect simulation, although moving too rapidly causes objects to blur slightly. Slowly, she grasps a microwrench with her "hand" on the screen and begins to loosen the first fastener on the amplifier's cover. Haptic feedback from the DataArm to her hand completes the illusion, and she winces as she realizes the bolt is rusty and will be difficult to remove without breaking.

Dr. Dunleavy, the community college vocational educator who serves as mentor to Karen and Phil, virtually monitors Karen's avatar as she struggles with opening the simulated device. He notes approvingly that she seems comfortable with the physical, hands-on parts of the job as well as the intellectual analysis; both sets of skills are important in a future engineer.

"Documenting a strong recommendation for Advanced Placement college credit via the Educational Testing Service will be easy in her case," he thinks, "but Phil is in danger of failing this unit. Maybe Ms. Tunbridge (the TransStar communications repair expert also serving as mentor for this experience) will offer him a job right out of high school, giving him some time to mature before he heads for college."

At his information appliance, Phil calls up the hypertext database for Electronics Repair. On the screen, a multi-colored, three-dimensional network of interconnections appears and begins to rotate slowly. Just looking at the knowledge web makes his eyes hurt. Since the screen resolution is excellent, he suspects that a lack of sleep is the culprit.

"Lesson 12," Phil says slowly, and a trail is highlighted in the network. He skims through a sea of stories, harvesting metaphors and analogies while simultaneously monitoring a small window in the upper-left-hand corner of the screen that is beginning to fill with data from the diagnostic sensors on Karen's DataArm.

Several paragraphs of text are displayed at the bottom of the screen. Phil ignores them. Since his learning style is predominantly visual and auditory rather than symbolic, he listens to the web as it vocalizes this textual material, and he watches a graphical pointer maneuver over a blueprint. Three figurines gesture near the top of the display, indicating that they know related stories. On the right-hand side of the monitor, an interest-based browser shows index entries grouped by issue, hardware configuration, and functional system.

Traversing the network at the speed Karen is working is difficult, given Phil's lack of sleep, and he makes several missteps. "Knowledge Base," Phil says slowly, "infer what the optical memory chip does to the three-dimensional quantum well superlattice."

The voice of his knowbot suddenly responds, "You seem to be assuming a sensor flaw when the amplifier may be the problem."

"Shut up!" thinks Phil, hitting the cutoff switch. He then groans as he visualizes his knowbot feeding the cognitive audit trail of his actions into the workstations of his mentors. He cannot terminate those incriminating records, and he cringes when he imagines his mentor's "avatar" delivering another lecture on his shortcomings. Mentally, Phil begins phrasing an elaborate excuse to send his instructors via e-mail at the end of the lesson.

For her part, Karen is exasperatedly watching the window on her AR display, where Phil's diagnostic responses should be appearing. "He's hopeless," she thinks.

Her knowbot's "consciousness sensor" (a biofeedback link that monitors user attention and mood) interrupts with a warning: "Your blood pressure is rising rapidly; this could trigger a migraine headache."

"Why," says Karen with a sigh, "couldn't I have lived in the age when students learned from textbooks?"

In a decade, entering college students who have experienced the types of distributed learning technologies described thus far are unlikely to be impressed by large lecture classes, multiple-choice tests, and sage-on-the-stage relationships with faculty. This will drive profound changes in higher education toward distributed learning.

Within a couple of decades, "distance education" may be an obsolete concept, as may the term "face-to-face education." Instead, all instruction within college and university settings will likely be a balance between classroom-based and distance-based learning interactions, as determined by subject matter, student population, and educational objectives. Such distributed learning demonstrates to students that education is integral to all aspects of life — not just schooling. This instructional approach also can build partnerships for learning among stakeholders in education (e.g., faculty and employers).

In the long run, distributed learning can potentially conserve scarce financial resources by maximizing the educational usage of information devices (e.g., televisions, computers, telephones, video games) in homes and workplaces. In addition, distributed learning enables shifts in the pattern of universities' investments. Less money is needed for physical infrastructure — buildings, parking lots — and more resources can go into ways of creating a virtual community for creating, sharing, and mastering knowledge.

Human and Organizational Challenges in Implementing Distributed Learning

Central to the effective utilization of advanced learning technologies via distributed learning is developing a reflective understanding of how each interactive medium shapes the cognitive, affective, and social interactions of participants. The creation, sharing, and mastery of knowledge is not simply an intellectual exercise; the emotional and psychosocial dimensions of learning are very important as well. Advanced interactive media enable an extraordinary range of cognitive, affective, and social "affordances" (enhancements of human capabilities) of great power for distributed learning — while at the same time also potentially limiting students' and instructors' expression and communication.

Much study is needed to develop the new kinds of rhetoric necessary to make these emerging media effective for learning and to design distributed learning environments appropriate to specific groups of learners for particular types of content and a given set of educational goals. While a great deal is known about instructional design in classroom settings to facilitate affective and social interactions, many emerging media are so new that little is understood about the emotional and collaborative affordances they provide — and lack. Understanding social, psychological, and emotional differences between how humans interact in physical environments compared with virtual environments, in which many direct sensory experiences can only be simulated or imagined, is critical for developing effective learning environments using advanced technologies.

The vignette that follows presents a deliberately dystopian portrayal of how emerging information technologies, if unreflectively applied, could enrich some aspects of higher education while also exacerbating some of its weaknesses (Dede 1995b). The scenario depicts the daily routine of a faculty member a couple of decades from now and illustrates some potential implications for colleges and universities of artifacts with embedded intelligence. (The ideas and situations in this image of the future draw heavily on a scenario developed by Weiser [1991].) The purpose of this image of the future is not to predict how colleges and universities will evolve, but instead to illustrate the types of smart devices that will permeate society in the future and some instructional capabilities that they will enable:

> Vesper is driving to work through heavy rush-hour traffic. She is a faculty member in computational engineering at a university located far from her home in the suburbs. Despite the long drive, the position was irresistible because the campus is noted for its usage of advanced networking technologies. She glances in the foreview mirror to check the traffic. (Commuters' automobiles are hooked into a large network that uses data sent by cars and highway sensors to monitor and coordinate the flow of traffic. The foreview mirror presents a graphic display of what is happening up to five miles in front of her car on Vesper's planned route to work.)

> Noticing a traffic slowdown ahead, Vesper taps a button on the steering column to check for alternate routes that might be faster. A moment later, she cancels the request for rerouting as the foreview mirror reveals the green icon of a food shop on a side street near the next exit from the freeway. The foreview mirror helps her find a parking space quickly, and she orders a cup of coffee while waiting for the traffic jam to clear.

> While drinking her coffee, Vesper calls up some work on the screen of her information appliance. (This device has the approximate processing power of supercomputers a decade from now and is about the size of a notepad. It is linked via wireless networking and fiber-optic cable to a large web of other information appliances, including those at Vesper's campus.) The university's diagnostic expert system for debugging prototype ULSI designs can handle the routine misconceptions typical of most senior engineering majors, but it is occasionally stumped by an unusual faulty procedure that some learner has misgeneralized.

> At this point in history, a computer program trained to mimic human experts can handle many routine aspects

of evaluating student performance, but complex assessments still require human involvement.

Vesper has an uncanny ability to recognize exotic error patterns by quickly scanning a complex schematic. She diagnoses three sets of student misgeneralizations before resuming her trip to school. Her knowbot (a semi-intelligent agent) automatically sends this new "bug collection" to the national database on design misconceptions to be entered into its statistical records. Her knowbot also forwards her diagnoses to the university's expert system on ULSI design, which incorporates the new bugs into its knowledge base and begins preparing intelligent tutoring systems modules to correct those particular errors. Later that day, this instructional material will be forwarded to the appropriate learners' notepads to provide individualized remediation.

As Vesper walks into the engineering complex on campus, her personalized identity tab registers her presence on the university's net of security sensors. (In a clip-on badge displaying her picture and name, a small device is embedded that broadcasts information about Vesper's movements. Such an identity screening procedure is part of the university's security system. In this future world, these elaborate precautions have unfortunately become necessary.)

A moment later, the machines in Vesper's office initiate a log-in cycle in preparation for her arrival. She realizes that she has left her car unlocked, but she does not bother to retrace her steps; from her office, she can access the network to lock her car via a remote command.

As Vesper gets to her desk, the telltale by her door begins blinking, indicating that the department's espresso machine has finished brewing her cafe au lait. (A telltale is a remote signaling device that can be triggered to blink or make a sound, advising people in its vicinity of some event happening elsewhere.)

Vesper drinks a cup of cafe au lait every morning on arriving. She heads down the hall to get the coffee; the espresso maker's brew will be much better than the vile stuff she had consumed at the food shop. On returning to her office, she instructs her knowbot to remind her not to stop there again. A copy of her evaluation is automatically forwarded to the food shop's manager and to the local consumer ratings magazine.

In the hour before class, as her senior students "arrive," they congregate in their various engineering labs to work on projects for their exhibition portfolios. (Of course, many of these students are not physically located on Vesper's campus; instead the facilities used by her students are geographically scattered all over the world, linked via broadband communications.) Vesper will "join" them in about half an hour to begin instruction. She takes a break from viewing her videomail to "surveil" the students' activities on their individual notepads. Valerie is still dallying too long before getting down to work; Vesper will have to speak with her. Ricardo has not arrived at his engineering complex, but no message has come in to indicate why he is later than usual.

Skimming an engineering education journal, she notices a case study that resembles a problem student in one of her colleague's classes. His apprentice appears to have a rare type of learning disability that interferes with developing a spatial sense of geometric relationships, an important skill in his branch of engineering. Vesper sends an excerpt from the article to her colleague's machine with voicemail appended explaining its significance. She tends to avoid videomail, even though its greater bandwidth empowers more subtle shades of meaning. It is too much trouble to assume a professional demeanor just to send a simple message. The knowbot in her journal-reading application notes that she found the article useful and reinforces the pattern recognizers that triggered its selection.

A small light on the edge of Vesper's glasses begins blinking. A phone call is coming in; must be from someone not on the network. "Activate," says Vesper (the only word her glasses can recognize). A voice begins speaking in her ear; it is Ricardo's girlfriend, informing Vesper that Ricardo is sick again. With a sigh, Vesper makes a note to prepare hardcopy homework that will be sent off by snailmail — what a hassle! She will be glad when all governments finally recognize that home access to basic network services is a fundamental right, even if it does mean subsidizing subscriptions for the poor.

Across campus, two graduates of local high schools are waiting their turn for individual consultations at the Admissions Office. Both have equivalent, above-average transcripts and want to attend college in this city, but Nick has no money to offer beyond the minimum subsidy this state provides, while Elizabeth has $150,000 from her parents to use on her postsecondary education. Nick will be offered four years of predominantly large-group classes, most from other higher education institutions taught by lecture/discussion across distance or via computer-based training software. However, he will have some local seminar classes in his junior and senior year. The campus will arrange for an unpaid internship with a regional employer, and Nick will receive a degree from this university.

In contrast, due to her financial contribution, Elizabeth will be offered mostly small-group classes, predominantly local (although many fellow students in those classes will attend across distance, as in Vesper's instruction). Elizabeth will also have a tele-mentoring relationship with a nationally recognized expert in whatever major she chooses and a senior-year apprenticeship guaranteed with one of her top five choices of employers.

Down the hall, the president of the university chairs a meeting on the school's forthcoming re-accreditation. Since the last accreditation a decade ago, major shifts have occurred. Many students who enroll in this university's courses live outside this region and will graduate from other colleges, while most local students take the majority of their courses across distance from other institutions, then have these counted toward their graduation. Due to excellent teaching, strong scholarly reputations, and distributed collaborations with industry, faculty members are better paid and have smaller classes — they command high fees in the competitive national market for distance course enrollments. However, determining "institutional quality" in this situation is a little confusing to the group preparing for accreditation: How does one describe this type of distributed virtual organization? Who counts as students? faculty?

Before walking down to the lab to join her students, Vesper decides to have a conversation with her colleague Dimitri. Both received notifications last week about next year's salary. Vesper got a 15 percent raise because the spirited bidding nationally for the limited distance-based enrollments in her classes drove up the university's revenue and thus the teaching part of her wages. Unfortunately, the opposite happened to Dimitri; his salary dropped 10 percent, as comparable faculty across the country showed greater increases in research visibility, student performance outcomes, and learners' ratings of teaching performance. This led to reduced fees being paid by prospective applicants to his classes and lower wages for him. Vesper is trying to cheer up Dimitri by suggesting ways he can reverse this trend. Being subject to the laws of supply and demand is upsetting to both instructors, but that is the price of progress.

As discussed earlier, this vignette's purpose is not to suggest that Vesper's world is the only possible future for higher education, but instead to illustrate the types of smart devices that will permeate society in the future and the human and organizational capabilities — and challenges — they will enable.

Many readers may find the above vignette unattractive from an affective and ethical perspective. Vesper's environment may seem implausible. Why would a person choose to live in such a machine-centered environment, with so little direct human contact? But how would today's world of cellular phones, facsimiles, electronic mail, voicemail, and streaming audio and video have seemed two decades ago? Further, in this hypothetical future, the power of interactive learning media has resulted in a market-driven, survival-of-the-fittest climate in higher education (comparable to what has happened in many other economic sectors). Also, the vignette deliberately incorporates a high level of surveillance; instruction is individualized by monitoring students' activities and intervening if these activities do not match some predetermined pattern.

From my perspective as an educator, such an evolution would be unattractive. However, I deliberately incorporated some dystopian aspects into this vignette, including concerns about equitable educational services in an era of greater access via distributed learning, to underscore that the design of powerful technologies must be carefully considered to avoid unfortunate side-effects. Of course, artifacts with embedded intelligence could be incorporated into education without the types of behavioristic manipulation that I have crafted into this future depiction. Whether the market-driven and inegalitarian impacts can be avoided is less clear. However, since other distributed learning vignettes in this chapter are optimistic portrayals, interjecting some pessimism into this vision seemed a good way to balance the scenarios and remove any "gee whiz" veneer on how emerging technologies will influence higher education.

Conclusion

The National Science Foundation (NSF) is currently studying how distributed learning communities aid in conducting research (Dede 1999b). Two years ago, NSF instituted a new multidisciplinary funding program to examine the potential of emerging information technologies in fostering "Knowledge and Distributed Intelligence" (KDI). This initiative [see http://www.ehr.nsf.gov/kdi/default.htm] was prompted by fundamental shifts that new interactive media are creating in the process of science. Scientists are moving away from investigative strategies based on reading others' research results in journal publications as a means of informing and guiding one's own scholarship. Instead, many scientists are engaged in virtual communities for creating, sharing, and mastering knowledge: exchanging real-time data, deliberating alternative interpretations of that information, using collaboration tools to discuss the meaning of findings, and collectively evolving new conceptual frameworks.

NSF calls this process "knowledge networking" and is funding a series of KDI investigations to study these virtual communities both in the context of science and as a generalizable process that could enhance many forms of reflective human activity. Through knowledge networking, an emergent intelligence appears in which the virtual community develops a communal memory and wisdom that surpasses the individual contributions of each participant. NSF is supporting studies of this process through its "Learning and Intelligent Systems" (LIS) initiative within KDI.

For example, Marcia Linn at the University of California-Berkeley is leading Project SCOPE: Science Controversies Online: Partnerships in Education. This project promotes knowledge networking among scientists and learners exploring current scientific controversies that connect to citizens' interests (such as evidence of life on Mars). The project's research combines expertise in natural science, pedagogy, technology, and classroom instruction from the University of California-Berkeley, the University of Washington, and the American Association for the Advancement of Science's *Science* magazine. Both national and international partners are involved in the distributed learning experiences. The investigators are creating new media as needed and using existing knowledge-sharing applications (for example, Linn's Knowledge Integration Environment [KIE] tools [http://www.kie.berkeley.edu/KIE/software/descriptions.html]).

Both knowledge networking and emergent intelligence are important new capabilities that can transform the learning process at every level of education. Knowledge networking involves creating a community of mind. Through sharing disparate data and diverse perspectives, a group develops an evolving understanding of a complex topic. Over time, the group's conception of the issues continually expands and deepens, at times broadening the range of fields and experiences seen as relevant. During these times, the membership of a networking community grows to include participants who bring new perspectives and backgrounds. Thus, a knowledge network is in longitudinal flux as an ever-larger cast of members redefines how to conceptualize the topic; this involves a constant collective acculturation into new ways of thinking and knowing. For example, in the context of improving higher education, the participants in a knowledge network might be faculty, administrators, parents, taxpayers, employers, politicians, researchers, accreditation agencies, and policymakers — each bringing differing perspectives and knowledge across multiple educational settings. Communal learning is at the core of the knowledge networking process.

This type of interaction is becoming routine in university scholarship, but unfortunately shifts in instruction lag far behind. For that matter, no one talks about "distance scholarship," but the academy is puzzled about how to handle "distance education," incorrectly seeing it as some minor variant of conventional teaching rather than as an exemplification of the much larger process of knowledge networking now reshaping civilization. In a few years, high-performance computing and communications will make knowledge utilities, virtual communities, shared synthetic environments, and sensory immersion as routine a part of everyday existence as the telephone, television, radio, and newspaper are today.

In this future, keeping a balance between virtual interaction and direct interchange is important (Dede 1996). Technology-mediated communication and experience supplement, but do not replace, immediate involvement in real settings; thoughtful and caring participation is vital for making these new capabilities truly valuable in complementing face-to-face interactions. How a medium shapes its users, as well as its message, is a central issue in understanding the transformation of distance education into distributed learning. The telephone creates conversationalists; the book develops imaginers, who can conjure a rich mental image from sparse symbols on a printed page. Much of television programming induces passive observers; other shows, such as

"Sesame Street" and public affairs programs, can spark users' enthusiasm and enrich their perspectives. As we move beyond naive "information superhighway" concepts to envision the potential impacts of knowledge networking and distributed learning, society will face powerful new interactive media capable not only of great good, but also misuse. The most significant influence on the evolution of higher education will not be the technical development of more powerful devices, but the professional development of wise designers, educators, and learners.

REFERENCES

Dede, Chris. 1995a. Emerging educational trends and their impact on the youth cohort in 2010. In *Future Soldiers and the Quality Imperative: The Army 2010 Conference*, edited by R. Phillips and M. Thurman. Fort Knox, KY: U.S. Army Recruiting Command.

Dede, Chris. 1995b. Artificial realities, virtual communities, and intelligent artifacts: Implications for engineering education. In *The Influence of Technology on Engineering Education*, edited by John R. Bourne, A. Broderson, and M. Dawant. Boca Raton, FL: CRC Press.

Dede, Chris. 1996. Emerging technologies and distributed learning. *American Journal of Distance Education*. (10)2: 4-36.

Dede, Chris, ed. 1998. Futures: Images of educational technology in the next millennium (pamphlet). Tallahassee, FL: Florida Educational Technology Corporation.

Dede, Chris. 1999a. *The multiple media difference*. Technos (8)1: 16-18.

Dede, Chris. 1999b. *The role of emerging technologies for knowledge mobilization, dissemination, and use in education*. Washington, DC: U.S. Department of Education.

Weiser, M. 1991. The computer for the 21st century. *Scientific American* 265(3): 94-104.

Chapter 4

Emerging Organizational Models: The Extended Traditional University

By Donald E. Hanna

During this century, traditional universities have been expected to serve outreach audiences through continuing education and public service programs. Universities become extended as they bring about internal change in administrative and academic arrangements regarding educational programs, priorities, budgets, and students in ways that are more responsive to students and their immediate and lifelong needs. In short, the basic idea of the extended traditional university, however it may be organized, is to enable the parent university to respond more ably and nimbly to what students, the adult marketplace, and the university publics generally say they want from their university. In doing so, the university will be less inclined to base important decisions about programs and priorities strictly upon considerations of content and program quality, or other largely internally driven criteria.

Hanna (1998) outlined characteristics of seven new or emerging organizational models of higher education that were contrasted with assumptions and characteristics of traditional universities, providing specific examples of each emerging model.[1] These emerging models were derived from analysis of

---

[1]   This chapter and chapters 5 and 6 expand upon this discussion.

trends, characteristics, and examples of emerging organizational practice. They included:

1. extended traditional universities;

2. for-profit, adult-centered universities;

3. distance education/technology-based universities;

4. corporate universities;

5. university/industry strategic alliances;

6. degree/certification competency-based universities;

7. global multinational universities.

Each of the seven models is designed to create a competitive advantage in a rapidly changing environment, recognizing the growing importance of rapidly developing learning technologies that are creating new possibilities for organizing learning for adults.

As described in chapter 1, these new and emerging models are both competing with and causing change in the traditional residential model of higher education. Benefits of this new competitive environment include removing barriers to existing educational programs, responding more effectively and quickly to emerging educational needs, improving educational quality, and achieving long-term cost efficiencies. Competitive advantages sought by universities that are experimenting with new forms and models include responsiveness, access, convenience, and quality at a reduced cost for students.

While these new forms will not replace the traditional campus and its emphasis on face-to-face classroom environments, they do offer the prospect of rapidly expanding the location, time sequences and schedules, teaching and learning processes, and purposes of higher education.

More universities in the United States are using technologies to deliver courses at a distance, and almost all universities with existing programs are planning expansion. These actions have been encouraged by recent predictions by notable authorities and respected higher education leaders such as James Duderstadt

(1999), Peter Drucker (1993), Eli Noam (1998), and Burks Oakley (1997) that universities will change radically or perhaps even cease to exist in the twenty-first century. Greater awareness and visibility for using technologies, especially for distance delivery, has also generated significant opposition within traditional universities, especially from the faculty (Educom Staff 1996; Margolis 1998; Noble 1998; Phipps and Merisotis 1999). This opposition has focused upon technologies and distance learning, but its foundation has to do with the very definition and shape of higher education in the future. As recently as 1992, Bergquist, in discussing the cultural dynamics of higher education institutions, included four primary cultures within the academy. According to Bergquist, these four cultures included:

1. The managerial culture, which finds meaning in the organization of work and conceives of the institution's enterprise as the inculcation of specific knowledge, skills, and attitudes in students who will become successful and responsible citizens.

2. The developmental culture, which finds meaning in furthering the personal and professional growth of all members of the collegiate community, primarily defined as existing within the campus environment.

3. The negotiating culture, which is concerned with and responsible for establishing and executing equitable and egalitarian policies and procedures for the distribution of resources and benefits in the institution. Here the focus is on either developing or maintaining systems that create negotiated and reasoned compromises in matters of personnel, reimbursement, and other distribution of rewards.

4. The collegial culture, which is the core of any institution, sustained primarily by faculty members. This culture finds meaning in academic disciplines, values faculty research, scholarship, and governance, and holds sway over the institu-

tion's most important assets – its curriculum and
its faculty.

There is now a fifth important culture – the entrepreneurial
culture – that has emerged as a powerful force in higher education in the few short years since Bergquist's book. The entrepreneurial culture values the ability to change and to change
quickly, to respond to market forces, to connect with and generate support from external audiences and constituencies, and to
introduce new ideas, programs, delivery mechanisms, goals, and
purposes into the other four cultures described by Bergquist,
which are focused more internally within the institution. It is no
wonder that this culture often generates significant political ill
will internally, especially within the collegial culture, while at
the same time deriving significant support from outside the university's other cultures.

Bergquist (1992, 6) explains why:

> Although most colleges and universities, and most fac-
> ulty and administrators, tend to embrace or exemplify
> one of these four cultures, the other three cultures are al-
> ways present and interact with the dominant culture (the
> collegial culture). This is a particularly important prem-
> ise for readers to consider, given that some analysts of or-
> ganizational culture believe that hybrid cultures are
> undesirable or symptomatic of a fragmented, troubled
> institution.

Tierney (1998, 2-21) states that "strong, congruent cultures
supportive of organizational structures and strategies are more
effective than weak, incongruent, or disconnected cultures." The
entrepreneurial culture is not only incongruous with the collegial culture, in particular, which Bergquist identifies as the normally dominant culture in higher education; it is also quite at
odds in a number of ways with the other three. Yet the entrepreneurial culture has become the bedrock of extending traditional
universities, and technology is both leading and forcing a renais-
sance of the concept of the university in service to society. Table
4.1 demonstrates the many ways in which the entrepreneurial
culture of extended traditional universities is different from —

and in some cases, in conflict with — assumptions of the traditional university.

Extended traditional universities are characterized by programs that are specifically organized and designed to serve a primarily adult audience that is usually non-residential in nature (Hanna 1998). The traditional university structure operates as a parent organization and serves as a sponsor for programs conducted for this "alternative or nontraditional" constituency or clientele (Knox 1981; Votruba 1981). Such programs do not necessarily threaten the basic academic organization of the university. But, as noted in table 4.1, they do serve an entirely different and more competitive market, one that is primarily external to campus-based courses and programs.

Most efforts of extended traditional universities have centered on delivering existing on-campus courses and programs to adult audiences. These activities have often been assigned to a continuing education or extension division, either at the institutional level or at a program level. The continuing education division or program within a traditional university operates with assumptions that diverge from the parent university organization in subtle but important ways. Continuing education organizations are embedded squarely within an entrepreneurial culture. They are typically much more dependent upon tuition and fees for their financial support than is the rest of the university, and as a result they are market-driven and open to changing processes, programs, and structures to fit changing circumstances. Their students usually attend part-time and are older working adults who are viewed by the dominant university culture as distinct from its major eighteen to twenty-two-year-old constituency. In order to compete in what is increasingly a competitive marketplace, continuing education organizations are typically focused upon meeting specific needs of the individual learner.

They make decisions that are more customer driven than content driven, and external needs of the community and the pro-

Table 4.1. Comparison of Traditional Residential Universities and Extended Residential Universities

Input	Traditional Universities	Extended Traditional Universities
Philosopy	Students come to campus	Campus goes to students
Mission	Mission defined by level of instruction	Externally focused, degree completion and workforce development
Funding	$ per full-time student	More self-sustaining and market-driven
Curricula	Relatively stable and comprehensive curriculum	More flexible curriculum; content for workforce competence and development
Instruction	Most courses are lecture-based	Greater variety of methods and use of student experience
Faculty	Primarily full-time faculty; academic preparation and credentials	Greater use of adjuncts with professional experience
Students	Selectivity at admission	Life and work experience is greater factor in admission
Library	Volumes in library	Access to specific documents and resources appropriate to program
Learning Technology	Enhance lecture-oriented instruction	Both lecture-oriented and used to extend access
Physical Facilities	Extensive physical plant	Still campus-based but less reliance on physical plant
Productivity Outcomes	Student credit-hours and degrees	Student credit-hours and degrees
Governance	Board of Trustees	Board of Trustees
Accreditation	Institutional by region; individual programs or disciplines are also accredited	Institutional by region as part of parent organization's accreditation; individual programs or disciplines are also accredited

gram's specific constituency receive greater priority in program decision making than do internal readiness or support.

As continuing education units gain experience in using technology to adapt programs to meet student needs for access, convenience, and flexibility, their influence can be expected to increase even more within the external community and society. And their value to the parent organization may also grow, especially in those universities that have committed themselves to long-term change and to integrating this entrepreneurial culture into the fabric of the university.

Alternatively, continuing education units represent a challenge to traditional, content-based organization and decision making — not to mention a potential economic threat — within the traditional university. And as technology permeates traditional institutions, a blurring of the boundaries between types of students, core-teaching locations, funding bases, and instructional methodologies is occurring. This blurring of boundaries is creating institutional stress. It is also opening up new opportunities for reframing and restructuring missions and programs. As a result, the distinctions that have been prevalent between continuing education organizations and programs and their parent institutions are breaking down, with both the role of the continuing education unit and the mission of the institution being changed in the process.

Extended Traditional University Strategies

Extended traditional universities are employing a number of strategies to position their programs to compete effectively for adult students. Most adults are working in or outside of the home, have children and other family and personal responsibilities, and are highly motivated to learn for personal development or career advancement. Accordingly, universities tend to select subcategories of individuals within the population to target with particular programs. These programs can be segmented according to characteristics of the learner, such as the learner's:

- location

- career
- organizational affiliation
- organizational level
- organizational function
- economic status
- social status
- academic background

From an institutional perspective, programs can be segmented also according to specific specialized curricula or technologies that provide certain advantages regarding accessibility, cost, or effectiveness. Programs can also be organized and marketed around a well-known "brand," such as a Harvard MBA, or around a particular set of services, such as outstanding student services directed toward building student self-confidence and success. All of these strategies are currently in play in the competitive higher education environment.

Strategies for Organizational and Program Growth

Extended traditional universities are employing multiple competitive strategies to grow successful extended programs. Among them:

Program duplication. Program duplication generally involves extending a traditional campus-based program and set of courses to other locations using resident campus faculty who travel physically to the extended location or who teach electronically via video or computer connections to one or more locations. Washington State University's extended degree in social sciences is an excellent example of such a mixed mode of delivering of what is essentially a single campus-based degree program staffed largely by faculty members resident on the Pullman campus of Washington State. The degree is flexibly designed, with options that include major and/or minor course concentrations in criminal justice, sociology, psychology, anthropology, history, human development, political science, and business (Washington State University 1999).

Program and institutional replication. Program replication involves developing a successful site-based program and recreating it across multiple locations, with each location forming a new base of operations for the program and operating somewhat independently from other locations. Typically, replication involves maintaining a stable curriculum and set of requirements but using different faculty to teach the program in each location the program is offered. As one example, this model has been employed successfully in both the United States and internationally by the University of Maryland University College; however, to date, University of Maryland University College international programs have served a targeted U.S. population composed largely of military personnel stationed overseas.

A future variation of this strategy will involve moving successful programs, and even institutions, from one country to another, as the British Open University is proposing to do with the creation of the Open University of the U.S. (Marklein 1999). Whether this global strategy of replication will be successful, given the enormous cultural differences from one country to the next, is yet to be seen. With technological and economic barriers falling, cultural differences and translation of concepts and content will become perhaps the most significant barrier to successful implementation of this strategy on a global basis.

Program diversification. Extended traditional universities are also diversifying the array of programs they offer at a distance. Old Dominion University, for example, has moved aggressively to duplicate a broad cross-section of its curriculum for delivery at a distance, at first concentrating on upper-division baccalaureate programs delivered via satellite throughout Virginia through linkages with Virginia's community college system. Such a strategy of program and location diversification works well to serve a broad cross-section of people with programs they need. And once programs are available on the satellite, the cost of adding new locations and students from other parts of the country becomes minimal.

As noted in table 4.2, Old Dominion's reliance on satellite technology give its programs a technological delivery niche and spreads the substantial fixed costs of course and program development and distribution of the video signal over a larger and larger student body. The university operates one of the largest distance learning by satellite programs in the United States, with seventeen degree programs available as of April 1999 through its Teletechnet programs. A detailed listing of programs and locations served is included in table 4.2, which outlines clearly Old Dominion's reliance upon the twin strategies of program diversification and niche technology programming.

Walden University (Minnesota) was founded in 1970 and has positioned itself as a graduate-level, distributed learning institution with no central campus. The university offers the Ph.D. in five fields: Applied Management and Decision Sciences, Education, Health Services, Human Services, and Psychology. The M.S. degree is offered in Education and Psychology. Current 1999 enrollment exceeds 1,300 students, of whom 35 percent are from minority populations and over 50 percent are women. The faculty numbers more than 160, 22 percent of whom are from populations traditionally underrepresented in their disciplines and fields. Students and faculty represent all fifty states and more than twenty foreign countries.

In addition to program diversification as a strategic approach, Walden also has developed a technology-based niche strategy, offering most of its programs electronically via the Internet. Doctoral programs use course-based and competency-based curricula. Instruction, assessment, mentoring, and the delivery of student services also rely extensively on the Internet. While Walden M.S. programs are, for the most part, entirely online, its doctoral programs require students to fulfill academic residency requirements that are designed to meet students' needs (Walden University 1999).

Niche Programming. Niche programming involves identifying programs of particular strength in areas in which the institution clearly has a comparative advantage over other providers, usually, although not always, on the basis of program quality or the uniqueness of the program and its resources.

**Table 4.2.
Old Dominion University,
Degrees Available Through Distance Learning, 1999**

Academic College	Distance Learning Location*
COLLEGE OF ARTS AND LETTERS	Blue Ridge Community College
B.A./B.S. in Criminal Justice	Southside Virginia Community College – Daniel
B.S. in Interdisciplinary Studies with Cerification in Elementary/Middle School Education	Central Virginia Community College Southwest Virginia Community College
B.S. in Interdisciplinary Studies – Professional Communication	Dabney Lancaster Community College Tidewater Community College – Portsmouth
COLLEGE OF BUSINESS AND PUBLIC ADMINISTRATION	Dahlgren (NSWC) Thomas Nelson Community College
B.S. in Business Administration – Accounting	Danville Community College Southwest Virginia Higher Education Center
B.S. in Business Administration – Finance	Eastern Shore Community College Virginia Western Community College
B.S. in Business Administration – Information Systems	Fort Lee Wallops Island
B.S. in Business Administration – International Business Chinese emphasis Europe emphasis Japanese emphasis Latin America emphasis	Germanna Community College Walter Reed Army Medical College J. Sargeant Reynolds Community College Wytheville Community College
B.S. in Business Administration – Management	John Tyler Community College Peninsula Higher Education Center
B.S. in Business Administration– Marketing	Library of Virginia Virginia Beach Higher Education Center
Master of Taxation	Lord Fairfax Community College
Master of Public Administration (certificate only)	Ford Motor Plant Mountain Empire Community College
DARDEN COLLEGE OF EDUCATION	Ingersoll-Rand
B.S. in Human Service Counseling	New River Community College
B.S. in Occupational and Technical Studies Environmental Protection emphasis General emphasis Information Systems Technology emphasis	Olympic College – Washington** Northern Virginia Community College – Annandale Trident Training Facility – Washington Northern Virginia Community College – Woodbridge
M.S. in Education – Special Education	Naval Station – Everett, WA

Academic College	Distance Learning Location*

M.S. in Occupational and Technical Studies
    Business and Industry Training
    Community College Teaching
    Middle and Secondary Teaching
	Paul D. Camp Community College
	Alliance for Higher Education – Dallas, TX
	Piedmont Virginia Community College
	Mount Olive College – North Carolina

COLLEGE OF ENGINEERING AND TECHNOLOGY	Quantico Marine Corps Base Pitt Community College – North Carolina
B.S. in Civil Engineering Technology	Rappahannock Community College – Glenns
B.S. in Electrical Engineering Technology	Southside Virginia Community College – Chris
B.S. in Mechanical Engineering Technology	
Master's of Engineering Management	
COLLEGE OF HEALTH SCIENCES	
B.S. in Health Sciences w/ minor in Human Services Counseling	* Not all degree programs listed are available at all locations listed.
B.S. in Health Sciences w/ minor in Management	
B.S. in Nursing (RN to BSN) M.S. in Nursing – Family Nurse Practitioner M.S. in Nursing	** Even though Old Dominion University is state supported, note that not all locations listed are located in Virginia, with approved locations as far away as Washington state.

Penn State University created the World Campus in 1998, beginning with several specific degree programs for which the university has special expertise. The World Campus, according to Penn State's president, Graham Spanier, will "not be built with brick and mortar but with the creative use of technology led by our faculty to extend selected programs nationally and internationally. Through this approach, we anticipate propelling Penn State's expertise not only to every citizen of Pennsylvania but potentially to new students globally" (The Penn Stater 1997). Initiated with the assistance of more than $2 million from the Sloan Foundation, the World Campus, at the beginning of 1999, offered five associate degrees, a dozen certificate programs, and a growing postbaccalaureate program. The World Campus projects that by 2002, more than thirty certificate programs, degree programs, and continuing professional education modules involving more than three hundred, individual courses will be available (Penn State University 1999b; Spanier 1997).

The World Campus has identified a number of niche programs that Penn State believes are of such eminent quality that students from across the globe will find them attractive. These programs include certificates in Turfgrass Management, Chemical Dependency Counselor Education, Customer Relations, Educational Technology Integration, Geographic Information Systems, Logistics and Supply Chain Management, Noise Control Engineering, and a variety of Electrical Engineering and professional engineering courses (Penn State University 1999a). Note that none of these programs:

- directly replicates or duplicates programs offered on the Penn State campus;
- is focused on general education at the baccalaureate level;
- is broadly accessible to the general population.

These program characteristics signal an alternative program and organizational growth strategy for the World Campus, one that relies heavily on addressing program-specific niches for which Penn State is ideally positioned.

Technology-based strategy. In selected situations, universities are developing programs using specific technologies and software that they hope will give them a competitive access or learning advantage with students. Such strategies generally rely upon an advantaged position with respect to a particular type of technology or software — a position that, because of rapid diffusion of advances in technology, is increasingly difficult to maintain.

Technology-based strategies were more common among universities when the investment required for technologies to deliver programs was exceedingly high, as was the case with satellite uplinks just a few years ago. Universities that were able to afford the up-front investment in these expensive technologies generally found the competition for their programs to be minimal. Their major challenge was to find a way, other than through program fees or cost recovery, to pay for their investment and thereby keep their competitive position (for which they had paid a high cost). They did this through grants from the federal government, states, and private industry.

Old Dominion is an excellent example of a university that has invested heavily and unilaterally in satellite technology to deliver programs on a statewide and now a national basis. To achieve this competitive position, the university and the State of Virginia have heavily subsidized both the program and the technology. However, there are few other examples of single universities that have primarily utilized a technology-based strategy and been able to sustain themselves over time, for reasons noted in the following section.

An excellent case study on the difficulties of sustaining technology-based strategies is the University of Alaska's Learn Alaska program, which was perhaps the most ambitious and successful example of this strategy in the 1980s. But the program was abandoned by the late 1980s, when economic conditions in Alaska and political winds within the legislature shifted, precisely at the same time. With the new low-cost communication capabilities of the Web, selecting a market niche based upon technology capabilities alone is likely to be even more risky in the future.

Program Aggregation. A few universities have developed strategies of program aggregation, whereby programs of other campuses are aggregated together with the institution's own programs for marketing and delivery. Increasingly, the strategy of aggregation has been developed by consortia and partnerships rather than under the rubric of a single institution. Aggregation as a specific program strategy is discussed in chapter 5, under the heading of "Interinstitutional Consortia and Partnerships."

Many other examples of exploratory strategies to serve a growing marketplace could be cited. But, despite examples of increased experimentation, most universities have not challenged traditional assumptions and approaches with respect to learning, students, and processes. A summary of strategies employed by universities as they seek competitive and comparative advantage is outlined in table 4.3.

Table 4.3.
Analysis of Competitive Strategies in Higher Education

Competitive Strategy	Course Level	Program Level	Institution Level	Classic Institutional Examples	Emerging Models
Duplication	Duplicate specific successful courses	Duplicate selected niche programs	Duplicate independent organizational model	Washington State University	British Open University
Replication	Identical courses across all locations	Multiple sites; single campus	Multiple campuses; franchising	University of Maryland University College	University of Phoenix
Diversification	Increase content areas offered	Increase programs offered	Increase program and course array	Old Dominion University	Walden University
Niche Programming	Identify specialty content areas	Select programs with narrow constituencies		Penn State University	Capella University
Niche Technologies	Build courses around technologies	Build programs	Tie program to particular technologies and delivery	Old Dominion University	Jones International University
Program Aggregation	Combine courses for marketing purposes	Combine programs and other services for marketing and delivery	Form consortia and inter-institutional partnerships		National Technological University American Distance Education Consortium

The Importance of Addressing Financial Assumptions and Models in Promoting Innovation

Traditional universities are having a very difficult time adapting their financial structures to accommodate the kinds of investment that new learning technologies require, and that enable and reward departmental and faculty behaviors that are responsive to dynamically changing needs. Academic departmental budgets are often relatively fixed, with little connection to enrollment growth or, more important, enrollment decline. This is the case because many faculty members are tenured and budgeted within the department, but it is also due to many other factors, including the fact that academic programs are built over time, with faculty as the primary determinant of quality. As a result, university administrators are hesitant to assess penalties that would result in a loss of faculty, tenured or not, in any program.

While penalties are eventually imposed on extreme laggards, few financial rewards are offered for growth within the mainstream academic budgeting process. Departments with growing enrollments end up subsidizing those with stagnant or decreasing enrollments for substantial periods of time. With this situation as an operating framework, it is little wonder that departments, left to themselves to operate within the traditional financial backdrop (and without additional financial inducement), see little value in adapting to technologies that will simply add to the individual workloads of faculty in at least three ways. First, the faculty member has the added burden of learning new instructional technologies. Second, adapting to new modes of instruction places a greater burden on the faculty member to provide one-on-one and "one-to-few" interactions rather than the "one-to-many" interactions so prevalent in lecture-style classrooms. Third, increased numbers of students with varying locations, schedules, and maturity demand flexibility. Adaptation presents new logistical as well as pedagogical challenges. All of these factors serve as powerful disincentives not only to faculty members, but also to academic departments, whose budgets control the academic structure of the university.

This lack of entrepreneurial orientation is deadly when combined with the escalating demand for higher education from adults, a growing competitive marketplace, and new financial requirements for investments in learning technologies. Because learning technologies are changing rapidly, they must be replaced much more quickly than ever before. They are also more dispersed, not only throughout the campus on faculty and student desktops, but also everywhere students may be, on and off campus. No longer can the university afford to gamble on a single technology, whatever the rationale. Multiple platforms and environments must be supported. And finally, investments in learning technologies are major capital expenditures that are increasingly difficult to fund from the relatively fixed budgets prevalent in most public and private universities.

The roughly straight-line changes of current university budgeting processes are simply incompatible with: 1) the requirements of new technologies, which emphasize systemic and interlocking changes across an entire organization; 2) the large up-front investments followed by the promise of major growth and the higher risk of failure; and 3) a more direct connection between dollars invested and productivity measures, whether of enrollments or tuition income.

To address this problem, the U.S. Department of Education's Fund for the Improvement of Postsecondary Education (FIPSE) launched the "Learn Anytime, Anywhere" program in 1999 to provide stimulus and incentive funds for institutions willing to experiment with the development of new models of instruction and uses of technology. According to the FIPSE grant guideline statement (FIPSE 1999):

> Technology now makes it possible to deliver education anytime and anywhere, but most educational institutions, including those providing distance education, continue to follow traditional practices. ... Technology provides the possibility that students will access courses and programs from almost anywhere, and this in turn has changed the ways institutions recruit students. *Even so, tradition, funding, institutional structures, and other factors constrain institutions to honor geographic boundaries that technology and learner demand may not respect* (author's emphasis).

In a very thoughtful analysis, Karelis (1999), the executive director of FIPSE, argued the following: Regardless of how learning technologies are budgeted and paid for by institutions —and no matter how great the overall benefits of utilizing these technologies C the use of technologies, with its requirement of extensive up-front capital investment, is not currently able to scale sufficiently to compete with basic face-to-face instruction in traditional universities. The only way it can do so, Karelis argues, is if enrollments exceed significantly those which are possible and/or conducive to creating quality teaching environments (termed the "scale barrier" in figure 4.1). Note here that the model of traditional classroom delivery selected by Karelis for comparison here is the traditional lecture (one-to-many) model widely used in universities today, which, as noted in chapter 2, is less than ideal in terms of producing effective learning for students. Nevertheless, the position articulated by Karelis in outlining this approach is inconsistent with the view of many (including Karelis himself) that employing technologies in higher education can and will save money in the long run. Karelis illustrates his point in figure 4.1, adapted from earlier models developed by Frank Jewett of the California State University System.

Karelis suggests that the funding gap between the intersect point and the maximum scale possible (The Scale Barrier) must be subsidized in one of two ways: 1) through direct institutional, state, or grant funding; or 2) through the formation of strategic alliances and partnerships with business and industry and with

Figure 4.1.
An Analysis of Return on Investment in Learning Technologies

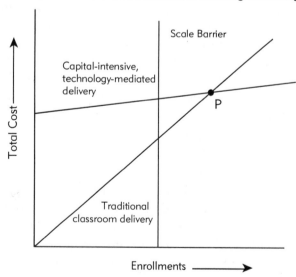

Source: Karelis (1999). Used with permission.

other universities, which helps to explain the tremendous growth in these organizational forms (see chapters 5 and 6). The funding implications of these two approaches are outlined in figure 4.2, which shows that, in both cases, subsidy and partnership, courses and programs can be offered that meet the test of quality and cost-effectiveness.

Karelis goes on to argue that the small, interactive, technology-enabled classroom described in chapter 2, while ideal, is simply too expensive to implement because it will always be more costly than face-to-face instruction, no matter what the enrollment. If the face-to-face model used for cost comparison is the traditional lecture approach to instruction, there is no doubt that this is the case. Karelis suggests that the most promising approach for delivering cost-effective instruction via technology is to deliver "low-cost, Internet-delivered instruction." His proposed

Figure 4.2.
An Analysis of Return on Investment in Learning Technologies, Factoring in Direct Subsidy or Benefits of Strategic Alliances

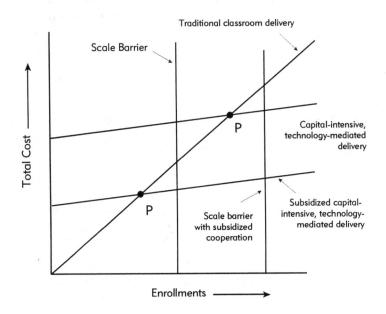

Source: Karelis (1999). Used with permission.

method of lowering costs is to substitute lower-paid teaching assistants, graduate assistants, and "people whose academic preparation does not qualify them for faculty positions" to handle classroom interaction and content delivery, while relying on faculty members for content development and overall guidance and coordination. This is a model that is being developed and employed at a number of for-profit and online universities, such as the University of Phoenix, Jones International University, and others. And of course, the idea of substituting low-cost instructors (graduate students) to increase efficiency is not unfamiliar to many research universities that regularly do so in staffing entry-level undergraduate courses.

The Role of Continuing and Extended Education

Through a combination of the strategies summarized in this chapter, continuing education programs and divisions operating in an entrepreneurial mode have achieved some success over the past decade in serving the adult market. Perhaps the most aggressive response to this dramatic change has come from a small number of largely urban, private, religiously affiliated universities, especially those universities affiliated with the Jesuit Order. Because these universities were not heavily oriented toward research and grant funding and also did not receive state-supported subsidies, they depended largely upon tuition for their annual budget needs. As a result, they were particularly vulnerable to enrollment declines among their traditional-age, student populations occurring in the early 1980s. One after another, private Jesuit universities such as St. Louis University, Loyola of New Orleans, Regis University, Gonzaga, the University of San Francisco, and others created colleges of Professional Studies or colleges of Lifelong Learning specifically to respond to growing demand from well-educated adults for greater access to applied graduate education. These universities used all of the strategies noted above in various combinations. However, they did not utilize technology extensively in their early efforts.

In some of these universities, the number of extended programs offered, degrees conferred, students enrolled, and part-time faculty members hired surpassed the equivalent numbers of the residential faculty and programs of the university. And, unlike most of the public universities, these universities generally did not attempt to merge this new market-focused entrepreneurial initiative into the fabric of the university's traditional structures. On the contrary, the leadership of these universities went to great lengths to keep such activities and programs separate with the express purpose of protecting both the entrepreneurial spirit on the one hand and the prevailing idea of "what a university is supposed to be" on the other. This strategy was an attempt to keep the clash of cultures from fragmenting the overall institution.

Instructional technologies have enabled many continuing and extended education units to expand their efforts to provide improved access to campus-based programs. But the impact of these efforts is not yet widespread throughout most traditional universities. Despite some success, core programs, operating assumptions, and values of the university remain relatively unaffected within Bergquist's four cultures, especially the collegial culture. The capacity of the entrepreneurial culture and of these organized units to adapt to changing markets is often resented rather than appreciated by campus-based faculty, staff, and students, many of whom see such efforts as diverting precious resources, offering lower-quality education, threatening time-honored conceptions of teaching and learning, and diminishing the status of the institution.

Olcott (1997, 2) states:

> ... [D]espite some remarkable success stories, the transformational capacity of technology to reshape the modern academy's teaching and learning processes has fallen well short of its earlier promise. Moreover, while the geographical boundaries of educational access have been rendered obsolete by technology, the "real" boundaries of turf and traditional service regions remain and are driven by political and economic factors rather than by educational priorities. Parochialism remains the dominant mindset for most institutions.

Unfortunately, leadership for development of the extended traditional university is originating most often from outside the core activities of the faculty and, in many cases, far away from the internal center of the institution, where the majority of learning and teaching occurs. As long as this is the case, traditional universities will be slow to embrace the integration of necessary changes required for academic departments and faculty to take advantage of new program opportunities. One of the most important and immediate but intensely challenging tasks for the traditional university is to develop additional strategies for building leadership capacity for change and decision-making structures that support change at the faculty level.

REFERENCES

Bergquist, William H. 1992. *The four cultures of the academy: Insights and strategies for improving leadership in collegiate organizations.* San Francisco: Jossey-Bass, Publishers.

Educom Staff. 1996. Should distance learning be rationed? Point/Counterpoint with Larry Gold and James R. Mingle. *Educom Review* 3(4).

Drucker, Peter Ferdinand. 1993. *Post-capitalist society.* New York: HarperBusiness.

Duderstadt, James J. 1999. Can colleges and universities survive in the information age? In *Dancing with the devil: Information technology and the new competition in higher education,* edited by Richard N. Katz. San Francisco: Jossey-Bass, Publishers.

Fund for the Improvement of Postsecondary Education. 1999. *Learning anytime anywhere partnerships* [Website]. Fund for the Improvement of Postsecondary Education. Available from < http://www.ed.gov/offices/OPE/FIPSE/LAAP/materials/invpriorities.html >.

Hanna, Donald E. 1998. Higher education in an era of digital competition: Emerging organizational models. *Journal of Asynchronous Learning* 2(1). Available from < http://www.alm.org/alnweb/ journal/jlan_vol2issue1.htm#hanna >.

Karelis, Charles. 1999. Education technology and cost control : Four models. [Website]. Fund for the Improvement of Postsecondary Education. Available from < http://www. Ed.gov/offices/OPE/FIPSE/LAAP/reading.html >.

Knox, Alan. 1981. The continuing education agency and its parent organization. In *Strengthening internal support for continuing education,* edited by James Votruba. San Francisco: Jossey-Bass Publishers.

Margolis, Michael. 1998. *Brave new universities* [Website]. First Monday. Available from < http://www.firstmonday.dk/issues/issue3_5/margolis/index.html#author >

Marklein, Mary Beth. 1999. Upstart college makes the grade and a profit. *USA Today,* 27 April: D1-2.

Noam, Eli. 1998. Will books become the dumb medium? *Educom Review* 33(2). [Website]. Available from < http://www.educause.edu/ pub/er/review/reviewArticles/33218.html >.

Noble, David. 1998. *Digital Diploma Mills.* [Website]. Available from < http://www.firstmonday.dk/issues/issue3_1/noble/index.html >.

Oakley, Burks. 1997. Will universities survive in the knowledge economy? *Interface,* IEEE Newsletter April.

Olcott, Donald John. 1997. Renewing the vision: Past perspectives and future imperatives for distance education. *The Journal of Continuing Higher Education* 45(3): 2-13.

Old Dominion University. 1999. *Distance learning at Old Dominion.* [Website]. Available from < http://web.odu.edu/webroot/ FrontEnd.nsf/pages/distlrn > or < http://web.odu.edu/webroot/ orgs/AO/clt/teletech.nsf/pages/undergrad >.

Penn State University. 1999a. *Programs and Courses.* [Website]. Penn State University. Available from < http://www.worldcampus.Psu. edu/pub/index.shtml >.

Penn State University. 1999b. World Campus observes successful inaugural year. [News Release dated 25 Feb. 1999]. Available from < http://www.worldcampus.psu.edu/pub/news/intercom. 2.25.99.shtml >.

Phipps, Ronald, and Jamie Merisotis. 1999. *What's the difference? A review of contemporary research on the effectiveness of distance learning in higher education.* Washington, DC: Institute for Higher Education Policy.

Spanier, Graham. 1997. 1997 President's State of the University Address, Penn State University. Available from < http://www.psu.edu/ ur/state/stateofuniv97.html >.

The Penn Stater. 1997. A Conversation With President Spanier. Available at < http://www.alumni.psu.edu/bnefits/Pennstater/penstater. html >.

Tierney, William. 1988. Organizational culture in higher education. *Journal of Higher Education* 59: 2-21.

Votruba, James. 1981. Strategies for organizational change. In *Strengthening internal support for continuing education,* edited by James Votruba. San Francisco: Jossey-Bass, Publishers.

Walden University. 1999. *Walden University* [Website]. Walden University. Available from < http://www.waldenu.edu/ >.

Washington State University. 1999. *Washington State University extended degree* [Website]. Washington State University. Available from < http://www.eus.wsu.edu/edp/index.htm >.

Chapter 5

The Distance Education/ Technology-Based Universities

By Donald E. Hanna

Universities have relied upon multiple technologies over time to provide the context for and to mediate a learning environment between the student and the instructor separated by distance and time. Until the 1930s, the technologies in use were largely the typewriter and the postal service, which provided the sole link between the individual instructor and the individual student. Courses were taught at a distance via correspondence, with the student accessing the professor and the teaching materials individually. In the United States, correspondence distance education programs were developed at many large state universities, with the University of Wisconsin-Madison, Penn State University, and others in the Midwest being early pioneers.

With the advent of radio, and later educational television and other forms of video, technology options for teaching at a distance were expanded. However, these correspondence programs serving off-campus constituencies were left largely isolated and undeveloped during the 1950s and '60s as the flood of traditional eighteen to twenty-two year-old students arrived on campuses. In the United States, energy and public resources went to building new campuses, expanding existing ones, and largely replicating the system of higher education already in place. In Europe and around the globe, however, new forms of institutions came into being, the first and most notable being the United Kingdom Open University (UKOU).

Approaches to Distance Education

In writing about this history of distance education, Keegan (1988) categorizes distance education universities as originating from two distinct traditions. The first of these traditions is correspondence study, involving only the student and the teacher in a two-party learning transaction, mediated by the technology of books and the postal service. The second is the extension of traditional classrooms to new locations through the use of new technologies such as satellite, broadcast television, cable television, and, more recently, compressed video and desktop video. This extension of the traditional classroom brought other students into the learning experience, complicated significantly the types of technology utilized, and dramatically increased the cost of reaching distance learners. However, it did not change or affect the overall dominant model of the teacher-centered classroom, described in chapter 2.

In the past five years, a third category of institution, the online university, has emerged. It does not fall neatly into either the correspondence or the extended-classroom models. Online universities take advantage of new computer-mediated conferencing systems and the emergence of the World Wide Web to enable asynchronous and synchronous interaction among students and the teacher, thereby offering a third, lower-cost model organized around a technological approach. With the development of the World Wide Web as an additional powerful learning tool, this model has significant potential for radically altering the learning environment in all settings by enabling and supporting interactive, socially constructed learning (described in chapters 2 and 12), and by dramatically increasing the educational resources, materials, and documents available to learners at the click of a mouse.

All distance education/technology-based universities are organized around one of these three approaches. The goal of each technology-based approach to learning is to minimize both the physical and psychological separation of the learner from the instructor. However, because each technology has certain strengths and weaknesses, the technology itself is interjected into the learning process, even as it makes the connection between the student and the teacher possible. Whether audio, video, or text, or a combination of all three basic technology devices, the technology chosen determines, to a great extent, what can and cannot be done in the learning environment among students and the instructor. Its presence is always a "fourth force" in the classroom, the other three forces being the content to be learned, the teacher, and the student. For many reasons, this fourth force of technology has, until recently, been employed primarily to extend the teacher rather than to empower the student, as was noted in chapter 2.

Distance education/technology-based universities tend to be more adult and workforce oriented, although the large national universities in many countries enroll substantial numbers of traditional-college-age students, largely due to the inability of traditional universities to accept all qualified applicants, especially in countries with rapidly growing populations. Table 5.1 notes major differences between the distance education/technology-based universities and both traditional and extended traditional universities. Table 5.2 captures major differences among types of distance education/technology institutions along selected characteristics and assumptions that serve to differentiate the types of institutions.

Table 5.2 illustrates selected differences among the three types of distance education/technology-based institutions with respect to funding, technologies employed, instructional approaches utilized, and productivity measures.

The Evolution from Correspondence to National Distance Education and Mega-universities

As noted earlier, many distance education universities developed from a print and correspondence tradition and were primarily established to increase access to higher education. Operated as governmental entities, national distance education universities were originally organized to serve a national development function. Their purposes were more immediately political than other models outlined in this book. They also suffer from significant government control and bureaucracy and are not able to accom-

Table 5.1.
**Comparison of Distance Education/Technology-based Universities
with Traditional Universities and Extended Traditional Universities**

Input	Traditional Universities	Extended Traditional Universities	Distance Education/ Technology-Based Universities
Philosophy	Students come to campus	Campus goes to students	Campus goes to students
Mission	Mission defined by level of instruction	Externally focused, degree completion and workforce development	Externally focused, degree completion and workforce development
Funding	$ subsidy per full-time student	More self-sustaining and market driven	Reduce cost of access to higher education
Curricula	Relatively fixed and comprehensive curriculum	More flexible curriculum; content for workforce competence and development	More flexible curriculum; content for workforce competence and development
Instruction	Most courses are lecture based	Greater variety of methods and use of student experience	Varies by type; see table 5.2
Faculty	Primarily full-time faculty; academic preparation and credentials	Greater use of adjuncts with professional experience	Some use of full-time faculty, but greater use of adjuncts with professional experience
Library	Volumes in library	Access to specific documents and resources appropriate to program	Access to specific documents and resources appropriate to program
Students	Selectivity at admission	Life and work experience is greater factor in admission	Life and work experience is greater factor in admission
Learning Technology	Enhance lecture-oriented instruction	Both lecture oriented and used to extend access	Varies by type; see table 5.2
Physical Facilities	Extensive physical plant	Still campus based but less reliance on physical plant	No physical plant; students are geographically separated from each other and the instructor

Input	Traditional Universities	Extended Traditional Universities	Distance Education/ Technology-Based Universities
Productivity Outcomes	Student credit hours and degrees	Student credit hours and degrees	Varies by type; see table 5.2
Governance	Board of Trustees	Board of Trustees	Varies by type; see table 5.2
Accreditation	Institutional by region; individual programs or disciplines are also accredited	Institutional by region; disciplines and programs also part of parent organization's accreditation	Varies by type; see table 5.2

modate change easily, let alone lead new developments and applications. While they are large and therefore significant, a major challenge for these universities is to adapt their traditional instructional approach, which relies heavily on correspondence study and a teacher-student relationship, to be more interactive and dynamic.

Daniel (1996) refers to the very largest of these national universities, many of which enroll more than 100,000 students annually, as "mega-universities." Most of these universities were established in the past thirty years, and they are rapidly adapting their content and delivery to new technologies, markets, and alliances. Their strategies for growth have focused primarily upon increasing access to existing programs (duplication) and upon increasing the types of programs offered (diversification).

The United Kingdom Open University (UKOU) is the best known of these national universities that utilize traditional distance learning methods such as correspondence, audiotapes, videotapes, and television. Generally, the pedagogical method employed by distance education national universities is a student studying independently of and in isolation from other students, working with an instructor who guides the student in his or her learning activities and courses. As a result, this process of education does not normally incorporate team-based, social constructivist learning models such as those emphasized in chapter 2. The term "open" is intended to communicate, according to Rumble and Harry (1982), the openness of the university

Table 5.2
Comparison of Major Differences among Types of distance
Education/Technology-based Universities

Input	Correspondence Tradition	Extended Classroom Tradition	Emerging Online/ Web-based Universities
Funding	National and state investments common	Industry often a driving force in funding programs; campuses use investments already made in campus instruction as a funding base	Tuition and industry contributions likely to drive funding
Instruction and Learning Modes	Most courses are print- and readings-based; interaction between instructor and student only	Greater variety of methods, including real-time student-student & student-instructor interaction, but still very teacher-directed instruction	Courses are online on the web. Interaction among students and with instructor occurs asynchronously and in real time using computer conferencing; use of other technologies as appropriate; jury is out on how teaching and learning will be organized online
Readings	Print syllabi and readings often provided; future includes use of multimedia and CD-ROM	Print syllabi and readings often provided	Online access to specific documents and resources appropriate to program
Productivity Measures	Costs per student compared with traditional higher education are lower	Dependent upon funding model selected, but access to instruction is a key consideration	Not yet established, but revenue generation and cost reduction are two probable criteria

Input	Correspondence Tradition	Extended Classroom Tradition	Emerging Online/ Web-based Universities
Learning Technology	Generally one-way technologies to enhance lecture-oriented instruction	Generally two-way technologies to enhance simulation of face-to-face classroom environment, but still instructor directed	Generally two-way interaction supplemented by online instructional references and resources

with respect to 1) people, since it would not deny admission to applicants based upon their lack of educational qualifications; 2) place, since learning would be home-based and not confined to classrooms and a campus; 3) new methods of teaching (note "teaching" not "learning") and 4) the examination of new and competing ideas.

The UKOU enrolls students from across the globe. In pursuit of its mission to be open to all students, the Open University has become an increasingly international institution. In 1998, there were more than 25,000 students taking Open University courses outside the UK. The largest concentrations of students enrolled were elsewhere in the European Union, in the former Soviet bloc (where courses are available in local languages), and Singapore (Daniel 1998). UKOU also offers growing numbers of programs in Ethiopia, Eritrea, South Africa, and India. In China, there are thousands of students at the Open University of Hong Kong taking UKOU courses within their Open University of Hong Kong curriculum.

The UKOU is adapting to new technologies, but its sheer size and previous substantial investments in fixed media inhibit its ability to shift its instructional approaches to recognize the more interactive features of the Internet and the World Wide Web. In 1999, only 50,000 of the 150,000 students enrolled in the Open University were even linked by computer to the university and to each other (Daniel 1999). While this number is still impressive and is growing rapidly (up from 42,000 in 1998 according to Daniel [1998]), it illustrates the immensity of the challenge. Numbers and growth say little about how those who are linked are actually using the connection to enhance their learning. The UKOU is currently making large investments in CD-ROM to integrate interactive multimedia technology into its courses. The university is experimenting with computer conferencing, but, as the data above indicate, it faces a major challenge in just connecting its students. Interestingly, it has been cautious in its approach to utilizing the World Wide Web for expanding access to its courses. Daniel (1998) outlines the reasons for this caution:

1. There is the copyright problem. The university's most precious capital assets are its intellectual property.

2. Text is — and will continue to be — a substantial component of university courses. So far, Open University students express a preference for printed paper as a main vehicle for study texts. They do not like reading a lot of material from a screen.

3. Many Open University students study on the move (e.g., in commuter trains, during air travel, and in hotels). The older media are still more convenient in these situations.

4. Most students' homes do not yet have computers, and few have the high bandwidth connections that allow the Web to be used to full effect.

The UKOU recently (1998) established the Open University of the United States with offices in Delaware. A search for its founding chancellor was completed in 1999. This experiment may be the ultimate test, and opportunity, to determine how the open university model can be adapted to take advantage of new technologies and a new competitive environment.

In North America, the largest of the national open universities is Athabasca University in Alberta, Canada. Established in 1972 using correspondence study and primarily non-interactive supplementary technologies such as audiotape and videotape, Athabasca now enrolls more than 14,000 students at a distance.

However, the university is rapidly shifting its focus to other technologies, especially the Internet and the Web.

In 1994, Athabasca's Centre for Innovative Management launched an online MBA. This program is currently Canada's sixth-largest MBA program, and its educational framework signals a direction likely to develop for other programs. The program emphasizes service to students, its ability to change courses and even the curriculum quickly to respond to changing circumstances and needs, and the development of student skill sets necessary for success in the corporate world. While the program currently is focused upon Canada and North America, courses are also offered in Japan, and discussions are under way to extend the program to other countries.

The university's MBA in Information Technology Management was announced in March 1999. This new program represents a unique collaboration between business and education to create Canada's first executive MBA focusing on IT management. Athabasca is partnering with companies such as Nortel Networks, IBM, PeopleSoft, and AT&T Canada to develop the program's courses.

In China, three distance education universities — the Shanghai TV University, Jiangsu Radio and TV University, and the China TV University System (CTVU) — enroll more than 1.5 million students annually. CTVU alone has graduated more than 1.5 million students during the past decade, which represents 17 percent of China's total number of college graduates during this period (Daniel 1996). Unlike many of the other distance education "mega-universities," students at CTVU attend scheduled classes broadcast to classrooms at their place of employment (Keegan 1994).

Sukhothai Thammathirat Open University (STOU) in Thailand is a government-sponsored university that enrolls almost 200,000 students annually in degree programs and an additional 300,000 in short training programs and single courses. More than three-fourths of the students are from rural areas of Thailand. Almost fifty baccalaureate degrees, three graduate programs, and a number of certificate programs are offered through STOU (Daniel 1996).

The Centre National d'Enseignement à Distance (CNED) operates under the authority of the Ministry of Education in France and is the largest distance teaching university in Europe. Using primarily a correspondence education approach at all educational levels, CNED uses satellite delivery to supplement its educational program via correspondence. "The reality appears to be that CNED is using its most glamorous technology, satellite video transmissions, to enrich, rather than fundamentally to change, its traditional correspondence teaching methods" (Daniel 1996, 10). Unfortunately, this block seems to be a characteristic one for the large national universities, most having adapted quite slowly to new and emerging interactive technologies.

In the United States, Empire State College in New York and Thomas Edison State College in New Jersey most closely resemble the national distance education university model common in Europe and Asia. Both receive state funds and are based upon an historical foundation of independent learning and self-study. Hall (1991) compares Empire State College with the United Kingdom Open University (UKOU) and acknowledges the direct influence of the UKOU on Empire State's development. He analyzes the approaches to the establishment of both institutions and finds few differences other than scale, with ESC being a state university and UKOU national in its orientation.

National distance education universities were established in many countries that are struggling to meet increasing demand from rapidly increasing populations and to pay for improved access to higher education necessary to compete in a new global economy. In that sense, these distance education universities function as a release valve for traditional, campus-based higher education, for which the number of available positions or student slots globally is woefully inadequate.

The Introduction of Extended Classrooms through Technology

Just as the national distance education universities were originally organized to take advantage of improved mail delivery, many universities have initiated programs based upon extending the traditional classroom by taking advantage of a particular delivery technology. The extended classroom model is based on the assumption that face-to-face instruction in traditionally structured classrooms, where students can interact with each other and with the instructor, is a preferred mode of learning, even at a distance. The extended classroom uses connective technologies such as satellite or two-way video and audio systems to connect learners who are separated from each other and the instructor.

The extended classroom tends to reinforce traditional, teacher-centered approaches to the learning environment; frequently the class members learning at a distance are simply connected to a regular on-campus classroom and are taught as part of the extended class. In all cases, the benefit is that the student does not need to commute to the campus. However, students and faculty members must generally conform to other requirements, such as designated meeting times, a schedule with fixed class meeting times, and, very often, a location to which students must commute in order to participate.

Numerous examples of the extended classroom tradition have developed across the globe over the past thirty years as technologies have increasingly enabled audio conferencing and two-way interactive video and audio communication among multiple locations. Early experiments with audio conferencing were conducted at the University of Wisconsin. In the 1970s, PeaceSat was formed to extend educational programs throughout the Pacific region via audioconferencing and an early form of text-based e-mail. Indonesia was also an early pioneer in the use of satellite for education, creating a system linking the many diverse regions and universities located throughout the island nation. The University of Alaska created Learn Alaska, also based upon satellite technology, to deliver educational programs to rural Alaska. And Washington State University and Ohio University created two of the first university-based, two-way-video, two-way-audio systems designed to deliver university-level credit courses to locations away from the main campus.

As a strategy for continuing education within traditional universities, the extended classroom has flourished, particularly in fields in which changing professional practices require continuous updating and those in which professionals are geographically dispersed. There are simply thousands of examples of the extended classroom model in traditional universities using two-way audio, one-way video/two-way audio, two-way video and audio, and other variations of technology. Campus-based courses and programs are duplicated through their extension to remote sites, with very little changed in the process. Course faculty, content, and approaches to teaching and learning remain relatively constant, and the extended classroom therefore presents a less dramatic departure from assumptions otherwise present in traditional universities.

While the cost of implementing these interactive technologies is high and cost recovery in most cases is not possible, many traditional universities with programs in selected fields of professional study have made these programs available through this extended classroom format within a specific area they serve. In most cases, they have justified costs by comparing this method of delivery with costs necessary to establish new full-service campuses and programs or with the costs of commuting faculty members and facilities. In many cases, traditional universities have contrasted these costs with the probable outcome of a decision not to respond. A few universities have independently initiated nationally offered curricula via satellite; however, because of the high cost of satellite delivery, the development of consortia and partnerships has emerged as the preferred method of organizing, coordinating, and delivering extended classroom programs on a national basis.

Interinstitutional Consortia and Partnerships

A number of consortia of universities have formed around the extended classroom model. One premier example is the National Technological University (NTU) which was originally framed around national satellite broadcast technology to deliver graduate-level master's degree programs in engineering to practicing engineers in business and industry. The program combines faculty expertise and course offerings from a number of leading U.S. colleges of engineering. By allowing courses from multiple universities to be organized and counted toward a degree, regardless of the institution originating the course, NTU meets a need for portability of credits toward a degree for mobile engineers who are frequently transferred across the country by their employers. NTU is more than a consortium; it is an independent university with its own accreditation and degree program authorizations. This makes it unique among the consortia described herein[1].

NTU courses are generally taught in a traditional lecture classroom format by affiliate institutions and faculty. Courses are delivered to groups of students who are employed at corporate locations; the technology simply allows for enlargement of the on-campus lecture hall across distance. An advantage of NTU's approach is that students can videotape lectures and view them at their convenience, an important feature for students working in industry who must travel and who otherwise are not in complete control of their schedules. NTU also has launched NTUOnline, bringing professional development, executive education, software applications, and technical training via the Internet. In addition to its own course offerings, NTU's online courses are delivered through three online course distributors: Broadcast.com, Digital Education Systems, and 7thStreet.com.

As noted above, NTU offers its own degrees and has been accredited to do so by the North Central Association since 1987. It also has expanded its programming by offering certificates, selected baccalaureate-degree programs, and noncredit professional development workshops. Other consortia in the United States have been organized to combine resources to deliver educational programs using the extended classroom, but none has been as successful as NTU. Nor has any other consortium developed its own accredited degree program.

The National Universities Degree Consortium(NUDC)[2] is a consortium of eleven separately accredited universities across

---

1   http://www.ntu.edu/. Affiliate members include: University of Arkansas, University of California-Berkeley, University of California-Davis, University of Colorado at Boulder, University of Delaware, University of Florida, University of Idaho, University of Illinois at Urbana-Champaign, University of Kentucky, University of Maryland at College Park, University of Massachusetts-Amherst, University of Michigan, University of Minnesota, University of Missouri-Rolla, University of Nebraska-Lincoln, University of New Mexico, University of Notre Dame, University of South Carolina, University of Tennessee at Knoxville, University of Washington, University of Wisconsin-Madison, Vanderbilt University.

2   Member institutions include: Colorado State University, Kansas State University, Mississippi State University, Oklahoma State University, University of Alabama, University of Idaho, University of Maryland University College, University of New Orleans, University of South Carolina, Utah State University, Washington State University.

the United States working together to offer over one thousand courses, three credit certificates, eighteen baccalaureate degree programs, and more than fifty graduate degree and certificate programs through distance education (National Universities Degree Consortium 1999). NUCD offers videotape and print-based independent study and correspondence courses as well as courses broadcast nationally via satellite networks. Most courses are available directly from the individual members. NUDC has not been able to generate programs that stand separately from its member institutions, although it has facilitated substantial cooperation in sharing courses, student services, and marketing.

A final example of consortial arrangements that have evolved from the extended classroom model is the American Distance Education Consortium (ADEC)[3], headquartered in Lincoln, Nebraska. With sixty institutional and affiliate members, ADEC is the largest consortium of those reviewed. Originally initiated in the late 1980s as AGSAT, the consortium has broadened its programming mission beyond agricultural programs offered through state university colleges of agriculture and has expanded its technological base beyond satellite. However, its current activities are still heavily focused in these content areas and dependent upon satellite delivery as a technology of choice.

[3] Member institutions include: Alabama A&M University, Iowa State University, North Carolina State University, Alcorn State University, Kansas State University, Ohio State University, University of Arizona, University of Kentucky, Oklahoma State University, University of Arkansas, Kentucky State University, Oregon State University, University of Arkansas at Pine Bluff, Lac Courte Oreilles Ojibwa Community College, Pennsylvania State University, University of California, Langston University, Purdue University, Clemson University, Louisiana State University, Rutgers University, Colorado State University, University of Maryland-College Park, South Dakota State University, Cornell University, University of Maryland-Eastern Shore, The University of Tennessee, CSREES-USDA, The University of Melbourne, Australia, Tennessee State University, University of Delaware, College of the Menominee Nation, Texas A&M University, Delaware State University, Michigan State University, Texas Tech University, Dine College, University of Minnesota, Tuskegee University, Dull Knife Memorial College, Mississippi State University, Utah State University, University of Florida, University of Missouri at Columbia, Virginia Tech University, Florida A&M University, University of Nebraska-Lincoln, West Virginia University, University of Georgia, University of Nevada-Reno, Washington State University, Haskell Indian Nations University, University of New Hampshire, University of Wisconsin-Madison, University of Idaho, New Mexico State University, University of Wyoming, University of Illinois, North Carolina A&T State University.

By aggregating the time demands of each participating institution into an overall package, ADEC can command significant purchasing clout for expensive satellite time, a factor that is part of the glue that holds it together. By sharing specialized courses in agriculture and other subject areas among members and affiliate members, ADEC can further justify the cost of purchasing satellite time. ADEC also functions as a clearinghouse for information and a convener of discussion and problem-solving activities among members. Finally, ADEC serves as a marketing arm for these universities and the programs under ADEC's purview, aggregating knowledge and information about nationally and internationally available programs in a single organizational location.

Emerging Online, Web-based Universities

With the development of computer conferencing systems and the World Wide Web, many new online universities have been established in just the past five years. These universities are coming into existence specifically to utilize new Web technologies that support learning independent of time, location, and distance but that allow students to study together. These institutions offer opportunities for students to learn through both synchronous and asynchronous interaction with each other and a faculty member. A classroom environment with student and faculty interaction is created, but students are not necessarily all in the classroom at the same time.

Online universities define their competitive market advantage based upon the convenience of the electronic, computer-based access they provide to specific programs. Unlike the national distance learning universities, which have a historical tradition tied to correspondence study and the post office, these new universities focus on the use of new technologies to provide not only improved access but also better interaction between and among students. While their numbers are relatively few and their structure is evolving rapidly, the following is a list of exclusively online universities and organizations bearing the title "university" that are currently on the Web:

1. Athena University

2. California Coast University

3. American Coastline University

4. Commonwealth Open University

5. Cyber State University

6. Greenleaf University

7. Jones International University

8. Kennedy Western University

9. International University

10. Open University

11. Southern California University of Professional Studies

12. Virtual Online University

Of the universities noted above, only Jones International University is regionally accredited (by the North Central Association of Schools and Colleges). The other universities are too newly established to receive accreditation, and some may never apply for or receive this certification of authenticity and legitimacy.

Jones International University is a for-profit institution owned by a for-profit company, Jones Cable. Jones International University was established by Jones Cable CEO Glenn Jones in 1995. It offers online undergraduate and graduate degrees in business communications. Enrollments in the program are small, but the university's affiliation with other Jones companies that market the program in the U.S. and Europe gives the university a substantial base for program delivery and enrollment growth. The university was approved as a candidate for institutional accreditation in March 1997 by the North Central Association, the regional accrediting organization for the Midwest states. It received accreditation in 1999, becoming the first entirely online institution to receive this status.

Magellan University was established in 1993 to use the tools of the Internet to deliver education beyond the boundaries of the conventional college campus. The institution's motto, "Excellence in Education, Anywhere, Anytime," undergirds its intention to make programs available worldwide. To date, only courses have been offered, but the intent is to develop degree programs in the future.

Will Distance Education/ Technology-based Universities Become Global Universities?

One of the subthemes of this book is the probable globalization of universities during the coming years. Mason (1998) concurs with Hanna (1998) that, as we enter the twenty-first century, there are no examples of truly global universities. While not able to offer specific examples of global institutions, both Mason and Hanna argue that the future is likely to include many examples of such institutions. Mason (1998, 11) defines a global university as featuring five interconnected criteria:

1. Students in more than two continents of the world are able to communicate with each other and with the teacher.

2. There is an express aim on the part of the teacher or institution to attract international participation.

3. Course content is devised specifically for transnational participation.

4. Support structures — both institutional and technological — exist to tutor and administer to a global student body.

5. Operations are on a scale of more than one program and more than one curriculum area, with more than one hundred students.

Mason (1998, 16) further suggests that:

> The distance teaching universities are obvious candidates for leading the field in the globalization movement. While the UKOU is one of the most prominent, many distance teaching institutions, whether dedicated or dual mode, have some partially global courses — franchising systems, arrangements with one or two other countries, or a few Web-based courses being piloted to test the global waters. Nevertheless, these institutions

also have entrenched attitudes, bureaucratic procedures, and general inertia to overcome before launching themselves as global institutions. Re-engineering an education institution to teach in new ways, with new media, to new kinds of students, is not an overnight task.

Hanna (1998) suggests that in order to compete effectively with rapidly developing for-profit entities and online organizations in a global environment, the large national distance learning universities must shed bureaucratic processes, and the extended traditional universities must adapt curricula, programs, courses, administrative processes, and technologies more quickly. What is very clear is that combined development of the Internet and the Web has enabled the first truly global educational interactions. We are now in the first five years of experience with this capability.

Summary

Many distance education universities developed from a print and correspondence tradition and were primarily established to increase access to higher education. Operated as governmental entities, these national distance education universities were originally organized to serve a national development function. Their purposes were more immediately political than other models outlined in this book. The largest of these universities are labeled "mega-universities" and enroll more than 100,000 students annually. They also suffer from significant government control and bureaucracy and are not able to accommodate change easily, let alone lead new developments and applications. Such institutions are generally organized within and focus upon a particular country as a whole. But, the geographic reach of some of these universities, such as the Open University of the United Kingdom, extends beyond national boundaries.

Distance education/technology-based universities in the United States are more diverse. Such institutions may be state funded (such as Thomas Edison in New Jersey), privately held (such as Jones International University), or organized as a consortium institution (such as National Technological University, which offers engineering degrees by satellite). Consortia have become popular means for some universities to collaborate, thus reducing the cost of technology acquisition and use and sharing the development of relatively expensive support systems such as marketing, student services, and, in some cases, courses and curricula.

A relatively recent phenomenon has been the establishment of a number of online universities that offer almost all of their curricula online. These universities are not yet a major factor in the overall scope of higher education; however, their growing presence has helped spark an amazing expansion of online course development and delivery among traditional universities. And there is little question that a dominant theme for the first decade of the next millennium will revolve around the nature, scope, and emerging organizational structures of online learning, and the impact this new form of learning will have upon all technology-based and extended traditional universities.

REFERENCES

Daniel, Sir John. 1996. *Mega-universities and knowledge media: Technology strategies for higher education.* London: Biddles Ltd.

Daniel, Sir John. 1998. Knowledge media for mega-universities: Scaling up new technology at the open university. Paper read at Shanghai Open and Distance Education Symposium, Shanghai, China.

Daniel, Sir John. 1999. An academic community spanning the world. Speech at Open University Alumni Dinner, Pomona, CA. [Website]. Available from < http://www.open.ac.uk/vcs-speeches/ >.

Hall, James W. 1991. *Access through innovation: New colleges for new students.* New York: American Council on Education & Macmillan.

Hanna, Donald E. 1998. Higher education in an era of digital competition: Emerging organizational models. [Website]. *Journal of Asynchronous Learning* 2(1). Available from < http://www.alm.org/alnweb/journal /jlan_vol2issue1.htm#hanna >.

Keegan, Desmond. 1988. On defining distance education. In *Distance education: International perspectives,* edited by David Sewart, Desmond Keegan, and Borje Holmberg. New York: Routledge, Chapman & Hall, Inc.

Keegan, Desmond. 1994. The competitive advantages of distance teaching universities. *Open Learning* 9(2):9-36.

Mason, Robin. 1998. *Globalizing education: Trends and applications.* London; New York: Routledge.

National Universities Degree Consortium. 1999. *National Universities Degree Consortium* [Website]. Available from < http:// www.sc.edu/ deis/NUDC/ >.

Rumble, Greville, and Keith Harry, eds. 1982. *The distance teaching universities.* New York: St Martin's Press.

Chapter 6

New Players on the Block: For-profit, Corporate, and Competency-based Learning Universities

By Donald E. Hanna

Thirty years ago, the concept of for-profit educational organizations was largely limited to truck-driving institutes, cosmetology schools, and correspondence schools that advertised on the back of a matchbook cover. Today, the matchbooks have disappeared, but the marketplace for adult learning is increasingly attractive to existing and new for-profit universities, organizations, and private businesses (Davis and Botkin 1994; Eurich 1985; Ghazi 1997; Ghazi and Irani 1997; Sperling and Tucker 1997). However, this transformation is not widely recognized in higher education today, even though the rapid expansion of for-profit institutions is increasingly difficult for even the most insular academic environments to ignore. Why are for-profit universities important in the mix of higher education models? Because they:

- have access to private capital and funds needed for start-up and expansion;

- can purchase, lease, or modify facilities quickly;

- focus upon a specific niche of the adult marketplace for education, namely, those knowledge workers who require high levels of education and whose employers can afford to pay the tuition for them in many cases;

- stay close to their customer base, thereby producing a high-quality educational product;
- are managed as well as governed;
- are focused upon making necessary changes as needed rather than as mandated;
- operate year-round;
- are experiencing significant enrollment growth overall.

The University of Phoenix now has the largest headcount of any private nonprofit or for-profit university (Sperling and Tucker 1997, 36).

Today's for-profit institutions of higher education have carefully delineated a focused educational market (Sperling and Tucker 1997). These institutions are substantially different than traditional nonprofit institutions of higher education, whether public or private, and they are much more sophisticated than earlier for-profit institutions. They are, in a word, entrepreneurial, and they carry with them the entrepreneurial culture that Bergquist (1992) omitted from his descriptions of the culture of traditional universities and colleges.

For-profit institutions derive almost all of their operating revenue from the tuition and fees that students or their employers pay. These institutions are also expected to return a dividend to investors who have provided the capital to create them. They are very responsive to the demands of the educational marketplace. Unlike the core traditional universities with eighteen to twenty-two-year-olds as the dominant set of learners, for-profit universities generally serve a market largely composed of older, career-oriented students who are interested in certification as well as degrees and who are focused upon practical application of content. In part, for-profit universities serve this market because there is money to be made. But they also serve it because this aspect of the higher education market has not been well or comprehensively served by existing not-for-profit institutions.

Because for-profit, adult-centered universities operate based upon the bottom-line, they are also particularly focused on developing and expanding programs that attract large numbers of students or that offer entry to or advancement in fields in which employment is both plentiful and lucrative.

For-profit universities develop market-driven programs with standardized curricula. Programs are then offered, in many cases, across multiple locations, using replication as a strategy for organizational growth. Programs are almost always career focused; and course offerings typically enable students to either enter a technical career or to advance to new management responsibilities. For-profit universities make minimal investments in expensive physical plants. Their student services are generally basic learning centers, with few frills. For better or worse, they sponsor no football team or intercollegiate sports program to rally the alumni/ae.

For-profit institutions also do not replicate many social aspects of universities. As a result, they offer neither a full complement of nor a direct alternative to the traditional university. Nevertheless, they are formidable competitors to universities (including, in this case, community colleges) that are, or that seek to become, responsive to the adult marketplace. Table 6.1 illustrates the dominant characteristics and assumptions of for-profit institutions in relation to both the extended traditional university and the traditional university.

The University of Phoenix

Perhaps the best known for-profit university in the United States is the University of Phoenix, which offers traditional classroom-based instruction at the undergraduate and graduate levels in many states (University of Phoenix 1999). With enrollment having grown from zero to more than 61,000 students in less than twenty-five years, it is the largest and most successful of the U.S.-based for-profit, adult-centered universities. Most students attend classes in learning centers located in urban areas in more than a dozen states, located primarily in the West (as shown in figure 6.1).

Table 6.1
Comparison of For-profit, Adult-centered Universities; Extended Traditional Universities; and Traditional Residential Universities

Input	Traditional Universities	Extended Traditional Universities	For-profit, Adult-centered Universities
Philosophy	Students come to campus	Campus goes to students	Campus and non-campus philosophy
Mission	Mission defined by level of instruction	Externally focused; degree completion and workforce development	Almost exclusively workforce focused
Funding	$ per full-time student	More self-sustaining and market driven	Market driven, workforce focused, and profit driven
Curricula	Relatively stable and comprehensive curriculum	More flexible curriculum content for workforce competence and development	Focused on workplace needs; adult oriented
Instruction	Most courses are lecture based	Greater variety of methods and use of student experience	Methods typically standardized across locations; greater use of student experience
Faculty	Primarily full-time faculty; academic preparation and credentials	Greater use of adjuncts with professional experience	Usually staffed with part-time faculty with professional experience
Students	Selectivity at admission	Life and work experience is greater factor in admission	Life and work experience is significant factor in admission
Library	Volumes in library	Access to specific documents and resources appropriate to program	Access to specific documents and resources appropriate to program
Learning Technology	Enhance lecture-oriented instruction	Both lecture oriented and used to extend access	Both lecture oriented and used to extend access
Physical Facilities	Extensive physical plant	Still campus based but less reliance on physical plant	Physical plant is provided in response to market demand
Productivity Outcomes	Student credit-hours and degrees	Student credit-hours and degrees	Bottom line is revenue generated compared with expenses/profitability
Governance	Board of Trustees	Board of Trustees	Board of Directors
Accreditation	Institutional by region; individual programs or disciplines are also accredited	Institutional by region as part of parent organization's accreditation; individual programs or disciplines are also accredited	Institutional by region; individual programs or disciplines are also accredited

Figure 6.1
The University of Phoenix Main Campus

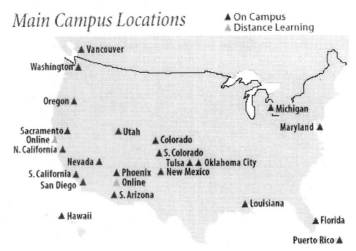

Locations as of July 15, 1999

Enrollment in the university's learning centers is growing by almost 28 percent per year, and enrollment in its online courses and programs grew 51 percent in fiscal year 1997. More than 3,200 students are enrolled in the universities online courses and programs, which includes one of the first online MBA programs in the United States.

The university is also rapidly expanding programs that serve corporations. For example, it has developed a contract with AT&T to provide academic programs to AT&T learning centers worldwide.

Recently, the university announced plans and received approval from the State of Pennsylvania to open campuses in Pittsburgh and Philadelphia, even though many in Pennsylvania believe that the state is already overpopulated with institutions of higher education. According to Mary Catherine Conroy-Hayden, vice president of program development and external relations at Carlow College in Pittsburgh, the University of Phoenix will be a significant force affecting student choice in the state and a "wake-up call" to many institutions (Blumenstyk 1999). "It has already forced some four-year institutions to develop articulation agreements with community colleges. Institutions that are flexible and innovative are going to survive. Phoenix appeals to adults who know what they want and how they want to get it" (Blumenstyk 1999, A43).

The University of Phoenix is owned by the Apollo Group, which trades on the New York Stock Exchange under the symbol APOL. For the second quarter of 1999, Apollo's net revenues increased by 28 percent, to $110.7 million in 1999 from $86.5 million in 1998, due primarily to a 24.1 percent increase in average degree student enrollments and tuition price increases averaging four to six percent (depending on the geographic area and program). Most of the company's campuses, including their respective learning centers, had increases in net revenues and average degree student enrollments from 1998 to 1999, although the overall percentage increase in both enrollments and revenues was less than in previous fiscal years.

Program replication has been the primary strategy the University of Phoenix has employed to achieve its organizational growth. Similar to the McDonald's Corporation's strategy of constant quality and equivalency across locations and outlets, Phoenix attempts to standardize courses and degree programs across locations as much as possible. Program growth is attributable to increasing enrollments at each campus location and to increasing the number of campuses. Decisions to launch new programs occur on an institution-wide basis to ensure uniformity of curriculum and course content.

Strayer University

Strayer University is a for-profit higher education institution offering undergraduate and graduate degree programs at twelve campuses in Washington, D.C., northern Virginia, and Maryland (Strayer University 1999). Strayer is owned by Strayer Education, Inc., which trades on the New York Stock Exchange under the symbol STRA. In November 1997, its board of directors awarded a 3-for-2 stock split on top of its regular annual dividend to shareholders. Its name was changed from Strayer College to Strayer University in 1998. Enrollment growth has been steady, with approximately a 5 percent growth rate expected for 1999. Strayer has begun an aggressive strategy of program and campus replication, with the opening of four new campuses in Maryland and Virginia in 1999.

Unlike the University of Phoenix but like many of its for-profit counterpart institutions, Strayer has not yet invested heavily in delivery by technology. However, the university recently announced that it would open an online division called Strayer Online in 1999. Strayer is not alone; 1999 has become the year of the online division in the for-profit university world. The dramatic rise of Internet commerce has convinced almost all businesses that they need to plan for an online presence, and for-profit higher education is no exception.

Education Management Corporation

Education Management Corporation operates for-profit educational programs that have provided career-related education for more than thirty-five years. The company offers associate and bachelor's degree programs and non-degree programs in the areas of design, media arts, culinary arts, fashion, and professional development. Its units include: The Art Institutes, The New York Restaurant School, The National Center for Paralegal Training, and The National Center for Professional Development.

For the nine months ended March 31, 1999, net revenues of the corporation had increased 17.8 percent, to $195.6 million, compared with $166.1 million for the comparable period in fiscal 1998. Net income had increased 31.6 percent, to $16.3 million, compared with the previous year (Educational Management Corporation 1999). The growth rate for Educational Management has been in double figures for several years, and the company has been traded on the New York Stock Exchange since 1997.

Like Strayer University, Educational Management Corporation has not invested heavily in online or distance learning. However, consistent with the overwhelming trend already noted, the company recently announced plans to open an online distance learning program in 1999.

Quest Education Corporation

Quest Education Corporation provides diversified, career-oriented postsecondary education to approximately 12,500 students in thirty schools located in eleven states. The company's schools offer bachelor's degrees, associate degrees, and diploma programs designed to provide students with the knowledge and skills necessary to qualify them for entry-level employment in the fields of health care, business, information technology, fashion and design, and photography.

Total student enrollment for Quest for the year ended March 31, 1999, had increased approximately 25 percent over the previous year, with 14 percent of the increase attributed to the recent purchase of five Iowa colleges and the opening of a new Hesser College location in Concord, New Hampshire. Enrollment otherwise increased from 10,008 as of March 31, 1998, to 11,088 enrolled in the same schools one year later, an 11 percent increase.

Recently, Quest announced that its Hamilton College and American Institute of Commerce (AIC) schools have received approval from the North Central Association of Colleges and Schools (NCA) for the following online associate degree programs: Applied Management and Interdisciplinary Studies, and for two, for-credit, online information technology (IT) programs; Microsoft Network Engineer and Microsoft Solution Developer.

According to its news release dated April 29, 1999, Quest indicated that "Hamilton and AIC are two of only a few colleges in the nation, and the first in the state of Iowa, to receive accreditation for online programs from NCA." While this statement fails to recognize the hundreds, if not thousands, of online degree programs already initiated and delivered in one form or another by extended traditional universities, it does communicate the perception of many leaders within for-profit entities regarding the promise of online education for the future. It also suggests that we are only beginning to see widespread interest, suggesting that increased investment in online programs is inevitable and likely to accelerate rapidly.

Sylvan Learning Systems

Sylvan Learning Systems, Inc., is a provider of educational services to families, schools, and industry. It also delivers computer-based testing for academic admissions as well as for professional licensure and certification programs, at more than 1,300 testing centers. The company also maintains a network of more than 640 Sylvan Learning Centers that provide personalized instructional services to students of all ages and skill levels. Sylvan also provides educational services under contract to public and private school systems through the Sylvan Contract Educational Services division. Moreover, it provides adult professional education and training through its Caliber Learning Network. Revenues for Sylvan Learning Systems grew by more than 43 percent as of the first quarter of the 1999 fiscal year, a growth rate that has been consistently reached over the past several years.

ITT Educational Services

ITT is a provider of technology-oriented postsecondary degree programs in the United States based on revenues and student enrollment. It offers associate, bachelor's, and master's degree programs and non-degree diploma programs to approximately 25,000 students. As of 1999, ITT operates sixty-seven institutes located in twenty-seven states. Programs are designed for individuals preparing for careers in various fields involving technology. As of December 31, 1998, approximately 99 percent of ITT's students were enrolled in a degree program, with approximately 74 percent enrolled in electronics engineering technology (EET) programs and approximately 23 percent enrolled in computer-aided drafting technology (CAD) programs.

ITT is traded on the New York Stock Exchange under the symbol ESI. It became a publicly traded company in 1994 after operating for years as a subsidiary of ITT Industries, an Indiana corporation. Student enrollment has increased gradually from 19,860 in 1993 to 25,608 at the end of 1998. Over this same period of time, total revenues increased 72 percent, from $169 million to $291.4 million, an 11.5 percent compound annual growth rate. Net income increased 179 percent, from $8.3 million to $23.2 million, a 22.7 percent compound annual growth rate.

ITT opened three new institutes in each of 1997 and 1998 and two new institutes in January 1999. In addition, in 1998 the corporation launched its first information technology program, Computer Network Systems Technology, at three of its institutes. The corporation plans to open two more new institutes in 1999. Strategies for growth include replication of existing programs through opening new institutes, as well as program diversification at existing campuses. The company does not yet appear to have developed a strategy for online education.

DeVry, Inc.

DeVry, Inc., owns and operates DeVry Institutes, Keller Graduate School of Management, and Becker CPA Review. DeVry is aggressively pursuing a growth strategy of acquisitions, as in the purchase of Educational Development Corporation, which operates Denver Technical College, and also the Fox Gearty CPA Review Course. The corporation also has an active strategy of geographic replication of programs and campuses, with plans to open a third campus in the Los Angeles area in 1999, a third campus in Chicago, and new locations in Arizona and Virginia for Keller Graduate School of Management. Net income is increasing, with third quarter 1999 net income increasing approximately 25 percent over the third-quarter of 1998.

Keller Graduate School of Management offers a systematic approach to replication of its curricula. Keller uses an approach called "System-Supported Teaching and Learning" (SSTL) to meet course objectives, which are oriented around a number of problem-based courses. SSTL is teacher directed and content focused, organized around the concept of mastery learning combined with a total quality approach, which permits distribution of mastery learning benefits to multiple sections, courses, and locations. The goal of the Keller Graduate School of Management is to move away from the concept of the individual course to one of commonality in all respects across all courses, and to a concept of standardization of content, which, by definition, is teacher directed. The school offers courses at twenty-eight sites in the United States, and, like almost every other for-profit university, it has initiated an Online Education Center. Keller centers are situated in major metropolitan areas and near transportation routes in order to reduce commuting time for adults. In this regard, they are a direct competitor with the University of Phoenix in markets where both are present.

As indicated by the strategies outlined in table 6.2, the entrepreneurial culture, discussed in chapter 4 as a new and not always welcome add-on for traditional universities, is well established in and provides foundational assumptions for for-profit universities. Organizational growth and expansion is a significant short- and long-term strategy for for-profit universities. This growth in programs, revenue, and campuses is occurring regionally, nationally, and, in a few instances such as Sylvan Learning Systems, internationally.

Unlike traditional universities, which, until recently, have largely limited their organizational development to a single campus community, region, or state (in the case of the large state universities), for-profit universities have not established boundaries based upon geography. This is a fundamental cultural and organizational difference between for-profit and traditional universities, and one that gives an advantage to the for-profit university in an era of potential globalization of education.

Corporate Employee Universities

During the 1980s, a number of corporations established umbrella organizations to provide for their comprehensive human resource development, education, and training needs. Their reasons for developing comprehensive training and educational programs included the needs to develop basic educational competencies in the workforce; acculturate employees into the company; improve cooperation; communication and competencies of individual employees and teams of employees; and improve recruitment, advancement, and retention incentives.

Many corporations labeled these education and training units or sub-units as universities, and a few of these units have developed academic degree programs that sought and received accreditation. Corporations that have created units designated as universities include American Express, Apple, Disney, First Bank of America, Intel, MasterCard, Motorola, Xerox, McDonald's, and Hart, Schafner & Marx. While corporate universities generally do not offer degrees, it is clear that these corporations view learning by employees as important to their future.

Thompson (1998, 6) suggests that the term "corporate university" be defined as "an educational institution that offers one or more accredited academic degree programs, and which is a wholly-owned subsidiary of a parent corporation whose core business is not education." This provides a working definition for corporate universities as described in this book.

Eurich (1985) identified at least eighteen corporations that, in 1985, offered academic degree programs. She predicted a dramatic increase in the numbers of corporations offering accredited degree programs in the future, possibly numbering in the hundreds. Nash and Hawthorne (1987) identified seven additional corporations in 1987 and also predicted dramatic increases for the future. This expansion has not happened, and accredited, degree-granting corporate universities are no more prevalent today than they were in the 1980s. A few of the corporate universities described by Eurich (1985) have become independent of their corporate parent organizations (DeVry from Bell and Howell, for example), and several others have either ceased to offer degree programs or have merged programs with existing universities. Other corporate universities that were projected by Eurich to evolve into degree-granting organizations have failed to do so. In fact, Thompson (1998) concludes that of the twenty-five universities identified by Eurich and by Nash and Hawthorne, only five continue to operate as distinctly corporate universities, and these five have not expanded in academic scope or enrollments to any great degree.

Table 6.2

For-profit Strategies For Growth and Expansion

Competitive Strategy	Course Level	Program Level	Institution Level	Esablished Institutional Examples
Duplication	Duplicate specific successful courses	Duplicate selected niche programs	Duplicate independent organizational model	University of Phoenix Online Strayer University
Replication	Identical courses across all locations	Multiple sites	Multiple	Keller School
Diversification	Increase content areas offered	Increase programs offered	Increase program and course array	Strayer University
Niche	Identify specialty content areas	Select programs with narrow constituencies		Educational Management Corporation
Niche Technologies	Build courses around technologies	Build programs	Tie program to particular technologies and delivery	Jones International University
Start-ups	Create new courses and curricula	Create new program	Found a new institution	Jones International University
Acquisition	Buy courses from other providers	Contract for specific programs	Purchase new content or locations	Sylvan Learning Systems
Spin-offs	Identify and sell profitable courses	Market and tailor specific programs for customers and other educational organizations	Create new forms of organizations with characteristics significantly different from parent	University of Wisconsin New York University University of Nebraska
Mergers	Combine courses and content across disciplines to form new content	Combine programs to cross organizational and disciplinary boundaries		

Thompson (1998) identifies three major reasons for this somewhat surprising outcome, given the optimistic predictions that were prevalent in the 1980s:

1. a growing tendency of corporations to focus their attention and resources upon their core business and to "outsource" corporate education;

2. the demands of the accreditation process; and

3. a growing willingness of colleges and universities to assist corporations in meeting their educational needs.

These conclusions relate directly to the expansion of options and programs noted earlier for extended traditional universities, and also to the dramatic expansion of university-industry partnerships, in which the strengths of the private sector and the universities are combined to form new structures and relationships.

Industry-University Strategic Alliances

Many businesses that are related either to emerging technology and communications applications or to mainline applications such as publishing companies are also testing the waters in the higher education marketplace, in a variety of ways. Market opportunities are developing around both content and access, with content being the special province of universities and their faculties. But with multiple forms of access becoming increasingly important, and with no one technology or mode of access dominating the market, companies with technologies that support learning that can be independent of time and location are finding the marketplace attractive.

Partnerships and strategic alliances are also developing between and among organizations that capture each organization's primary strengths. Increasingly, these partnerships marry for-profit organizations and universities in ways that force contact and interaction between very different cultures, goals, and operating principles and assumptions. For example, UOL Publishing, a publisher of interactive and on-demand Web-based courseware for the academic and corporate education markets, assists community colleges, proprietary colleges, and extension and continuing education programs in meeting the growing demand for distance learning. UOL course development and delivery software is intended to enable institutions that wish to take advantage of the growing markets for adult learning to get courses up and running very quickly and reliably. Real Education, another company that specializes in assisting colleges and universities to develop online courses, changed its name in 1999 to eCollege.com to reflect the growing emphasis on higher education. The corporation has also formed an alliance with Pearson Education, combining resources to build course learning environments. The combined resources of the two companies are intended to provide universities and corporate training units with all of the means to create an online educational program, including:

- a reliable infrastructure, seamlessly integrating technology with traditional teaching methods;
- customized teaching and learning environments in which students have access to all of the learning resources they have come to expect;
- a complete, globally accessible online learning program in which students can depend on quick delivery of course content;
- high-quality course content, which supports the instruction of the independent distance learner.

One potential benefit of this interaction is the opportunity for both the corporate and university organizations to acquire much-needed information and knowledge from the other, and also to change some of the unexamined practices that may be inhibiting the respective organizations from developing a successful strategy in a changed marketplace. Another view, offered by Sir Douglas Hague of Great Britain (Hague 1991, 13), is that, speaking of universities in the United Kingdom, universities must develop partnerships in order to survive the onslaught of competition:

To avoid being driven out of activities which they have imagined their own by right, the universities will have to make substantial changes in what they do and how they do it. Where they find that difficult, one solution will be to form alliances with the interlopers. Increasingly, the choice will be alliance or annihilation.

Finally, as described in chapter 4, the development of partnerships and alliances can be a way to spread and share the substantial capital investment and risk associated with developing and employing new learning technologies (Karelis 1999).

Universities are also forming strategic alliances with major companies in fields such as publishing (Addison, Wesley and Longman), communications (Echo Star, Prime Star), entertainment (Disney), and telecommunications (AT&T, GTE). In most of these partnerships, the university brings content and faculty to the enterprise, and the company contributes technology, marketing, packaging, and business knowledge and thinking. Whether these alliances will work is still to be discovered. But new contracts, limited liability companies, and other approaches are being organized every day.

A growing number of corporations are also establishing strategic partnerships with colleges and universities to jointly develop degree programs tailored to meet their specific corporate needs (Meister 1994). Thompson (1998) outlines AT&T's activities in conjunction with a number of universities, detailing relationships with universities such as Penn State, Indiana, Wisconsin, George Washington School of Business and Public Management, Virginia Tech, Rhode Island, Georgia Tech, Arizona State, Rutgers, Columbia, the Wharton School of Business, and the University of Phoenix.

Competency-based Organizations

Organizations are also emerging to take advantage of recent changes in the labor market brought about by the increasing pace of change, especially in technology areas. With learning a requirement to stay current, and with workers changing both careers and employers more often than ever before, individuals need to certify and re-certify their competencies on a regular basis. In the professions, this has become a requirement known as "mandatory continuing professional education" (Nowlen 1988). In information technology, the categories of certification include various network certifications, software competencies, and system capabilities. Mechanisms for ensuring that individuals have requisite knowledge, abilities, and experiences, and that they are able to perform critical functions, are being developed in many professional fields. It is inevitable that these approaches are now being applied to higher education.

Whether mandated by law or by the marketplace, individuals, their current and prospective employers, and the public increasingly rely on certification to document an individual's knowledge and his or her ability to apply knowledge in real situations. For-profit companies have developed around the need for certification, primarily in the area of corporate training, and new nonprofit organizations are developing with certification and competency-based learning as major products. Certifying learning and knowledge through assessment appears to be a growth opportunity, one that existing higher education organizations have little experience or infrastructure to develop and have largely ignored. However, these measurements will increasingly need to reflect and measure abilities to apply content to real situations, and to gauge skills that are more difficult to measure, such as synthesis and application, problemsolving, teamwork, and creativity.

The challenge to traditional colleges and universities offered by organizations such as these is captured by Olcott (1997, 2), who suggests the following:

> Particularly if colleges and universities are to be competitive in the marketplace, future models of financing must be reconstructed to recognize diverse sources of learning (outside the traditional academic environment) that are not defined by FTE, credit-hour, or clock-hour restrictions. A competency-based approach strikes at the heart of traditional funding structures in higher education. For example, legislative appropriations are tied to FTE formulas while vocational funding is defined in terms of student clock-hours.

Certification assumes that people need to be able to demonstrate knowledge and mastery, whether acquired through life experiences, self-directed learning, employer-based learning, or university classes. Especially in information technology areas, the need for certification has grown dramatically as technology shifts rapidly and on-the-job experience becomes a more widely accepted method of acquiring knowledge and skills.

One example of certification applied to higher education is credit for proficiency based on life experience, which is now awarded by many institutions as part of their academic degree programs. Such credit is awarded for experiences and knowledge gained on the job and in other ways that can be demonstrated through testing, portfolio assessment, and other evaluation mechanisms. Credit earned can then be applied toward certification or a degree, usually in limited numbers. This approach is very different from the model of a degree-granting institution that awards the degree based upon assessment of the student's mastery of core skills and competencies and demonstrated critical knowledge.

New York's Regents College, which advertises itself as "America's First Virtual University," is an example of an institution offering a complete baccalaureate degree program by examination. Regents has no physical campus and teaches no courses. Students engage in a variety of guided activities in preparation for examinations that are intended to measure the knowledge necessary to be awarded a degree. Upon passing the appropriate exams, regardless of how the student developed his or her knowledge base, the student is awarded a Regent's degree. A standard for graduation supplants a standard for admission. Regents recently formed an international partnership with the Rima Group of Colleges in Kuala Lumpur, Malaysia, to make its programs available to the Rima Group's graduates (Regents College 1999).

Another example of an organization that has initiated a competency-based certification degree is Western Governors University (WGU). Formed by the governors of thirteen western states in 1996, WGU defines the skills and competencies of particular degree programs and awards an accredited degree to students who demonstrate these skills and competencies. Unlike the examination model of Regents College, competency is judged through a variety of mechanisms, including completion of coursework from traditional universities, portfolio assessments, examinations, and evaluation of workplace experience. Competencies necessary for degrees are defined by WGU using faculty specialists, who develop the degree program assessment process.

WGU has developed an extensive advising and assessment process that guides students in a very personal and tailored way to appropriate learning resources, materials, and institutions, theoretically enabling the student to take the shortest and least-costly path to demonstrating competencies required for the degree. While the model is too new to be assessed, early enrollments were less than expected. It may take some time for the assessment, competency, and performance model described by Nowlen (1988) to take effect in colleges and universities. The western governors clearly intend to push the envelope, and by doing so they are very likely to have an effect upon traditional universities. Clearly, WGU has been a wake-up call for many university faculty members, as well as university leaders, as demonstrated by the letter sent to Governor Gary Locke of Washington by more than eight hundred University of Washington faculty members protesting the state of Washington's participation and funding of WGU.

Characteristics of competency-based univrsities with degree-granting authoroity are described in detail in table 6.3.

The Role of Accreditation

Accreditation plays a vital role in establishing the long-term viability of all these models. Accreditation is generally concerned with measuring traditional inputs to instruction, as earlier discussed. This approach emanates from traditional universities, and institutional accreditation processes now in place in the United States are geared to assessing the attributes of traditional residential universities. While numerous universities offer online educational programs, these programs are accredited as part of the institution's regular cyclical accreditation process.

Table 6.3
Characteristics of Degree/Certification,
Competency-Based Organizations

Input	Characteristics
Philosophy	No physical campus
Mission	Externally and market focused
Funding	Intended to be self-sustaining and market driven
Curricula	Defined by competencies and knowledge, not courses offered
Instruction	Emphasizes students' independent learning and initiative
Faculty	No full-time, teaching faculty; advising and support services are assumed by professional advisors
Students	Life and work experience is major factor in admission; graduation standards more important than admissions standards
Library	No library; access to materials through cooperative relationships with other institutions
Learning Technology	Access to information about courses and programs provided using technology; technology important in providing the maximum access to learning resources
Physical Facilities	No physical plant
Productivity Outcomes	Student assessments, competencies acquired, degrees awarded
Governance	Varies, from administrative board to consortial representative board
Accreditation	Institutional by region, although Western Governors University is seeking accreditation from four regional accreditation agencies in one process

All of the models discussed in this chapter differ in fundamental ways from those of traditional institutions, as earlier discussed. Because universities are increasingly offering programs internationally, regional accrediting associations are under increasing pressure to change the way they accredit institutions and the criteria they use to establish eligibility for accreditation. Only recently, with the establishment of for-profit universities and new models such as Western Governors University's competency-based model, have accrediting agencies been challenged to review their accrediting processes.

An excellent example of this major challenge for accreditation is the establishment of Western Governors University. WGU is based upon measuring student learning outcomes in very personal and direct ways, and its quality must be assessed based upon how well it accomplishes this goal. WGU also intends to serve students across a wide geographic base. These characteristics, among others, challenge the traditional regional accreditation process for institutions. The response of the accrediting associations has been, in the case of Western Governors University, to convene a cross-regional accreditation team to develop guidelines for evaluating and assessing this new institution.

These processes, as described in chapter 2, have generally been organized around a campus, a campus regional service area, and inputs to the educational process.

Western Governors University represents an excellent example of this major challenge for accreditation, because its effectiveness is based upon the assessment of student learning outcomes rather than reviewing institutional inputs. Because Western Governors University's mission focuses on producing these measurable learning outcomes for its students, its quality must be assessed upon how well it accomplishes this goal.

Note also that the models framed by this and preceding chapters do not capture all aspects of every institutional model. There are many variations, and they are organized in increasingly diverse ways. Of particular note are the numbers of universities that intend to or are established to capture a global rather than a regional or national market for university education.

A Global University?

The marketplace for learning is becoming global (Duderstadt 1997; Mason 1998). With new technologies, neither language nor distance is a barrier to access, although cultural norms and patterns are among the formidable obstacles to learning across political and cultural boundaries.

There are currently few examples of universities that are truly global and multinational in character, although there are hints of what such a program might look like. San Diego-based National University has developed a "global MBA," offered online, that is available in Argentina, Turkey, Mexico, Ecuador, and Portugal. The program establishes linkages with local host institutions; these institutions provide faculty members and services for enrolled students on a contractual basis. Other universities are also attempting to expand from a national to an international base of operation.

As a signal of the new global environment, two aggressive organizations have teamed up to form a standards review for educational programming that crosses international boundaries. This new organization is the Global Alliance for Transnational Education (GATE), formed in 1996. GATE's purpose is to be a source of information on educational programs and certifications worldwide for corporate human resource professionals and higher education officers and students. Its goal is to maximize information and assure quality in a rapidly globalizing education and human resource market. GATE's programs and services are designed to:

- explore current issues that companies face in international hiring and that universities face in international admissions;

- network across national borders with other corporations and educational associations and institutions;

- access global information on educational systems, institutions, and transnational educational offerings;

- develop principles of good practice and recognition for quality international education and training.

While GATE does not offer programs, it was formed in recognition that the number of educational programs offered on a worldwide basis is about to explode, and that some mechanism for global information sharing and quality standards needed to be established. According to GATE literature, there is a need for the organization because:

> The global marketplace and new technologies are contributing to the rapid globalization of higher education. Today's business environment draws its professional work force from all corners of the globe. Human resource development divisions of multi-national corporations face the increasing challenge of evaluating courses and degrees from other countries when identifying personnel. Further, higher education is no longer provided solely within national borders. Provided both by the higher education and corporate sectors, transnational education can be found in multiple forms, provided both electronically and through traditional instruction and training programs. Issues of quality, purpose, and responsibility abound in this new borderless educational arena and the time is ripe for an international alliance of business, higher education, and government dedicated to principled advocacy for transnational educational programs (Global Alliance for Training and Education 1999).

GATE represents an early pioneering effort to develop international standards for quality that recognize that higher education is no longer a local or regional or even national enterprise. It also promotes the use of technology in expanding global access. The organization may be the foundation for a new form of institutional assessment and accreditation on a global basis, or it may be no more than a clearinghouse for globally accessible higher education.

As the millennium comes to a close, there are no concrete examples of fully operating global universities that have been established purposefully to operate in a global context. But the examples offered here demonstrate some future possibilities.

Each of the models and corresponding examples presented in this chapter has been developed to create a competitive response in a rapidly changing and growing higher education market-place. With rapidly developing learning technologies creating new possibilities for organizing learning for adults, these models are both competing with and causing change in the traditional, residential model of higher education. The potential benefits of this new competitive environment include removing barriers to existing educational programs, responding more effectively and quickly to emerging educational needs (especially of adults), improving educational quality, and achieving long-term cost efficiencies. The potential risks include an overemphasis on the bottom line, an efficiency model of higher education that ignores what we know about effective learning, the standardization and establishment of homogeneous approaches to education and learning that do not fit in a multicultural world, and the possibility that the wealthier will gain even greater advantages over the poor as the speed of knowledge access and distribution increases with the exponential growth of the World Wide Web.

REFERENCES

Bergquist, William H. 1992. *The four cultures of the academy: Insights and strategies for improving leadership in collegiate organizations.* San Francisco: Jossey-Bass, Publishers.

Blumenstyk, Goldie. 1999. In a first, the North Central Association accredits an online university. *The Chronicle of Higher Education,* 19 March: A27.

Davis, Stanley M., and James W. Botkin. 1994. *The monster under the bed: How business is mastering the opportunity of knowledge for profit.* New York: Simon & Schuster.

Duderstadt, James. 1997. The future of the university in an age of knowledge. *Journal of Asynchronous Learning Networks* 1(2). [Website] Available at < http//www.aln.org/alnweb/journal/jaln_Vol1issue2. htm#Duderstadt >.

Educational Management Corporation. 1999. Report of EDMC's third quarter fiscal results. Pittsburgh, PA: Educational Management Corporation.

Eurich, Nell. 1985. Corporate classrooms: The learning business. In *A Carnegie Foundation Special Report.* Princeton, NJ, Lawrenceville, N.J.: Carnegie Foundation for the Advancement of Teaching. (Copies available from Princeton University Press.)

Ghazi, Kian. 1997. *The adult education market: A comprehensive guide.* New York: Lehman Brothers Education Services.

Ghazi, Kian, and Isabelle. Irani. 1997. *Emerging trends in the $670 billion education market.* New York: Lehman Brothers.

Global Alliance for Training and Education. 1999. *GATE vision: Achieving worldwide access to quality education and training* [Website]. Global Alliance for Training and Education. Available from < http://www.edugate.org/vision.html >.

Hague, Sir Douglas. 1991. *Beyond universities: A new republic of the intellect.* London: Institute of Economic Affairs.

Karelis, Charles. 1999. *Education technology and cost control: Four models* [Website]. Fund for the Improvement of Postsecondary Education. Available from < http://www.ed.gov/offices/OPE/FIPSE/LAAP/ reading.html >.

Mason, Robin. 1998. *Globalizing education: Trends and applications*. London; New York: Routledge.

Meister, Jeanne C. 1994. *Corporate quality universities: Lessons in building a world-class work force*. New York: Irwin.

Nash, Nancy, and Elizabeth Hawthorne. 1987. Formal recognition of employer-sponsored instruction: Conflict and collegiality in post-secondary education. College Station, TX.: Association for the Study of Higher Education.

Nowlen, Philip M. 1988. *A new approach to continuing education for business and the professions: The performance model*. New York: Macmillan Publishing Company.

Olcott, Donald John. 1997. Renewing the vision: Past perspectives and future imperatives for distance education. *The Journal of Continuing Higher Education* 45(3).

Regents College. 1999. *Regents College* [Website]. Regents College. Available from < http://www.regents.edu/ >.

Sperling, John G., and Robert W. Tucker. 1997. *For-profit higher education: Developing a world-class workforce*. New Brunswick, NJ: Transaction Publishers.

Strayer University. 1999. *Strayer University* [Website]. Strayer University, 12. Available from < http://www.strayer.edu/ >.

Thompson, G. 1998. *Unfulfilled prophecy: The evolution of corporate colleges*. University of Saskatchewan. Publication forthcoming.

University of Phoenix. 1999. *University of Phoenix Campuses* [Website]. University ofPhoenix. Available from < http://www.uophx.edu/uop /_campus.htm >.

Chapter 7

Leadership in the Age of Knowledge

By Janet Poley

In this knowledge-based economy, the new coin of the realm is learning. Working in the Age of Knowledge requires abilities to recognize patterns, maintain a broad set of relationships, share ideas with communities of interest, and pull value out of these relationships. Learning to master these skills becomes even more critical as collaboration and mutual advantage become the essence of most organizations (Reich 1998).

Shared leadership is not a new proposition for higher education, but the academy has not been as adept, human, or fundamentally humane in its leadership practices as the future requires. It is time for university leadership to take the high road — and quickly. The greatest challenges facing universities may not be how to raise more money or reshape undergraduate education in isolation from institutional reform, but rather how to become flexible, resilient, speedy, creative, just, and concerned.

The Jobs of Leadership – the Future Is Already Here

Xerox Parc guru John Seely Brown says the new job of leadership is not about making money but making meaning (Reich 1998). In a twist of purposes, universities, which have for centuries proclaimed to "make meaning," now want to "make money." Ironically, U.S. foundations are awash in money, but higher education does not seem to be able to tap these funds in a "big-picture" way. *Newsweek* calls it "an embarrassment of riches" as foundations parcel out the 5 percent they are required to give away each year (Spragins 1999). There is little evidence that higher education leaders have been able to make the case that they have in place or could have in place the appropriate strategies, structures, and technologies to meet the important educational challenges ahead. And an increasingly important part of the money requirement in higher education today is the need to keep pace with respect to technology (American Association of State Colleges and Universities 1999b):

> Colleges and universities spent a total of $2.8 billion on computer hardware and software for this school year. Public institutions averaged $149 per student, and private institutions averaged $283 per student. There is a reason for this spending frenzy. Results of the annual survey show substantial growth in the use of technology for academic work. The number of courses using electronic mail rose more than 11 percent (to 44 percent) since last year, while the number using Web pages for class materials and resources reached 22.5 percent, up nearly 8 percent. Responding to this demand, nearly a third of institutions have formal plans to use the Internet in distance education, an increase of about 25 percent .

In "The Future That Has Already Happened," management author Peter Drucker (1998) writes that we can see the shape of things to come. According to Drucker, inevitable upcoming events include the raising of the retirement age, the growth of the economy solely from the productivity of knowledge workers, and the absence of any single, dominant world economic power. The changing demographics mean that lifelong, continuing education for adults may become the fastest growth industry in the United States. Drucker argues most organizations are stuck in nineteenth-century models, but that we are evolving toward structures in which rank means responsibility, not authority, and in which leaders do not command, but persuade.

Drucker (1996) cites four simple characteristics of leaders:

1. they have followers;

2. they get results;

3. they set visible examples;

4. they recognize that leading is a responsibility.

Bennis and Biederman (1997) state that leaders are often pragmatic dreamers and scientists with poetry in their souls. Leaders act as maestros — orchestrating congruence toward an attainable vision while assuring that all contributors are free to do exceptional work.

Small Relationships and Big Effects

The Internet and networks increase the size and scope of the system and accelerate the pace of change within that system. Many in senior leadership posts in higher education are unprepared for the fact that in today's business ecosystem, relationships at all levels are critical, and small changes can have large effects. Leaders must have a complex understanding of everything about the organization — its internal and external environments — and intervene only as appropriate and necessary to stimulate creativity and productivity (Poley 1998).

No one individual today can have all of the knowledge required for complex problem solving. The era of the "bwana kubwa" (the "big man" in Kiswahili) is over. Increasingly, organizations require lateral leaders to congeal the partial insights or knowledge of individuals and groups into "robust social knowledge" (Hargrove 1998).

Structural Implosion and Merely Go Round

Because the world is round, university leaders that leave the boxes and pyramids to history and adopt a circular model (the wheel of fortune) with a center but no top or bottom are more likely to succeed. Leadership will be increasingly fluid, mission focused, values based, and demographics driven. Followership is trust (Hesselbein 1999).

Many of our universities are working on artificial intelligence, computer-mediated communication, computer science, meta-data, geographical information systems, human/computer interaction and interface design, neural networks, standards, software development, programming, and educational technology of many types. Creative play abounds at our institutions, but there is little alignment in terms of strategy, structure, technology, and budget. Some, like John Perry Barlow of the Electronic Frontier Foundation, as well as businesses desiring to compete with U.S. higher education, advocate the deconstruction of the academy and its cultures. Others, like Chris Dede, information technology and education professor at George Mason University in Virginia and the author of chapter 3, propose dramatic modifications to leadership, strategy, structures, and culture to use technology appropriately in ways that engage students and faculty and prepare learners for *both* the workforce and to think and learn (American Association of State Colleges and Universities 1999a).

New technologies are both pushing change and holding it back. The phenomenal growth of the Internet — there may be as many as 329 million users by 2002, up from 82 million in 1997 — is clearly a change driver (Gens 1999). And those using the Internet increasingly look more like Americans demographically, even though they have miles to go before they look anything like the world.

The challenge for leaders over the next ten years will be to speed the transition from the static boxes of the twentieth century value chains to the anarchic network of the twenty-first century model (Omae 1983). People, technology, finances, marketing, and geography are already taking on changed roles and meaning in higher education systems.

Learning How to Do and How to Be

The higher education leadership challenges and choices emerging in this Age of Knowledge are substantial. Leadership is now about learning — both how to do and how to be.

On the question of what and how to do, leadership from public higher education is essential to ensure a rapid, smooth, and extendable transition to the flat, round world of tomorrow's organizations, including universities. These knowledge technology transformations will affect (President's Information Technology Advisory Committee 1999):

- how we communicate;
- how we store and access information;
- how we become healthier and get medical care;
- how we learn;
- how we conduct business;
- how we work;
- how we design and build things;
- how we conduct research;
- how we sustain a livable environment;
- how we manage our government.

There are also profoundly important questions about free exchange of information and access to knowledge. How we define the public interest and when it should override free-market considerations on the knowledge frontier will influence what's in our refrigerators and medicine chests and how much these goods will cost. Knowledgeable people who are able to work together must exercise leadership to ensure that we do not privatize essential knowledge. Vital intellectual resources must be shared, lest we choke productivity, magnify social inequalities, and erode our democratic institutions (Shulman 1999).

Bogue (1994) argues that effective leadership is as much a test of character as a test of intellect. He calls leadership a conceptual, moral, and performing art form — effective leaders integrate knowledge, values, and skill in exercising positive power and influence in diverse settings. He highlights how important honor, dignity, candor, compassion, and courage are to real leaders. For these leaders, organizational outcomes and the development of a sense of direction and belonging among organizational members are more important than personal positioning and power.

Can a bad person be a good leader? Aristotle and Parsons would answer "no." Character and virtue are transparent and self-evident through one's actions; therefore, a bad character is incapable of good leadership (Parsons 1999). Some in authority positions in higher education are not leading or serving their organizations or publics well in preparing for the Knowledge Age. They are inward looking, leading nothing and hopping from job to job trying to climb a pyramid set to crumble. All the while, they quietly move from one side of the boat to the other, trying to preserve tranquility in a sea not likely to return to such a state anytime soon.

Just as leaders' high expectations can have a Pygmalion effect on constituents, so the expectations of constituents can influence the behavior of leaders. When people feel unique, competent, secure, empowered, and connected to the people around them, they are generally more able to leverage change. Fiedler's (1967) theory of contingency leadership reinforces the fragility of leadership in higher education, where task structures are low and position power is weak. In these circumstances, leadership is truly an art form, and the relationships of the leader with his or her constituencies really do matter.

When leaders believe that they *can* learn, that belief will influence their ability to learn. The resulting learning may improve leadership capacity (Kouzes and Posner 1999). It is ironic that too many of today's leaders within higher education admit to technology illiteracy and then do nothing to correct the situation. This can no longer be tolerated; according to Varn (1999, 74-75):

> Higher education should not be where we passionately and methodically search for new insight into how we learn, how to use technology, and the factors and methods of human organization and success, just so we may ignore such insights when it comes to our own programs. We must practice what we teach.

In an interview with staff of the *Educom Review* (1998), Michael Schrage echoes these same themes. On the one hand, he notes that institutions of higher education are surrounded with insurmountable opportunities, and that technology will become a dominant way that universities embody their values of scholarship, teaching, learning, and community. But, he adds, a lot will happen by default. He credits Tom Malone, Sloan School professor, for saying, "The more choices you have, the more your values matter." Malone observes today that there are more choices than anyone knows what to do with. He thinks the most successful universities will establish design sensibilities that create new ideas for marketplaces as well as marketplaces for ideas.

Arguments about whether leaders shape the organization or organizations shape the leader (and to what extent) will keep social scientists busy well into the future. Bergquist (1992) in *The Four Cultures of the Academy*, shapes a powerful argument for the importance of context and culture in examining the leadership question. He says that leadership may emerge from any of the following: traditional academic culture, management culture, developmental culture, and negotiating culture. Individuals gravitate toward one of the four cultures depending upon their personality, knowledge, and experience. In an organizational pyramid, traditional hierarchical structure, one would assume that the top leader would nearly always be standing on shaky turf, unless he or she is extremely skillful in the practice of situational leadership and organizational politics.

It is interesting to consider the challenge of new technologies in relationship to these four distinct cultures and how, within each context, there are differences of perspective. The academic culture is primarily concerned with knowledge, the managerial culture with money, the developmental culture with people, and the negotiating culture with bargaining within itself and with the other three cultures. The new technologies create discomfort, dissonance, and increased ambiguity in each sphere.

It is a fallacy to believe that technology will automatically change a culture or cultures. Although technology allows and, in some ways, reinforces the flattening of organizations, it does not do so by itself. Organizational leaders must have the will to make the necessary cultural changes, and then technology can help make it easier. A better computer network will not buy instant collaboration and a culture of sharing. If people think their power continues to rest in hoarding their knowledge, they are not likely to start giving it away (Dyson 1999).

Getting from Here to Around

While shared leadership is increasingly gaining attention, the individual at the top of the pyramid positionally is still too frequently the primary focus of leadership study and development. Increasingly, leaders must attend to individual relationships, eliminating barriers to communication to create a positive environment appropriate to the Knowledge Age.

Several developments have already occurred. Electronic communication networks have permeated higher education, breaking vertical and horizontal boundaries. Respected leaders today are excellent and broad communicators, which includes reading and answering unfiltered e-mail as a number one priority. They understand that strong educational providers, in order to engage in collaborative research and education, must foster development of excellence in communities of interest that cross institutional and national borders and boundaries. They do not seek to control knowledge, nor do they bar faculty and staff from communicating with powerful others directly rather than through the chain of command. Flattened organizational structures are increasingly the norm in organizations, including universities, and traditional leaders are frequently referred to as the eaters, meeters, and greeters, whose value added is increasingly devoted to external fund-raising — an activity that may be counterproductive in terms of the overall health of the institution.

Despite the challenges of technologies, funding, restructuring, and increasing expectations in a new world where businesses and industry depend more than ever before upon the knowledge generated and the knowledge workers coming out of higher education, tomorrow's leaders within higher education will have to do better than the performance of many in this cadre during the last decade. Too many of today's college leaders have succumbed to the numbing process of inaction and maintenance of the status quo, due to:

- a flawed sense of role — condition of empty vision;

- a contempt for ideas — condition of empty mind

- a neglect of constructive value — condition of empty heart;

- a retreat from servant ideals — condition of empty spirit;
- a violation of cultural norms — condition of empty sensitivity;
- a sacrifice of honor — condition of empty character (Bogue 1994).

Leadership research continues to show that leadership does not depend on mystical qualities or inborn gifts, but rather on the capacity of individuals to know themselves, their strengths, and their weaknesses, and to learn from the feedback they get in their daily lives — in short, their capacity for self-improvement (Kouzes and Posner 1999).

Who Are the Leaders Anyway? Moving with, Moving against, Moving Away

A promotional flyer from the *Academic Leader* newsletter asks whether the deans and department chairpersons on your campus are the leaders they can be. Has the campus developed its collective leadership potential? The newsletter goes on to say that studies show that chairpersons make 80 percent of the decisions that must be made to keep institutions of higher education functioning.

Tom Peters repeats time and again in his seminars that leadership and hard work are the keys to making organizations thrive. In an advertisement for one of his seminars, he says, "It is all about sheer determination and genuine teamwork, a firm belief that everyone can make a difference ... ." Ken Blanchard, author of the *One-Minute Manager*, states in that same marketing piece: "We all know that the days of looking to a single leader to figure it all out are days long gone. It takes the commitment and enthusiasm of everybody." The higher education community is, in general, head oriented — preferring abstract conceptualization to feelings of growth and learning. Too often, realities like feelings and energy are considered soft, illogical, and irrational. Yet leadership development programs strongly emphasize the development of the "soft track" dimensions as important in complementing the "hard track" skills: persuading, reasoning for and against, and bargaining. Many leadership trainers use a positive power and influence model developed over the past twenty-five years by Roger Harrison, David Berlew, and Bill LeClere that includes diagnostic materials based on Karen Horney's work to assess influence skills using an energy model. All skills, hard and soft, are considered important for leaders to use in appropriate situations. Leaders are considered to be "moving with" others as they listen, empathize, bridge, and network; they are "moving against" others as they lead using persuasion and bargaining. The model also includes use of "moving away" in a strategic sense. There are times when leaders will need to let things cool off, disengage, break the tension, and allow time for reconsideration.

Elaine Showalter (1999), a professor of English, states that it is time to tame incivility in academia. She says that many scholars during the last decade have asked why there is so much incivility among academic thinkers. She writes: "In *We Scholars*, David Damrosch ... argues that academic life looks for — and reinforces with rewards — traits of isolation, competitiveness, and 'associability.' He writes that 'we have been selecting for certain kinds of alienation and aggression on campus.' Thus departments are 'clubs of the unclubbable,' and controversy degenerates into hostility. Damrosch asks whether this tribal culture can be changed to a communal one: 'Alienation and aggression are distasteful grounds for an educational system; further, I wish to argue that they are now also historically outmoded and intellectually counterproductive,' he writes."

Academics all need to learn more about the skills the business world calls emotional intelligence: the human capacities of empathy, self-awareness, and self-regulation, and the ability of leaders to reward and motivate themselves and others. "Emotional competence is particularly central to leadership and for star performance in all jobs. In every field emotional competence is twice as important as cognitive abilities and it can be taught and learned" (Showalter 1999, B4-B5).

No one can write about leadership without mentioning vision and charisma. Everyone thinks leaders have special qualities to see, use language, inspire, energize, motivate, and engage others to follow. The whole is more than the sum of the parts. The totality, the package becomes important. In "Ten Lessons for Leaders" she learned from writing about U.S. presidents, historian Doris Kearns Goodwin found the following were important to Roosevelt, Kennedy, and Johnson (Goodwin 1999). Each lesson includes suggested applications for leading, coping with challenges, and making choices in higher education.

Lesson One:
Timing is (almost) everything

Leadership application

Nearly thirty years ago, an individual (who shall remain nameless) advocated for a university consortium to provide distance education on a collaborative basis. Considerable funds were invested in this effort, as were time and energy. While the collapse of the enterprise was not totally due to poor timing, similar efforts today fall on much more fertile ground, as Hanna notes in chapter 4. In large measure, networking tools to increase the frequency and level of communication and to build trust were unavailable in the 1960s and 1970s.

Too often, leaders fail to test their ideas thoroughly with respect to timing. A well-honed sense of timing comes from being highly other directed as well as environmentally and culturally sensitive. Working in nonlinear fashion and paying attention to multiple "circus tents" and performers also increases the possibility of right timing for the right target — not just the immediate linear target at hand. Long-range thinking is essential.

Lesson Two:
Anything is possible if you share the glory

Leadership application

Leaders simply cannot do enough encouraging and appreciating. Credit is the one thing that is infinitely sharable and serves as yeast in relationship energy. Real leaders are never so self-absorbed in worrying about where next to be and what to say that they miss hundreds of small hourly opportunities to compliment, reward, and build the human competencies that are the real value of a university. Tearing down individuals, groups, and everyone who ever came before "this leader/savior" as a personal marketing strategy is doomed to failure. The leaders who are capable of finding the good things, the positive things, the things ripe for shared development can build far beyond expectations with sustained effort.

Lesson Three:
Trust, once broken, is seldom restored

Leadership application

Leaders must tell the truth if they want to be trusted. They cannot always "put a good face on it." Leaders today are far too susceptible to using organizational hype and cutting deals to get a better deal on a computer system or network, and then spinning "the solution." Most often, "the solution," whether it's Lotus Notes, Microsoft Word, or two hundred online classes by next year, will set off a religious war and badly damage the organization's trust in the leader.

Trust grows when people see leaders translate their personal integrity into organizational fidelity. At the heart of fidelity lie truth telling and promise keeping. Truth is not power (De Pree 1997).

Lesson Four:
Leadership is about building connections

Leadership application

Michael Schrage (Educom 1998) argues that communication and collaboration require shared space. He says, "You have pea-brained executives who believe that if you call a meeting and assign tasks that you are successfully running a project." The questions that should be asked: Where is the shared space? What is the medium to manage the collaboration? Schrage argues that innovative prototypes generate innovative teams. Innovative people build a model and then show it to others who might comment. A community of interest grows. The prototype drives the process. It attracts people. The shared space is where the value is created. The issue in collaboration is not just creative individuals, but creative *relationships*.

Business and industry leaders have been urging higher education throughout the last decade to pay more attention to these communication, collaboration, and connection skills. The traditional higher education process emphasizes individualism and competition rather than collaboration and connections. Today's world requires people to work together in face-to-face as well as networked modes. There are few job descriptions seeking bright lone rangers. New technologies offer creative possibilities for improving upon this important dimension.

Lesson Five:
Leaders learn from their mistakes

Leadership application

For better or worse, leaders who use the Internet to communicate with faculty, staff, colleagues, and constituents cannot avoid learning about their mistakes. The fast, powerful nature of instant messaging stings painfully and with regularity. Learning leaders cannot just mutter obscenities and hit the delete key. They must have their own learning relationships, people to whom they can go to get advice and gain clarity on situations as well as to brainstorm possible solutions. There is tremendous need for training and technical assistance for senior leaders who need to discover how to apply these powerful tools to their own learning.

Lesson Six:
Confidence — not just in oneself — counts

Leadership application

Leaders with ascribed power — the top job — can learn a lot from leaders without such ascribed power.

Hope and expectant confident prophecies are critical ingredients in all organizational change efforts. There is much banal rhetoric and verbal hand wringing going on at universities about everything from the Y2K bug to competition from the private sector to poor faculty to the cost of doing business in an Age of Knowledge. One would think that an Age of Knowledge could stir the souls of leaders concerned with development and learning. U.S. universities are the best in the world and have incredible potential to live up to their great history. No institution should hire a senior leader who denigrates the faculty, the students, the citizens supporting the institution, the business community, and the alumni/ae. No leader should allow externals to practice this type of denigration unchallenged. Long-term possibilities for publishing individual accomplishments through the Web should strike terror into the hearts of every leader playing the game of "the place was awful 'til I came."

Lesson Seven:
Effective partnerships require devotion to one's partners

Leadership application

The recent rise and fall of the California Virtual University suggests that CVU's leaders may have missed this important lesson. The readiness of the university partners to support this effort long term was obviously not assessed by Governor Wilson when he proposed it.

Scott Rosevear's (1999) research shows that planners who want to establish a virtual university or organization should answer these questions: What is the state's technological infrastructure? How prepared are the traditional colleges and universities to support virtual learning environments? Do they all have equal technological capabilities? What is a reasonable prediction for how long it will take before the virtual university is operational? What are the resource gaps, and how will they be filled? Such questions could be studied by an outside consultant.

The answers to these questions can eliminate problems before the formation of the alliance. The successful ADEC distance education consortium is an example of the importance placed on building partnerships — placing a high priority on reciprocity and devotion to one's partners. This concept is strongly linked to the importance of connections and relationships and trust building.

Lesson Eight:
Renewal comes from many sources

Leadership application

While the Internet offers an enhancement to renewing activities such as letter writing, playing games, reading, and chatting, increasingly leaders recognize that they need some unplugged renewal time. Learning when and how to disconnect may be a greater future problem than the problems some universities have today with "clueless" leaders. The whole notion of "virtual" may be overemphasized. We may need to think more about "how can my network connectedness enhance the pleasure I take in husbanding my garden?" "How can I establish communication patterns that are authentic for me, rather than becoming a slave to 'you've got mail.' "

Lesson Nine:
Leaders must be talent brokers

Leadership application

It is now possible for leaders to retain lifelong relationships on a far wider and broader scale than ever before. This means that mentoring possibilities are large, staying in touch over time is possible, and the networks for talent brokering are now global. Again the relationship factor becomes clear. Extraverted communicators with broad talent networks will increasingly be more valued in universities. The most important job in the next ten years will not be fund-raising but people raising.

Lesson Ten:
Language is one's most powerful tool

Leadership application

The tools of the Knowledge Age are already giving voice to many more who might become leaders. Good writers and good thinkers who can use the Internet, as well as other communication media, have a larger stage upon which to play. Some leaders have a greater gift for language than others. In fact, an important goal for many in higher education leadership would be to understand the importance of the words *and* the music. Words themselves make music; they hit the right or wrong note or tone depending upon cultural reasons. A phrase like "pull up your socks" carries meaning in one place and not another. Being able to select the right words for the right time and the right place is a gift. As writing becomes so much more important in building relationships, those with the ability to see, hear, and predict the impact of their words on others will have an advantage. Whole new areas of study will unfold as the Internet and World Wide Web actually become worldwide.

As Importance of Knowledge Grows, Demands Increase for and upon Higher Education

Information technology has become essential to workplace knowledge. For more and more businesses, knowledge *is* the business. Today, information technology is transparent to the user, ubiquitous, and more capable than ever of capturing knowledge as opposed to mere data or words. Times of rapid change require leaders, but business in general is not satisfied with the pace nor the intensity of change in higher education. Business wants leaders with a clear vision and the ability to develop coalitions — leaders who can ensure that attention is focused on the most important priorities over the long term. "Episodic and short-lived initiatives must give way to a more holistic approach" (Oblinger and Verville 1998):

> In business we know that an outstanding manager can lead a mediocre team to great success; conversely, a mediocre manager will quickly lead an outstanding team to mediocre performance. The overwhelming improvement that is required necessitates massive restructuring. In business we call it re-engineering/ re-inventing ourselves by re-evaluating all that we do, eliminating unnecessary or unproductive practices, and developing new methods of delivering improved products to global markets. Who does the hard work of re-engineering? Senior management.

Summary

Leaders of the future must be integrators who can look beyond obvious differences among organizations, sectors, disciplines, functions, or cultures. They must be diplomats capable of conflict resolution and able to exercise positive power and influence. They must be cosmopolitans who are comfortable operating across borders and capable of implementing visions that will expand the pie for everyone, not pit group against group. They must have strong networking skills and partnering abilities. They must be cross-fertilizers, bringing the best ideas from one place to another. Finally, they must be deep thinkers who are smart enough to see new possibilities and conceptualize them (Kanter 1995). Without question, higher education needs more deep-thinking, diplomatic, cosmopolitan, cross-fertilizing integrators in its leadership ranks.

Since knowledge is inextricably tied to growth and change and is unmistakably a cornerstone of successful development, it is critical that institutions of higher education be looking for leaders, leadership structures, and strategies that will result in an increase in the institution's ability to adapt, interpret, and generate knowledge.

REFERENCES

American Association of State Colleges and Universities. 1999a. Experts challenge higher ed presidents. [Website]. *Converge*. Available from <http://www.aascu.nche.edu/news/>.

American Association of State Colleges and Universities. 1999b. Keeping pace or not keeping pace. [Website]. *Converge*. Available from <http://www.aascu.nche.edu/news/>.

Bennis, Warren G., and Patricia Ward Biederman. 1997. *Organizing genius: The secrets of creative collaboration.* Reading, MA: Addison-Wesley.

Bergquist, William H. 1992. *The four cultures of the academy: Insights and strategies for improving leadership in collegiate organizations.* San Francisco: Jossey-Bass, Publishers.

Bogue, E. Grady. 1994. *Leadership by design: Strengthening integrity in higher education.* San Francisco: Jossey-Bass, Publishers.

Damrosch, David. 1995. *We scholars: Changing the culture of the university.* Cambridge, MA: Harvard University Press.

De Pree, Max. 1997. *Leading without power: Finding hope in serving community.* San Francisco: Jossey-Bass, Publishers.

Drucker, Peter. 1996. The leader of the future. In *The leader of the future,* edited by Frances Hesselbein, Marshall Goldsmith, and Richard Beckhard. San Francisco: Jossey-Bass, Publishers.

Drucker, Peter. 1998. The future that has already happened. *The Futurist* 32(8): 16-18.

Dyson, E. 1999. Aligning corporate culture to maximize high technology. In *Leader to leader: Enduring insights on leadership from the Drucker Foundation's award winning journal,* edited by Frances Hesselbein and Paul Cohen. San Francisco: Jossey-Bass, Publishers

Educom. 1998. Technology, silver bullets, and big lies: Musings on the Information Age with author Michael Schrage. [Website]. *Educause.* Available from <http://www.educause.edu/pub/er/review/review Articles/ 33132.html>.

Fiedler, Fred. 1967. *A theory of leadership effectiveness.* New York: McGraw-Hill.

Gens, F. 1999. Anticipating IT's cyberspace Odyssy: On the road to a billion users. *International Data Corporation Information Industry and Technology Update, 1998-1999.*

Goodwin, Doris Kerns. 1999. *Ten lessons from presidents*. San Francisco: Jossey-Bass, Publishers.

Hargrove, Robert. 1998. *Mastering the art of creative collaboration*. New York: McGraw Hill.

Hesselbein, Francis. 1999. Managing in a world that is round. In *Leader to leader: Enduring insights on leadership from the Drucker Foundation's award winning journal*, edited by Frances Hesselbein and Paul Cohen. San Francisco: Jossey-Bass, Publishers.

Kanter, Rosabeth Moss. 1995. *World class: Thriving locally in the global economy*. New York: Simon & Schuster.

Kouzes, James M., and Barry Z. Posner. 1999. *Encouraging the heart: A leader's guide to rewarding and recognizing others*. San Francisco: Jossey-Bass, Publishers.

Oblinger, Diana, and Anne-Lee Verville. 1998. *What business wants from higher education*. Phoenix, AZ: ACE/Oryx Press.

Omae, Kenichi. 1983. Strategy in a world without borders. In *Leader to leader: Enduring insights on leadership from the Drucker Foundation's award winning journal*, edited by Frances Hesselbein and Paul Cohen. San Francisco: Jossey-Bass, Publishers.

Parsons, Gerald. 1999. Leadership ethics is an oxymoron. *University of Nebraska-Lincoln Institute of Agriculture and Natural Resources First Quarter Newsletter*, 4 March.

Poley, Janet. 1998. Creating shared leadership environments in institutional and international settings. *The American Journal of Distance Education* 12(2): 16-24.

President's Information Technology Advisory Committee. 1999. *Report to the President: President's Information Technology Advisory Committee*. Washington, DC: National Coordination Office for Computing, Information, and Communications.

Reich, Robert. 1998. The company of the future. *Fast Company* (19): 124.

Rosevear, Scott. 1999. Virtual University: Lessons for developing a partnership-based virtual university. [Website]. *The Technology Source*. Available from < http://horizon.unc.edu/TS/vu/1999-04.asp >.

Showalter, Elaine. 1999. Taming the rampant incivility in higher education. *The Chronicle of Higher Education*, 15 January: B4-B5.

Shulman, Seth. 1999. We need new ways to own and share knowledge. *The Chronicle of Higher Education*, 19 February: B4-B5.

Spragins, Ellyn E. 1999. What a nice problem: The bull causes some overendowment. *Newsweek*, 22 March.

Varn, Richard J. 1999. Higher education: From industrial age to information age education. *Converge*, February: 74-75.

Chapter 8

Who Owns Knowledge in a Networked World?

By John Tallman

Who owns knowledge? The question is broad. We will discuss it within narrower parameters: in a university[1] setting, who owns knowledge on the World Wide Web that is communicated on the Internet[2]? Though we examine the question in a particular setting and with reference to relatively new and emerging digital technologies, the answer involves many traditional issues concerning intellectual property.

Just what is intellectual property? It has been defined (*Merriam Webster's Dictionary of Law* 1996) as "property that derives from the work of the mind or the intellect."

An exploration of who owns knowledge has several dimensions. There are questions that relate to the creation of information and to its use. What rights do creators have when they publish works on the Web? When are their works protected? What restrictions are there on the use of information created by others that is obtained from the Web? When is consent of a creator necessary?

---

[1]   Throughout the chapter, "university" includes colleges and other institutions of higher education.

[2]   The terms "Internet" and "World Wide Web," or "Web" are frequently used interchangeably. In fact, they are different in form and substance. The Internet consists of the computers and their connections in the United States and throughout the world that constitute the highway to get you to where you're going. The Web contains the content, the knowledge, that you are looking for.

How free should access be to information available on the Internet? Some argue that in the United States, historically there has been a balance struck between the interests of creators and users of intellectual property. Digital technology introduces a weighty factor that can upset that balance, they say (Lehman 1995). Therefore, a paramount question is: *in a technological environment in which it is easier to publish information and easier to get at it than ever before, how should the rights of creators and users be balanced?*

What significance does the question "Who owns knowledge in a networked world?" have in an employment context? A faculty or staff member is an employee of the university. What rights and obligations might both a university employee and the university employer have when information is communicated using the Internet and the Web? What about someone who is not an employee of the university but whose services are commissioned by the university to create a work?

There are liability issues. Today, many universities are on-line "service providers." They offer the technology to their faculty, staff, and students to gain access to the Internet and the Web. Is a college or university liable if a faculty or staff member or a student obtains material from the Web and in the process violates a creator's rights?

Works on the Internet cross national boundaries. What are the important issues that involve the transmission of knowledge internationally?

Here we will explore these questions from a variety of perspectives.

Significance of Intellectual Property

Just how important is intellectual property in our country and other countries throughout the world? Particularly with the growth of the Internet and the Web[3], which are relatively recent

---

[3]   For background on the development of the Internet, see Barry M. Leiner et al. *A Brief History of the Internet.* Available from < http://www.isoc.org/internet/history/brief.html >; and Needham Boddie, II et al. 1998. A review of copyright and the Internet. *Campbell Law Review*, 20(2): 193-272.

phenomena, there is growing public interest in the subject of protection of intellectual property (even if that term itself isn't commonly used in the discussions and debates). Maybe intellectual property is being talked about more, but the subject is not new in the United States. It has been important from the very beginning of the nation. It was so important, in fact, that it is addressed in the U.S. Constitution. Article I, Section 8, Clause 8 of the Constitution provides that "The Congress shall have the power ... [t]o promote the progress of science and useful arts, by securing for limited times to authors and inventors the exclusive right to their respective writings and discoveries."

The sequence of the clauses in the constitutional provision is significant. By starting the section with reference to promoting the progress of science and arts, the founding fathers were stressing, first and foremost, the vital importance of the public interest in scientific and artistic advances.[4] To be sure, they established incentives for individuals to create new works by granting exclusive rights to them, but for a limited period of time. The constitutional provision is designed to encourage individuals to create and invent, but always in the context of advancing greater societal interests.[5]

The subject of intellectual property is important worldwide as well. The World Intellectual Property Organization (WIPO) is the international organization responsible for administering treaties relating to intellectual property. The fact that there are more than 150 countries, including the United States, which are members of WIPO indicates the importance of intellectual property to nations throughout the world (Lehman 1995).

Intellectual property covers a broad range of works. What are the basic legal forms of protection of intellectual property? Given the subject of this chapter, we are interested in the forms of protection covered mostly by federal law. Essentially, there

4 Twentieth Century Music Corp. v. Aiken, 422 U.S. 151, 156 (1975); Fox Film Corp. v. Doyal, 286 U.S. 123, 127 (1932).

5 Harper & Row, Publishers, Inc. v. Nation Enterprises, 471 U.S. 539, 558 (1985); Sony Corporation of America v. University City Studios, 464 U.S. 417, 429 (1984); Twentieth Century Music Corp. v. Aiken, id.

are three.[6] Patents are available for inventions.[7] Trademarks are words, names, symbols, or devices, or a combination of those, that identify and distinguish goods or services in the market-place.[8] The subject that is most relevant to our exploration is copyright, the legal protection extended to creations by "authors," such as books and computer software programs.

Copyright Basics and Internet Issues

General Copyright Requirements and Conditions

Copyright in the United States is governed principally by federal law. Congress has enacted legislation concerning copyright throughout our history. A significant revision of U.S. copyright law occurred with the adoption of the Copyright Act of 1976.[9]

Though the United States has a long history of statutory regulation of copyright, the introduction of information on the Internet has fostered an impression that if a creator puts material on the Internet that is so easy to access and, after that, to copy and circulate, it must not be protected by copyright law (Boddie et al. 1998). This impression is wrong. Because of technological advances, the way information can be shared may be changing profoundly. But, in general, the application of copyright law to digital technologies has not. Except where U.S. copyright law specifically carves out an exception for works that involve digital technologies, copyright law applies to the works on the Web as it does to "traditional" forms of copyrightable works.[10]

---

6   Protection of "trade secrets" can be considered a fourth form. By and large, they are covered by state law, not federal law. Furthermore, a right of privacy and a right of publicity, both governed by state law, may establish limitations on the exploitation of intellectual property.

7   35 U.S. C. § 101.

8   15 U.S. C. § § 1051 et seq.; *Gilbert/Robinson, Inc. v. Carrie Beverage-Missouri, Inc.*, 758 F. Supp. 512 (E. D. Mo. 1991); *Paramount Pictures Corp. v. Video Broadcasting Systems, Inc.*, 724 F. Supp. 808 (D. Kansas 1989).

9   Codified in 17 U.S. C. § 101 *et seq.*

10   *Religious Technology Centers. v. Netcom Online Communication Services, Inc.*, 907 F. Supp. 1361 (N. D. Cal. 1995); *Playboy Enterprises, Inc. v. Starware Publishing Corp.*, 900 F. Supp. 433 (S. D. Fla. 1995); *Sega Enterprises Ltd. v. Maphia*, 857 F. Supp. 679 (N. D. Cal. 1994); *Playboy Enterprises, Inc. v. Frena*, 839 F. Supp. 1552 (M. D. Fla. 1993).

If that is the case, what is the starting point? A first question to ask: when is copyright protection available? Section 102 of the Copyright Act provides that "[c]opyright protection subsists ... in *original* works of authorship *fixed* in any tangible medium of expression, now known or later developed, from which they can be perceived, reproduced, or otherwise communicated, either directly or with the aid of a machine or device [emphasis added]."[11] The statute establishes that the basic requirements of a work, in order to receive copyright protection are: *originality* and *fixation*.

The Act does not define originality. Its characteristics have developed through experience over time and case law. To be original, a work simply must be one of independent creation, not copied from another, with "some minimal degree of creativity."[12] Novelty is not a requirement.[13] Neither is artistic merit.[14]

If the amount of originality in a work is small in order to qualify for copyright protection, what are examples of work for which even minimal creativity has been absent and therefore copyright protection has been denied? Courts have held that fragmentary words or phrases do not involve enough creativity to enjoy copyright protection. [15] Because words and phrases cnnot be copyrighted does not mean that they are without protection. They may qualify as trademarks. The same is true for "white pages" of a telephone directory.[16] Words and phrases such as titles[17] and slogans[18] do not involve enough originality to

---

[11] 17 U.S. C. § 102.

[12] *Feist Publications, Inc. v. Rural Telephone Serv. Co., Inc.*, 499 U.S. 340, 345 (1991).

[13] Feist, *id.*, p. 345 ; *E. Mishan & Sons, Inc., v. Marycana*, 662 F. Supp. 1339, 1340-43 (S. D. N. Y. 1987).

[14] *Bleistein v. Donaldson Lithography Co.*, 188 U.S. 239, 250 (1903).

[15] *Arica Institute, Inc. v. Palmer*, 770 F. Supp. 188, 191-92 (S. D. N. Y. 1991), *aff'd*, 970 F. 2d 1067, 1072 (2d Cir. 1992); *Magic Marketing, Inc. v. Mailing Services of Pittsburgh, Inc.*, 634 F. Supp. 769 (W. D. Pa. 1986); *Smith v. George E. Muehlebach Brewing Co.*, 140 F. Supp. 729 (W. D. Mo. 1956). Because words and phrases cannot be copyrighted doesn't mean that they are without protection. They may qualify as trademarks.

[16] Feist, *supra*.

[17] *Arthur Retlaw & Associates, Inc. v. Travenol Laboratories, Inc.*, 582 F. Supp. 1010, 1014 (N. D. Ill. 1984).

[18] *Sebastian International, Inc. v. Consumer Contact (PTY) Ltd.*, 664 F. Supp. 909 (D. N. J. 1987), vacated on other grounds, 847 F.2d 1093 (3rd Cir. 1988).

be copyrightable. A manufacturer's parts numbering system,[19] a reproduction of U.S. mechanical banks,[20] mere reproductions of illustrations created by another that had been in the public domain,[21] and minimal or trivial alterations of a logo provided by another[22] do not qualify, either.

The second essential requirement of a work to qualify for copyright protection is fixation. The Copyright Act doesn't define originality, but it does establish requirements for fixation. To be fixed, a work must be sufficiently embodied in a medium of expression, such as print or videotape, for example, to allow perception, reproduction, or communication for more than a transitory period of time.[23] When works are communicated via the Internet, at what point are they fixed? Under current law, a work that is merely transmitted is not fixed.[24] "Live" transmission must be simultaneously fixed to enjoy copyright protection. If a transmission also involves embodiment in a copy or phono record that is "sufficiently permanent or stable to permit it to be perceived, reproduced, or otherwise communicated for a period of more than transitory duration,"[25] it will meet the fixation test.[26] If the creator makes a copy of the work to disk at the time it is transmitted, it will be fixed because it becomes embodied in a medium of expression from which it can be perceived, reproduced, or otherwise communicated for a period of more than transitory duration.

At what point does a qualified work — one that meets the tests of originality and fixation – enjoy copyright protection? Many believe that a work becomes copyrighted only when it is produced containing a copyright notice. A typical copyright

[19]   *Toro Co. v. R & R Products Co.*, 787 F.2d 1208, 1212 (8th Cir. 1986).

[20]   *L. Batlin & Son, Inc. v. Snyder*, 536 F.2d 486 (2d Cir. 1976).

[21]   *Hearn v. Meyer*, 664 F. Supp. 832, 840 (S. D. N. Y. 1987).

[22]   *Moore Pub., Inc. v. Big Sky Marketing, Inc.*, 756 F. Supp. 1371 (D. Idaho 1990).

[23]   17 U.S. C. § 101.

[24]   Nimmer and Nimmer 1998, § 203[B][2]; Lehman 1995, 27.

[25]   17 U.S. C. § 101.

[26]   *Trenton v. Infinity Broadcasting Corporation*, 865 F. Supp. 1416, 1423-25 (C. D. Cal. 1994).

logo might read: © 1999 John Tallman.[27] Does the absence of copyright information on a work mean that it does not have a valid copyright? No. Until 1989, U.S. copyright law required that a copyright notice had to be present on a work to enjoy copyright protection. The United States is a member of an international treaty called the Berne Convention. Under the Berne Convention, a copyright notice does not have to be included in order for a work to be copyrighted. The U.S. enacted legislation to comply with that provision.[28] As result, works published in the United States as of March 1, 1989, receive copyright protection the moment two conditions are present — originality and fixation — whether or not a copyright notice appears on the work. Thus, if a copyright notice is not present on such a work, it is not safe to assume that the work is not copyrighted. In fact, it is safer to assume just the opposite.

Even if a copyright notice is not required for works created after 1989, there are good reasons to include it. It is a familiar reminder to someone who is examining the work that a copyright claim is being made. Also, without a copyright notice, it makes it unnecessarily difficult for someone to ask permission to copy or use the work. Without the notice, whom do you ask for permission?

Registration of copyright for a work created in the United States with the federal Copyright Office isn't required to obtain copyright protection, either.[29] But registration is simple and inexpensive and affords additional protections in the event a copyright dispute winds up in court.[30] It also provides protection for works made available outside the United States, a circumstance that is more and more applicable to distance education.

[27] 17 U.S. C. § § 401 (b), 402(b). More precisely, a copyright notice must include: the letter "c" in a circle, ©, or the word "copyright," or the abbreviation "copr."; the year of first publication; and the name of the copyright owner.

[28] *Berne Convention Implementing Act,* Pub. L. 100-568, 102 Stat. 2853, October 31, 1988.

[29] 17 U.S. C. § 406(a); see *Arthur Rutenberg Homes, Inc. v. Drew Homes, Inc.* 29 F.2d 1529 (11th Cir. 1994).

[30] See 17 U.S. C. § § 407 - 412. Copyright registration information is available on the U.S. Copyright Office web site: < http://lcweb.loc.gov/copyright/ >.

If copyright protection is not available to all types of intellectual property, what types are covered by copyright protection? Table 8.1 outlines categories of works protected by copyright.

Table 8.1
Works covered by copyright protection

Literary works	Pantomimes and choreographic works	Pictorial, graphic, and sculptural works
Musical works	Sound recordings	Motion pictures and other audiovisual works
Dramatic works	Architectural works	

All works on the Internet are in digital form. Works that exist in digital form are "literary works" for purposes of U.S. copyright law.[31]

By contrast, what kinds of work are not copyrightable? There are seven categories of works that aren't: (1) an idea; (2) a procedure; (3) a process; (4) a system; (5) a method of operation; (6) a principle; or (7) a discovery.[32] Ideas for game concepts,[33] general plot ideas,[34] and selecting or ordering the presentation of facts[35] are other examples of types of works that are not copyrightable.

It is important to understand conceptually what copyright covers and what it does not cover. As we have seen, ideas are not protected by copyright. The *expression* of ideas is.[36] Say you are a

---

31   The Computer Software Copyright Act of 1980, Pub. L. 969-517, §10, 94 Stat. 3015, applied the Copyright Act of 1976 to computer programs; see *Atari Games Corp. v. Oman*, 888 F.2d 878, 885, n. 8 (D. C. Cir. 1989); *Apple Computer Inc. v. Franklin Computer Corp.*, 714 F. 2d 1240, 1249 (3rd Cir. 1983); *Corsearch, Inc. v. Thomson & Thomson*, 792 F. Supp. 305, 322, n. 10 (S. D. N. Y. 1992); *Yost v. Early*, 87 Md. App. 364, 589 A.2d 1291, 1302, *cert. denied*, 324 Md. 123 (1991).

32   17 U.S.C. § 102 (b). These may be types of works that can't be copyrighted. But discoveries and processes, for example, may find protection through patents.

33   *M. Kramer Mfg. Co, Inc. v. Andrews*, 783 F.2d 421 (4th Cir. 1986); *Williams Electronics, Inc. v. Bally Mfg. Corp.*, 568 F. Supp. 1274 (N. D. Ill. 1983).

34   *Berkic v. Crichton*, 761 F.2d 1289 (9th Cir. 1985), *cert. denied*, 106 S. Ct. 85 (1985).

35   *Walker v. Time Life Films, Inc.*, 615 F. Supp. 430 (S. D. N. Y. 1985), *aff'd*, 784 F.2d 44, *cert. denied*, 476 U.S. 1159 (1986).

36   *Mazer v. Stein*, 347 U.S. 201, 214 (1954).

faculty member in animal medicine. You have an idea for an article — life, events and relationships in the turbulent environment
of the emergency room of a veterinary clinic that specializes in
dogs. You share that idea with a colleague. Months later, you
happen upon an article in a journal in your field. The article is entitled *Puppy Trauma!* and deals with the same idea you shared
with your colleague. In fact, she is listed as the principal author.
You talk with her and complain that she has illegally stolen your
idea. You are not going to be able to make a claim of a copyright
violation. Your *idea* for the article is not copyrightable. You and
anyone else are free to use that idea. Her expression of that idea,
in the form of the article, is protected by copyright (assuming
that the script meets the test of originality; it is already fixed).
You are free to create your own expression of your idea.

Facts cannot be copyrighted, either.[37] You cannot copyright
the facts of Martin Luther King, Jr.'s life. Your expression of his
life, in the form of your original contributions in a biography
that you might write is copyrightable.[38] You cannot copyright
the fact that the Titanic sank. Your expression of that tragic
event, in the form of, say, a blockbuster motion picture, is
coyrightable.

Who owns a copyright? With an important exception, the
author of a work owns it. If there is more than one creator, all of
them own the copyright jointly.[39] The important exception is in
an employment setting, which is particularly relevant for higher
education. The general rule is that an employer owns
"works-made-for-hire."[40] Copyright law recognizes two forms
of a "work-made-for-hire." The first is that the employer is the
"author" of a work created by an employee within the scope of

[37] *Walker v. Time Life Films, Inc., supra;* M. Kramer Mfg. Co., *Inc. v. Andrews, supra;
Cooling Systems and Flexibles, Inc. v. Stuart Radiator, Inc.* 777 F. 2d 485 (9th Cir. 1985);
Miller v. Universal Studios, Inc., 650 F2d 1365 (5th Cir. 1981); *Peckarsky v. American
Broadcasting Co. Inc.,* 603 F. Supp. 688. (D. D. C. 1984).

[38] Note that original contributions in a biography are protectable; recitation of
mere facts are not. See, for example, *Harper & Row, Publishers, Inc. v. Nation Enterprises,* 732 F.2d 195 (2d Cir. 1983), rev'd on other grounds, 471 U.S. 539 (1985).

[39] 17 U.S. C. § 201(a).

[40] 17 U.S. C. § 201(b).

his or her employment.[41] Therefore, the employer owns the copyright of the work.

Ownership of copyright of works created by faculty and staff at a university deserves special attention. Occasionally, some have claimed that a university owns the copyright to faculty lectures.[42] Cases have held, however, that a professor who creates his or her own lectures (assuming they meet the tests of originality and fixation[43]) owns the copyright in his or her works. The employer does not.[44]

Aside from lectures, faculty and staff at a university create a vast array of other types of copyrightable works within the scope of their employment. It is generally accepted that a university does not own the copyright to books, articles, and equivalent expressions of creations authored by faculty.

The second form of a "work-made-for-hire" is when an employer commissions an independent contractor who, by definition, is not an employee, to create a work.[45] In both cases, in order for the university to claim ownership of a work-made-for-hire, the parties must agree to the arrangement in writing.[46]

The digital technology environment has created a number of copyright issues that have important implications in university settings. Courses created by faculty that are made available on the Internet raise a particularly significant issue: who owns

---

[41] 17 U.S. C. § 201(b).

[42] See, for example, *Williams v. Weisser,* 78 Cal. Rptr. 542 (1969).

[43] If lectures are merely delivered orally, they are not copyrighted because they have not been fixed. See Daniel, Philip T. K. 1998. Copyright, fair use, and the internet: Information for administrators and other educational officials. *The College Law Digest,* 28(7). If they are reduced to writing under the authority of their creator, the fixation requirement is met.

[44] *Hayes v. Sony Corp of America,* 847 F.2d 412, 416 (7th Cir. 1988); Williams, supra.

[45] 17 U.S. C. § 201(b). For factors that should be evaluated to determine whether a work is a "work-made-for-hire" by an independent contractor, see *Community for Creative Non-Violence v. Reid,* 490 U.S. 730 (1989). In both forms of a "work-made-for-hire" — a work created by an employee within the scope of employment or by an independent contractor — the employer owns the work unless the parties have entered in a written agreement to the contrary.

[46] Id.

them? The university or the faculty member? A university and its faculty have a number of options.

Given the vast resources the university invests in the creation of an online course, it is understandable that a university will claim its ownership. One university, Drexel, has promulgated a draft of a policy that takes this position.[47] Faculty reaction has been predictable. In essence, many have said that they will not participate in the university's distance education program if they cannot own the courses they create. However, if faculty create an online course that is deemed to be within the scope of their employment — and therefore the university claims ownership of it C they receive a potential significant benefit: they are covered by the university's liability protection. It may thus be in the interests of the faculty to have the university own the copyright to online courses. In that event, it is also in the university's interests to consider granting nonexclusive licenses and entering into royalty sharing agreements that are generous to faculty as incentives for them to participate in online course development.

On the other hand, the traditional acknowledgment that faculty own the copyright to books, articles, and the like can be extended to online courses as well. In that case, faculty own the copyright to such courses. University interests in the courses can be recognized through nonexclusive licenses and royalty arrangements.

It is not necessary that *only* the university or *only* the faculty member own the copyright to online courses. There is a middle ground. Considering the significant interests of a university and faculty in online course development, the parties can own the copyright jointly. As joint copyright owners, each of the parties is free, among other things, to license the courses without the consent of the other. The parties are accountable to each other, however, for a share of the profit derived from the commercial exploitation of online courses.

That universities have realized that the Internet has opened vast economic potential for the marketing and selling of copy-

---

47   See: A debate over ownership of on-line courses surfaces at Drexel U., *The Chronicle of Higher Education*, 45(31).

righted works created at their institutions has raised another important issue: universities are entering into agreements, sometimes private, with private sources to market and sell copyrightable instructional materials outside the university. A number of universities have entered into confidential agreements, purportedly without consultation with their faculties. It has been reported that UCLA and the Home Education Network, the University of California at Berkeley and America Online, and the University of Colorado and Real Education have entered into such agreements (Noble 1998). This circumstance has set off alarms in some quarters. Critics contend that by entering into such agreements, universities are usurping faculty control over the heart and soul of a university: course materials. One commentator states: "With the commoditization of instruction, this transformation of academia is now reaching the breaking point" (Noble 1998). Developments of this type suggest the seismic impact the Internet can have on traditional copyright polices and practices in American universities. They also demonstrate that universities need to approach with great care how they might exploit economic opportunities that the Internet creates for works created by faculty and staff at their institutions.

Does publishing, or "posting," copyrighted work on the Internet mean that an author has completely surrendered his or her rights as a copyright owner? No. The method of conveying information may be new, but the general principles of copyright law are not. If an author owns the copyright in a work, the owner does not surrender all of his or her copyright by posting it on the Internet.[48] To underscore the point, even if law does not require it, an author should include a standard copyright notice on the posted work. With limited exceptions, a copyright owner of works posted online is entitled to exercise certain "exclusive" rights, authorize others to exercise any of the exclusive rights, and prevent others from exercising those rights in the same way that any other copyright owner can (Lehman 1995, 46).

---

[48] *Religious Technology Centers v. Netcom Online Communication Services, Inc.,* supra; *Playboy Enterprises, Inc. v. Starware Publishing Corp.,* supra; *Sega Enterprises Ltd. v. Maphia,* supra. See, also, Kurz, Raymond A., and Celine M. Jimenez. 1996. Copyrights online, *Howard Law Journal,* 39(2) and Price, Joseph R. 1996. Colleges and university as internet service providers: determining and limiting liability for copyright infringement, *The Journal of College and University Law,* 23: 183-229.

The Rights of Copyright Owners

The owner of a copyright has five exclusive rights,[49] commonly known as a "bundle of rights":[50]

- the right to reproduce copies of the work;
- the right to prepare derivative works;
- the right to distribute copies;
- the right to perform the work publicly;
- the right to display the work publicly.

If a creator owns the copyright to a work, unless an exception authorized by law applies, a user must obtain the consent of the copyright owner to use the work if the use involves any of the exclusive rights.

Here is a brief look at each of the five exclusive rights.

The right to reproduce copies of the work

Common sense should tell us that if a user prints a document from his or her computer, the person is making a copy of it. The same goes for copying a document to disk and loading it into the computer's memory.[51] It has been held, however, that merely viewing a document on a computer screen also involves copying, for copyright purposes.[52] When a person browses the Internet, the images on a computer screen exist by virtue of a copy that has been reproduced in the computer's memory.[53] In one case, the court stated that a work placed in the computer's memory constitutes a reproduction or copying of that work because it may be, as the Copyright Act provides, "perceived, reproduced, or ... communicated with the aid of a machine or device."[54]

---

49 17 U.S.C. § 106.

50 *Stewart v. Abend,* 495 U.S. 207, 220 (1990).

51 MAI Systems Corp. v. Peak Computer, Inc., 991 F.2d 511, 519 (9th Cir. 1993).

52 *Id.,* p. 518.

53 Id.

54 *Id.*

If that is the case, it would follow that if the Web material is copyrighted, unless the viewer has the consent of the owner or another legal exception to consent applies, viewing constitutes a copyright infringement. Nevertheless, it seems unlikely that a copyright owner who posts material on the Internet would cry foul simply because someone looks at it. If an author puts a copyrighted document on the Internet, at a minimum he or she should expect that it will be viewed. Why else would someone put it there in the first place?

Simply viewing a copyrighted work on a computer may not pose a serious threat to a copyright owner's interests. But there are other instances when computer transactions result in making copies and present more serious copyright considerations for a copyright owner. In 1993, President Clinton created a working group to study and make recommendations on intellectual property and the national information infrastructure. The working group issued a final report in 1995, *Intellectual Property and the National Information Infrastructure: The Report of the Working Group on Intellectual Property Rights*, commonly known as the "White Paper" (Lehman 1995, 65-66). The White Paper identified a series of common computer transactions that it stated constituted copying:

- When a work is placed into a computer, whether on a disk, diskette, ROM, or other storage device or in RAM for more than a very brief period, a copy is made.

- When printed work is "scanned" into a digital file, a copy — the digital file itself — is made.

- When other works — including photographs, motion pictures, or sound recordings — are digitized, copies are made.

- Whenever a digitized file is "uploaded" from a user's computer to a bulletin board system (BBS) or other server, a copy is made.

- Whenever a digitized file is "downloaded" from a BBS or other server, a copy is made.

- When a file is transferred from one computer network user to another, multiple copies are made.

Under current technology, when an end-user's computer is employed as a "dumb" terminal to access a file resident on another computer such as a BBS or Internet host, a copy of at least the portion viewed is made in the user's computer. Without such copying into the RAM or buffer of the user's computer, no screen display would be possible.

If these transactions are done without the consent of the copyright owner or unless they are otherwise permitted by law, they constitute the type of activities that strike at the heart of a copyright holder's copyright interests.

Because the copyright reproduction right is so important, regulating or controlling the copying of copyrighted material on the Internet is crucial for a copyright owner to protect his or her rights. There are a number of technologies available to users to control access to and use of their copyrighted works on the Internet. They include encryption, electronic copyright management systems, digital objects, proprietary viewers, watermarks, dispersed works, and real-time audio and video (Hardy 1998).[55]

Aside from technological advances that help control access and use of copyrighted materials on the Internet, there is a law, recently enacted in the United States, that is designed to give copyright owners legal tools to enforce their rights. On October 28, 1998, the Digital Millennium Copyright Act of 1998 (DMCA) went into effect in the United States.[56] The act includes provisions of special interest and importance to universities. One section of the act deals with the subject of so-called anti-tampering devices, technological measures used by a copyright owner to protect his or her copyrighted works. The act rec-

---

[55] A technical description of each of these technologies is beyond the scope of this chapter. There may be ways to control initial copying of a copyrighted work, but a copyright owner may not be able to control further copying of the work. See *Pye v. Mitchell*, 574 F.2d 476, 481 (9th Cir. 1978); Boddie 1998, 225.

[56] Pub. L. 105-304, 112 Stat. 2860.

ognizes two categories of technological measures, those that prevent unauthorized access to a copyrighted work, and those that prohibit unauthorized copying of a copyrighted work. Making or selling devices used to circumvent either category is prohibited if (U.S. Copyright Office 1998):

- they are primarily designed or produced to circumvent;

- their purpose or use is commercially insignificant except to circumvent; or

- they are marketed for use in.

For universities, there is an exception to the prohibition of devices or products designed to circumvent technological measures used by a copyright owner to prevent unauthorized access to copyrighted works. Nonprofit libraries, archives, and educational institutions may circumvent such measures, but only to make a good-faith determination whether to obtain authorized access to the work.[57]

The right to prepare derivative works

The right to prepare derivative works means that a copyright owner has the right to control the abridgement, adaptation, translation, revision, or other transformation of his or her work.[58] If a work is downloaded from the Internet and is modified — by annotating, editing, translating, or otherwise significantly changing it — a derivative file is created.

One commentator provides several examples of relatively simple computer transactions that may involve derivative rights. A user might download a copyrighted graphics work, alter it somewhat, then post it on the Internet. Or, a user might translate a computer software program from one language to another. Both examples might well involve copyright infringement of a copyright owner's exclusive right to make derivative copies of the original copyrighted work (Kurz 1996, 574).[59]

[57] DMCA § 1201(d).

[58] 17 U.S. C. § 106(2).

[59] In both instances, depending upon the facts of the cases, violations of the reproduction, distribution, performance, and display rights may also be involved.

Though creation of derivative material without the consent of the copyright owner constitutes a copyright violation, once again the context of the act presents a situation unique to Internet transmission. It is not likely that the owner of a copyright will even be aware that a derivative work has been prepared if a user simply makes the derivative work and stores it in his or her computer. The likelihood that the copyright holder will discover the derivative work has been created will increase if the user transmits it over the Internet.

Moreover, computer technologies allow for rapid and frequent changes of an original copyrighted work. Therefore, in short order, a work derived from original copyrighted material can be so different from the original that its origin is lost (Boddie et al. 1998, 225-226).

Absent effective restrictions to the access and use of copyrighted materials on the Internet, enforcement of derivative rights becomes the issue.

The right to distribute copies

The right to distribute copies of a copyrighted work allows the copyright holder to sell it, lease it, lend it, and give it away (Lehman 1995, 67).[60]

Internet transmissions might involve a copyright owner's right to distribute copies. For example, the right could be infringed simply by viewing the copyrighted material "because browser technology requires that a copy be 'distributed' for storage in the memory of the user's computer" (Major 1998, 99).

The right to perform and display a work

Copyright owners have two other exclusive rights: the rights to perform a work publicly and to display a work publicly. There are several issues associated with these rights as they may apply to Internet communications. Does reading or viewing a digital ex-

---

[60] 17 U.S.C. § 109(a). A copyright owner's right to distribute, however, is qualified by what is known as the "first sale" doctrine. In essence, a copyright holder controls only the first transfer of his or her copyrighted work. The owner does not control subsequent transfers of a lawful copy of the work.

pression on a computer screen involve a "performance" or a "display"? If so, is the reading or viewing of it "public"?

A performance is defined as reciting, rendering, playing, dancing, or acting a work, directly or using any device or process, "or, in the case of a motion picture or other audiovisual work, [showing] its images in any sequence or [making] the sounds accompanying it audible."[61] For purposes of the Internet, a display of a work means "to show a copy of it, either directly or by means of a ... television image, or any other device or process."[62]

It has been suggested (Price 1996, 200-204) that when a digitized motion picture is shown on a computer, there is a "performance." It may also constitute a display.

For both a performance and a display of Web material in a university setting, "public" means to perform or display a work "at a place open to the public ..."[63] When the images of the work are shown in sequence so that users can watch it, even if the transmission is not copied, a "performance" has occurred.[64] It has been held that "public" includes instances in which a group of viewers watch a work being performed or displayed at different times and at different locations.[65] When a user browses the Internet viewing copies of works, a public display occurs (Major 1998), because when the work was posted it was made available to the public (Price 1996).

The performance or display of works in the context of distance education at nonprofit educational institutions has some protections under the Copyright Act. Under section 110 (2), a work may be *displayed* and a non-dramatic literary or musical work may be *performed* through transmissions if they are a regular part of systematic instruction at the institution, if they di-

---

[61]   17 U.S. C. § 101.

[62]   17 U.S. C. § 101.

[63]   17 U.S. C. § 101.

[64]   *Columbia Pictures Industries, Inc. v. Aveco, Inc.* 800 F. 2d 59, 62 (3rd Cir. 1986); *Playboy Enterprises, Inc. v. Frena, supra*; *On Command Video v. Columbia Pictures*, 777 F. Supp. 787 (N. D. Cal. 1991).

[65]   *Columbia Pictures Industries v. Aveco*, id.; *Columbia Pictures Indus. v. Redd Horne, Inc.*, 749 F. 2d 154 (3rd Cir. 1984); *On Command Video Corp. v. Columbia Pictures*, id.

rectly relate to teaching content, and if they are received in classrooms or similar places. (Transmissions also may be received by persons because of their disabilities or other special circumstances[66].) This provision raises a particular issue relating to transmissions on the Internet for educational purposes. Since education through the Internet increasingly takes place in a student's room, does that — or a similar location — constitute a "classroom" or a similar place "normally devoted to instruction," so that such transmissions may be made without violating a copyright owner's performance and display rights?

Relevant exceptions to the requirement to obtain a copyright owner's consent

As we have seen, the general rule is that if you want to use a copyrighted work, you must secure the permission of the copyright owner. Especially as they relate to this discussion of copyright issues and the Internet, there are several instances when consent is not required.

Public domain

"Works may be in the public domain if they do not meet the original requirement for copyright protection, if copyright protection has expired, or if they fall into certain classes of works that are not copyrightable, such as the white pages of a phone book ..." (Boddie et al. 1998, 5-6, 219). We have previously reviewed the copyright requirement for originality. We have also discussed examples of works that have been deemed not copyrightable.

Works whose copyright has expired are in the public domain. They may be used by anyone.

For works created as of January 1, 1978, copyright law has provided that a copyrighted work is protected for fifty years after the death of the author,[67] or, in the case of joint works, fifty

---

[66] 17 U.S. C. § 110 (2).
[67] 17 U.S. C. § 302(a).

years after the death of the last surviving author.[68] As of October 27, 1998, the duration of a copyright was extended twenty more years.[69] Now, therefore, copyright protection for works created on or after January 1, 1978, endures for the life of the author, or the last surviving author, plus seventy years.

Implied License

A user who wants to make use of copyrighted material from the Internet without seeking the copyright owner's permission may argue that he or she has an implied license to use it. The Copyright Act establishes that a copyright owner may grant an exclusive license to another to use his or her copyrighted works, but if so it must be in writing.[70] The act does not address the subject of nonexclusive licenses. Therefore, nonexclusive licenses may be granted orally. They may also be implied from the conduct of the parties.[71] To determine whether the parties' conduct creates an implied license, one must examine the intent of the parties.[72] Whether or not an implied license exists is determined on a case-by-case basis.[73]

To argue successfully that a user has an implied license, a person must show two things: one, that the creator voluntarily submitted the work to the user for publication;[74] and two, that there was a meeting of the minds.[75] There is a sound argument that by posting material on the Internet, the owner is granting users a nonexclusive license, albeit a narrow one, that restricts the user to use the materials for personal purposes only and not to redistribute or modify it.

---

[68] 17 U.S. C. § 302(b).

[69] Sonny Bono Copyright Term Extension Act, Pub. L. 105-298, October 27, 1998.

[70] See 17 U.S. C. § § 101, 204.

[71] *Effects Associates, Inc., v. Cohen,* 908 F. 2d 555 (9th Cir. 1990), *cert. denied,* 498 U.S. 1103.

[72] *Johnson v. Jones,* 921 F. Supp. 1573, 1584 (E. D. Mich. 1996).

[73] *Apple Computer, Inc. v. Microsoft Corp.,* 821 F. Supp. 616, 627 (N. D. Cal. 1993), *aff'd,* 35 F.3d 1435 (9th Cir. 1994), *cert. denied,* 1155 S. C t. 1176 (1995).

[74] *Herbert v. United States,* 32 Fed. Cl. 293, 298 (1994).

[75] *N. A. D. A. Services v. Business Data of Virginia,* 651 F. Supp. 44, 49 (E. D. Va. 1986).

Fair Use

Fair use is a concept in U.S. copyright law that for many years was developed through court cases. In 1976, it was embodied in the Copyright Act. While ordinarily you need the consent of the copyright holder to use copyrighted material, if you are making fair use of it you do not need permission. Fair use of a copyrighted work for such purposes as criticism, comment, news reporting, teaching, scholarship, or research does not constitute a copyright violation.[76] There are four tests that are applied to evaluate whether a use is fair:

1. *What is the purpose and character of the use?* Are you using the original, copyrighted work for a different purpose or in a different manner? Merely assembling works into an anthology by downloading copies of articles from the Web, for example, does not really change the original.[77] Does your use of the work involve commercial benefit for you?

2. *What is the nature of the copyrighted work?* Is it fact or fiction? Factual works are considered to have more public value. Therefore, greater use of them will be tolerated. Works of fiction often involve more subjective impressions of the creator. It is believed that they deserve more protection.

3. *What is the amount and substantiality of the portion used in relation to the copyrighted work as a whole?* This test has both qualitative and quantitative aspects. For example, the amount of material you plan to use may not be much — say, a paragraph or so of a long article. However, if that paragraph presents the thesis, or main idea, of the work, then the use may not be fair. Or, you may want to use 95 percent of the work. The more you plan to use, the less fair the use may be considered.

---

[76] 17 U.S. C. § 107.

[77] See *Basic Books, Inc. v. Kinko's Graphics Corp.*, 758 F. Supp. 1522 (S. D. N. Y. 1991).

4. *What is the effect upon the potential market for or value of the copyrighted work?* In other words, does your use involve a diminishment of commercial value to the copyright owner?

All four factors must be analyzed in a fair use consideration. One of the tests is not necessarily more important than the others, but the greater commercial benefit the use will be to you, the more suspect your use as fair use is likely to be.

Fair use is as available to a user of Web material as it is for any other copyrighted work. One commentator (Price 1996) suggests a number of arguments relating to fair use of copyrighted materials on the Web. Concerning the first fair use factor, the *purpose and character of the use*, he suggests that it weighs in favor of a public or nonprofit university because of the essential nonprofit educational purpose of the institution, the benefits a university brings to the public by contributing to the functioning of the Internet, and the Internet access universities offer.

The commentator argues that the second and third factors, the *nature of the work* and the *amount and substantiality of the portion used in relation to the whole*, are not really relevant to Internet transmissions. As to the *nature of the work*, he suggests that a university is merely facilitating the posting of materials. Their nature, therefore, is not relevant to a fair use analysis (Price 1996). For *amount and substantiality*, regardless of the amount of a copyrighted work on the Internet that is copied, a university just forwards postings to the Internet automatically. It does not screen them. As a "conduit," the university itself is not concerned with how much material is being used. Therefore, this factor should have no impact on a fair use claim.

The commentator concedes (Price 1996, 225), however, that the fourth factor, potential *effect on the market*, favors a copyright owner. Internet transmission of copyrighted works potentially has direct impact on the market interests of a copyright holder.

Because fair use must be analyzed in relation to facts presented on a case-by-case basis, it is not possible to assess the strengths of the commentator's fair use arguments in all instances. His observations are examples, however, of how a fair use analysis needs to be conducted whenever a user will seek to make fair use of a copyrighted Web document without the consent of the owner. In the final analysis, fair use of a copyrighted work on the Internet invites a traditional question: "*Would a reasonable copyright owner have consented to the use?*"[78] If the answer is yes, then the use would likely be considered fair.

There is fair use guidance for nonprofit educational institutions concerning two important educational activities: classroom copying of books and periodicals,[79] and use of educational multimedia.[80] By conforming to the standards set forth in the guidelines for each of these subjects, a user will be considered to have a "safe harbor." The use will be deemed fair; it will not involve copyright infringement.

Infringement

Infringement occurs when any rights of a copyright owner have been violated.[81] To show infringement, a copyright holder must show that he or she has a valid copyright in a work and that an alleged violator has "copied" the work.[82]

There are three forms of copyright infringement liability: direct, contributory, and vicarious. A user who makes digitized copies of a copyrighted photograph or other copyrighted works without the consent of the copyright owner would have direct liability for infringement (Price 1996, 206-207). The person engaging in the infringing activity is held to a strict liability standard.

---

[78]   Harper & Row Publishers, *supra*.

[79]   The Guidelines for Classroom Copying are available at <http://lcweb.loc. gov/copyright/ circs/circ21>. As stated, the guidelines are written in relation to nonprofit educational institutions. *Fair use* is available to any user, however, including for-profit educational institutions.

[80]   The Guidelines for Educational Multimedia are available at <http://www. med. virginia.edu/instructions/fairuse.html>.

[81]   17 U.S. C. § 501.

[82]   *See Walker v. University Books, Inc.* 602 F.2d 859 (9th Cir. 1979); *Johnson v. Jones,* supra; Religious Technology Centers, *supra; Playboy Enterprises, Inc. v. Frena, supra; Apple Computer, Inc. v. Microsoft Corp, supra.* The White Paper (Lehman, 1995, 101) also notes that courts use the term "copying" as a shorthand for a violation of any of the copyright rights.

Therefore, the infringer's knowledge or intent is irrelevant, except as they might relate to establishing damages. If a party induces, causes, or materially contributes to the infringing activity of another, the party may be contributorily liable.[83] A university service provider may be subject to contributory liability, for example, if it has knowledge of infringing activity and "substantially participates" in it (Price 1996, 212). Finally, if a party has the right and ability to exercise control over the activities of its subscribers and reaps a direct financial benefit from the infringing activity, it becomes vicariously liable (Price 1996, 212). If a university service provider has a policy that governs employee use of the Internet and an employee promotes university online courses that bring revenue to the university, but the Internet activity involves copyright infringement, the university may become vicariously liable.

There are civil and criminal penalties for copyright infringement.[84]

The issue of online server provider liability has been hotly debated in the past several years in the United States. In the White Paper (Lehman 1995), for example, the working group concluded that "it is — at best — premature to reduce the liability of any type of service provider in the [national information infrastructure] environment." In the recently enacted Digital Millennium Copyright Act of 1998 (DMCA),[85] however, Congress decided to provide limits on liability for copyright infringement by online service providers.[86] One of the limits is of special interest to university service providers, defined simply as those that provide online services.

The DMCA establishes that a public or nonprofit university service provider will not be liable for the copyright infringing activities of its faculty and graduate student teachers when the activities occur while they are "performing a teaching or research function," so long as:

[83] *Religious Technology Centers, supra,* 1373-75.

[84] See 17 U.S. C. §§ 504 - 506.

[85] DMCA, Pub. L. 105-304, 112 U.S. C. 2860, October 28, 1998.

[86] DMCA § 512.

- the infringing activities do not involve providing online access to instructional materials "required or recommended" in a course taught by the faculty member or graduate student within the last three years;

- the university has not received more than two complaints that the faculty member or graduate student has engaged in copyright infringement within the last three years; and

- the university provides its system users with materials that accurately describe and encourage compliance with copyright law.[87]

Given the conditions that apply in order to gain exemption from liability, just how effective is this limitation on liability? For example, what value is the limitation if it excludes instructional materials that have been required or recommended for the last three years? Moreover, the university may have received more than two complaints in the last three years that a faculty member or graduate student has violated a copyright owner's rights. But under the statute, mere receipt of complaints is the test, not whether complaints have merit. Thus, whether or not complaints are true, the liability limitation does not apply if the university simply receives them.

International Issues

Historically, copyright has been governed by national law. Each country that has chosen to recognize and protect intellectual property has enacted its own copyright laws. International treaties have recognized the primacy of national copyright law. The principal international copyright treaty is the Berne Convention (Lehman 1995). The Berne Convention establishes a number of international standards for copyright protection. One of its provisions says that countries that are members of the convention may not require a copyright notice to be present on a work in or-

---

87 The Digital Millennium Copyright Act, 1998. "Joint Explanatory Statement of the Committee of Conference," 74-75.

der for it to enjoy copyright protection. To comply with that provision, it was necessary for the United States to enact its own legislation. As we have seen, the United States did so, effective in 1989. In other words, the Berne Convention established basic copyright requirements. To become effective, a nation has had to enact its own legislation.

In October 1998, the United States enacted the DMCA. The main section of the act was designed specifically to implement two treaties of the World Intellectual Property Organization: the WIPO Copyright Treaty and the WIPO Performances and Phonograms Treaty, each adopted in 1996.[88] As we have seen, among the subjects included in the DMCA the United States has implemented provisions concerning protection of a copyright owner's anti-tampering systems[89] and the limitations, albeit arguable, on the liability of public and nonprofit universities for the infringing activities of its faculty and graduate student teachers.[90] Again, the WIPO international treaties set the general standards. A country has to adopt its own legislation to implement them.

The Internet is an international means of fast and easy transmissions and communications. The technology is not necessarily limited by national borders. The universal nature of digital technology presents legal problems that are unique to the Internet. The DMCA recognizes the international character of the Internet by establishing that persons of other countries that have joined international copyright treaties will receive copyright protection of their works in the United States.[91]

A host of other international issues have not yet been addressed by international treaties or the laws of the respective nations. Because of the interactive nature of digital technologies, it may be hard to determine precisely where a work was posted or where it has been used. Even if the location of these activities can be determined, if they occur in different countries, whose law

---

[88] DMCA, "Joint Explanatory Statement of the Committee of Conference," p. 63.

[89] DMCA § 1201; *see* pp. 17-18, *supra*.

[90] DMCA § 512; *see* p. 28, *supra*.

[91] DMCA, §102.

will apply?[92] Will each country respect the laws of another? This issue could be potentially significant for online courses. Unless a creator is able to build in effective technological restrictions on access and use, if a student in another country allegedly violates U.S. copyright rights of online course materials, will the other country recognize the laws of the United States to address these violations?

Can copyright interests in materials on the Internet continue to be effectively protected by the laws of the separate nations? Some argue no.[93] Some state that a new international treaty establishing copyright standards and monitoring provisions that apply to all its members without further national enactments is necessary.[94] Still others suggest that it is not realistic to expect nations of the world to accept international copyright standards and enforcement mechanisms anytime in the near future.[95] The question is whether the countries of the world are ready for uniform international legal standards and enforcement mechanisms for an area of law that more traditionally has been addressed through the laws of the respective nations.

Summary

Works created by "authors" that are original and fixed receive copyright protections. A copyright notice is not required to be present on a work in order to obtain copyright protection. Copyright protections apply when a creator publishes, or posts, his or her copyrighted works on the Internet. A copyright owner has five "exclusive" rights. Perhaps the most important one is the right to reproduce copies. Internet technologies make it easy to post works online. They also make access, and therefore use,

---

92 It is important to note the jurisdictional problems are not just international issues. If a work has been created in Wisconsin, but copyright infringement occurs in Texas, the law of which state will apply?

93 See, for example, Barbara Cohen. 1996. A proposed regime for copyright protection on the internet, *Brooklyn Journal of International Law*, 22(2): 401-435.

94 Cohen, *id.*

95 See, for example, Andreas P. Reindl. 1998. Choosing law in cyberspace: Copyright conflicts on global networks, *Michigan Journal of International Law*, 19(3): 799-871.

easy. To protect a copyright owner's rights, new technologies have been developed to restrict access and, to some extent, to restrict use of copyrighted works on the Internet. Once a user has a copy, however, controlling the creation and use of subsequent copies presents a more difficult situation.

Copyright law provides, in general, that works created by employees within the scope of employment belong to the employer. That provision has particular relevance to the creation and delivery of online courses at a university. A university may claim that online courses are created within the scope of a faculty member's employment, and that, therefore, the university owns them. There are reasonable grounds for a university to claim such ownership. There are also reasonable bases for faculty to claim ownership. It may be possible to avoid contention if the parties agree to own copyright of online courses jointly.

In October 1998, the United States adopted two laws relating to copyright, several provisions of which are especially pertinent to universities. First, for the past several decades, copyright protections for works created on or after January 1, 1978, have endured for the life of the author plus fifty years. Under one of the new laws, protections will extend an additional twenty years.

The second new law, the Digital Millennium Copyright Act, establishes prohibitions of devices that circumvent technological measures used by a copyright owner to prevent unauthorized access to or copying of his or her copyrighted work. There is a limited exemption from the prohibition on devices relating to control of access for nonprofit educational institutions, libraries, and archives. The act also limits the liability of nonprofit educational institutions for copyright infringement of faculty and graduate student teachers when certain conditions are met. The conditions are such, however, that the value of the limitation is debatable.

Internet transmissions are not restricted by national boundaries. Digital technologies make it easy to transmit and receive materials on the Internet quickly and easily. The international nature of the Internet creates significant legal issues. Among them is the question of defining just when copyright infringement occurs. Does it occur in relation to where a document is created? Where it is posted? Where it's received? Or perhaps where it is used?

There is also the issue of jurisdiction. Whose copyright laws will apply in a copyright infringement claim? There are a number of suggestions to address the issue, including the development of international laws that will have international application and enforcement. Will the nations of the world agree to subject themselves to international laws and enforcement mechanisms that apply uniformly to those who join the treaties?

Resolution of copyright issues in the United States and internationally will involve a consideration of circumstances that are unique to the Internet. In each instance, lawmakers will have to wrestle with a question of balance. How will the rights of creators be protected in a technological environment when users will demand and expect easy and ready access to information that flows freely on the Internet?

REFERENCES

Cases Cited

Apple Computer Inc. v. Franklin Computer Corp., 714 F. 2d 1240 (3rd Cir. 1983)

Apple Computer, Inc. v. Microsoft Corp. 821 F. Supp. 625 (N. D. Cal. 1993) *aff'd.*, 35 F. 3d 1435 (9th Cir) 1994)

Apple Computer, Inc. v. Microsoft Corp., 821 F. Supp. 616 (N. D. Cal. 1993), *aff'd*, 35 F.3d 1435 (9th Cir. 1994), *cert. denied*, 1155 S. C t. 1176 (1995)

Arica Institute, Inc. v. Palmer, 770 F. Supp. 188, 191-92 (S. D. N. Y. 1991), *aff'd*, 970 F. 2d 1067, 1072 (2d Cir. 1992)

Arthur Retlaw & Associates, Inc. v. Travenol Laboratories, Inc., 582 F. Supp. 1010 (N. D. Ill. 1984)

Arthur Rutenberg Homes, Inc. v. Drew Homes, Inc. 29 F.2d 1529 (11th Cir. 1994)

Atari Games Corp. v. Oman, 888 F.2d 878, 885 (D. C. Cir. 1989)

Basic Books, Inc. v. Kinko's Graphics Corp., 758 F. Supp. 1522 (S. D. N. Y. 1991)

Berkic v. Crichton, 761 F.2d 1289 (9th Cir. 1985), *cert. denied*, 106 S. Ct. 85 (1985)

Berne Convention Implementing Act, Pub. L. 100-568, 102 Stat. 2853, October 31, 1988

Bleistein v. Donaldson Lithography Co., 188 U.S. 239, 250 (1903)

Columbia Pictures Indus. v. Redd Horne, Inc., 749 F. 2d 154 (3rd Cir. 1984)

Columbia Pictures Industries, Inc. v. Aveco, Inc. 800 F. 2d 59 (3rd Cir. 1986)

Community for Creative Non-Violence v. Reid, 490 U.S. 730 (1989)

Cooling Systems and Flexibles, Inc. v. Stuart Radiator, Inc. 777 F. 2d 485 (9th Cir. 1985)

Corsearch, Inc. v. Thomson & Thomson, 792 F. Supp., 305, 322 (S.D.N.Y. 1992)

E. Mishan & Sons, Inc., v. Marycana, 662 F. Supp. 1339, 1340-43 (S.D.N.Y. 1987)

Effects Associates, Inc., v. Cohen, 908 F. 2d 555 (9th Cir. 1990), *cert. denied,* 498 U.S. 1103 (1991)

Feist Publications, Inc. v. Rural Telephone Serv. Co., Inc., 499 U.S. 340, 345 (1991)

Fox Film Corp. v. Doyal, 286 U.S. 123 (1932)

Gilbert/Robinson, Inc. v. Carrie Beverage-Missouri, Inc., 758 F. Supp. 512 (E. D. Mo. 1991)

Harper & Row, Publishers, Inc. v. Nation Enterprises, 732 F.2d 195 (2d Cir. 1983), rev'd on other grounds, 471 U.S. 539 (1985)

Hayes v. Sony Corp of America, 847 F.2d 412, 416 (7th Cir. 1988)

Hearn v. Meyer, 664 F. Supp. 832, 840 (S. D. N. Y. 1987)

Herbert v. United States, 32 Fed. Cl. 293, 298 (1994)

Johnson v. Jones, 921 F. Supp. 1573, 1584 (E. D. Mich. 1996)

L. Batlin & Son, Inc. v. Snyder, 536 F.2d 486 (2d Cir. 1976)

M. Kramer Mfg. Co, Inc. v. Andrews, 783 F.2d 421 (4th Cir. 1986)

Magic Marketing, Inc. v. Mailing Services of Pittsburgh, Inc., 634 F. Supp. 769 (W. D. Pa. 1986)

MAI Systems Corp. v. Peak Computer, Inc., 991 F.2d 511, 519 (9th Cir. 1993)

Mazer v. Stein, 347 U.S. 201, 214 (1954)

Miller v. Universal Studios, Inc., 650 F2d 1365 (5th Cir. 1981)

Moore Pub., Inc. v. Big Sky Marketing, Inc., 756 F. Supp. 1371 (D. Idaho 1990)

N.A.D.A. Services v. Business Data of Virginia, 651 F. Supp. 44 (E. D. Va. 1986)

On Command Video v. Columbia Pictures, 777 F. Supp. 787 (N. D. Cal. 1991)

Paramount Pictures Corp. v. Video Broadcasting Systems, Inc., 724 F. Supp. 808 (D. Kansas 1989)

Peckarsky v. American Broadcasting Co. Inc., 603 F. Supp. 688 (D. D. C. 1984)

Playboy Enterprises, Inc. v. Frena, 839 F. Supp. 1552 (M. D. Fla. 1993)

Playboy Enterprises, Inc. v. Starware Publishing Corp., 900 F. Supp 433 (S. D. Fla. 1995)

Pye v. Mitchell, 574 F.2d 476 (9th Cir. 1978)

Religious Technology Centers v. Netcom Online Communication Services, Inc., 907 F. Supp. 1361, 1373-75 (N. D. Cal. 1995)

Sebastian International, Inc. v. Consumer Contact (PTY) Ltd., 664 F. Supp. 909 (D. N. J. 1987), vacated on other grounds, 847 F.2d 1093 (3rd Cir. 1988)

Sega Enterprises Ltd. v. Maphia, 857 F. Supp. 679 (N. D. Cal. 1994)

Smith v. George E. Muehlehach Brewing Co., 140 F. Supp. 729 (W. D. Mo. 1956)

Sony Corporation of America v. University City Studios, 464 U.S. 417 (1984)

Stewart v. Abend, 495 U.S. 207, 220 (1990)

Toro Co. v. R & R Products Co., 787 F.2d 1208 (8th Cir. 1986)

Trenton v. Infinity Broadcasting Corporation, 865 F. Supp. 1416 (C. D. Cal. 1994)

Twentieth Century Music Corp. v. Aiken, 422 U.S. 151 (1975)

Twin Books Corp. v. Walt Disney Co., 83 F.3d 1162 (9th Cir. 1996)

Walker v. Time Life Films, Inc., 615 F. Supp. 430 (S. D. N. Y. 1985), *aff'd*, 784 F.2d 44 (2d Cir. 1986), *cert. denied*, 476 U.S. 1159 (1986)

Walker v. University Books, Inc. 602 F.2d 859 (9th Cir. 1979)

Williams Electronics, Inc. v. Bally Mfg. Corp., 568 F. Supp. 1274 (N. D. Ill. 1983)

Williams v. Weisser, 78 Cal. Rptr. 542 (1969)

Yost v. Early, 87 Md. App. 364, 589 A.2d 1291, 1302, *cert. denied*, 324 Md. 123 (1991)

Statutes Cited

15 U.S. C. § § 1501 *et seq.*

17 U.S. C. § § 101 *et seq.*

35 U.S. C. § § 101 *et seq.*

Digital Millennium Copyright Act, "Joint Explanatory Statement of the Committee of Conference"

Digital Millennium Copyright Act, Pub. L. 105-304, 112 Stat. 2860

Sonny Bono Copyright Term Extension Act, Pub. L. 105-298, October 27, 1998

The Computer Software Copyright Act of 1980, Pub. L. 969-517, 94 Stat. 3015

U.S. Copyright Office Summary of the Digital Millennium Copyright Act, December 1998

Books, Websites, and Journals

Author. 1999. A debate over ownership of on-line courses surfaces at Drexel U. *The Chronicle of Higher Education*, 9 April.

Boddie, II, Needham, et al. 1998. A review of copyright and the internet. *Campbell Law Review* 20(2).

Cohen, Barbara. 1996. A proposed regime for copyright protection on the Internet. *Brooklyn Journal of International Law* 22(2).

Daniel, Philip T. K. 1998. Copyright, fair use, and the Internet: information for administrators and other educational officials. *The College Law Digest* 28(7).

Fair Use guidelines for educational multimedia. [Website]. Available from < http://www.virginia.edu/instructions/fairuse.html >.

Guidelines for classroom copying in not-for-profit educational institutions with respect to books and periodicals. [Website]. Available from < http://lcweb.loc.gov/copyright/circs/circ21 >.

Hardy, I. Trotter. 1998. Project looking forward: Sketching the future of copyright in a networked world: Final report. U.S. Copyright Office.

Kurz, Raymond A. and Celine M. Jimenez. 1996. Copyrights on-line. *Howard Law Journal* 39(2).

Lehman, Bruce A. 1995. Intellectual property and the national information infrastructure: The report of the working group on intellectual property rights [White Paper]. Washington, DC: Information Infrastructure Task Force.

Leiner, Barry M., et al. 1998. A brief history of the internet. [Website]. Available from < http://www.isoc.org/internet/history/brief.html >.

Major, April M. 1998. Copyright law tackles yet another challenge: The electronic frontier of the world wide web. *Rutgers Computer and Technology Law Journal* 24(1).

Merriam Webster's Dictionary of Law. 1996. Springfield, MA: Merriam-Webster, Inc.

Nimmer, Melville E. and David Nimmer. 1998. *Nimmer on copyright.* New York: Matthew Bender & Co.

Noble, David F. 1998. *Confidential agreements between universities and private companies pose serious challenge to faculty intellectual property rights.* [Website]. Reprinted with permission. Available from < http://communication.ucsd.edu/dl/ddm2.html >.

Price, Joseph R. 1996. Colleges and universities as internet service providers: Determining and limiting liability for copyright infringement. *The Journal of College and University Law* 23.

Reindl, Andreas. 1998. Choosing law in cyberspace: copyright conflicts on global networks. *Michigan Journal of International Law* 19(3).

University of wisconsin system administration general administrative policy paper # 27, ownership of instructional materials. [Website]. Available from < http://www.uwsa.edu/fadmin/gapp/gapp27.htm >.

U.S. Copyright Office. 1998. *Summary of the digital millennium copyright act.* [Website]. Available from < http://lcweb.loc.gov/copyright/ >.

Chapter 9

Ethics and Technology: Challenging Issues, Enlightened Choices in a Technoethic Society

By Donald Olcott, Jr.

Today, we embrace technology as the inevitable evolution of modern science. And yet, our preoccupation with pushing back the "technological" frontiers of knowledge has created an ostensible delusion that permeates our social conscience and conveys the message that technology is synonymous with progress. We embark upon each new endeavor with the illusion that technology can expurgate any problem ... efficiently, economically, and without impending social consequences (Olcott 1997, 22).

Introduction

It was springtime ... a time for life, a time for hope, and indeed a time for renewal of the human spirit. The year was 1945, and the war in Europe was over. From Paris to New York and Moscow to Vienna, VE celebrations ushered in a new era filled with promise and hope, and an uncertain future (Stromberg 1992). Charles Dickens' prophetic words rung true: "It was the best of times, it was the worst of times."

Amidst these celebrations there were echoes everywhere of the role the ubiquitous use of technology had played in this devastating, inhumane tragedy. Technology had transformed the weapons of war, industry, transportation, and communications that created the destructive capacity leading us from Pearl Harbor to Omaha Beach. The dictum of "technology as progress" that emanated from the Industrial Revolution had matured from an idealistic vision to a destructive reality — a destructive progress that would culminate in the New Mexico desert and on the Japanese mainland in the summer of 1945.

As the realities of the post-war world settled across the great capitals of Europe, the new age of technology was creating a crisis of conscience among prominent scientists in an unknown town in the mountains of New Mexico that the world would come to know as Los Alamos (Goodchild 1981).

The Manhattan Project to develop the first atomic bomb had begun in the early 1940s and had brought these gifted scientists to Los Alamos. But in the spring of 1945, the war in Europe was over, the Germans had never been close to developing the A-bomb, and the Japanese did not have the scientific expertise or resources to do so (Stromberg 1992).

Two billion dollars later, the military wanted a product and the scientists wanted moral absolution. Trinity would become reality, absolution for the scientific elite would remain eternally (Goodchild 1981).

There was, in retrospect, a question of whether or not there had been a justifiable reason to unleash the basic power of the universe. But technology and science and the military had prevailed. In the early morning hours of July 16, 1945, ethical and moral reflection became subservient to technology as progress. Following the test, J. Robert Oppenheimer, the director of Los Alamos, told reporters, "A scientist cannot hold back progress because of fears of what the world will do with his discoveries" (Halberstam 1993).

At the time of the explosion, however, Oppenheimer's words were more tempered with introspection. Quoting a passage from the *Bhagavad-Gita*, Oppenheimer said, "If the radiance or a thousand suns were burst into the sky, that be like the splendor of the Mighty One ... I am become Death, destroyer of worlds" (Halberstam 1993, 34). Hiroshima and Nagasaki would become the echoes of this progress, and the world would never be the same.

Future historians will very likely draw many analogies concerning the dramatic transformational role of technology on society between the periods 1940-45 and 1990-1995. The axiom of technology as progress will, in retrospect, be viewed as a dominant intellectual paradigm during both periods of the twentieth century. And while drawing ethical and moral comparisons between the Atomic Bomb and the Internet or Uranium 235 and the Web is extreme at a minimum, the implications of failing to reflect on the ethical implications of the impact of technology in the Knowledge Age will bring many unanticipated educational, social, and cultural consequences.

As in the summer of 1945, the momentum of rapid technological change has resurfaced in the Knowledge Age and challenges us to reflect on what we are creating. The question for the information generation is not whether history repeats itself, for it does not — foolish people repeat history. The challenge and responsibility for avoiding this mistake in the Information Age is ours, and ours alone.

This chapter will examine the ethical ramifications of technology in the Knowledge Age. Topics will include defining technoethics; critical issues in a technoethic environment; a decision-making framework for technoethic issues; a case study analysis; implications for practice; and recommendations for educators. The purpose of this chapter is to create a framework for understanding the ethical ramifications of technology use and adoption and the consequences of our technological choices. These choices range across all levels of education and to society in general.

Defining Technoethics

The general term "ethics" has been defined as "the systematic exploration of questions about how we should act in relation to others" (Rhodes 1986, 21). This is particularly evident in situations in which the actions of others may cause harm. A related component is the concept of ethical sensitivity, which describes an individual's awareness that his or her actions can affect the welfare of others (Bebeau, Rest, and Yamoor 1985).

Rest (1982) developed a four-component model of the psychological processes associated with morality. These components are:

1. interpreting the situation;
2. interpreting the ideal course of action;
3. deciding what values are most important;
4. executing and implementing what one intended to do.

These processes begin with an awareness or perception that something one might do or is doing can affect the welfare of someone else, either directly or indirectly, by violating a general practice or a commonly held social standard. "Failure to behave morally can result from deficiencies in any of the four components" (Bebeau, Rest, and Yamoor 1985, 26). By combining the elements of Rest's model and the concept of "ethical sensitivity," it becomes readily apparent that educators at all levels face issues around the ethics of technological choices.

Technoethics can be broadly defined as the relationship between technology choices and the ethical consequences of these choices. Building upon Rest's (1982) model, technoethics examines the following questions:

1. What are the ethical issues associated with technological choices?
2. What decision-making parameters do we use to analyze and balance technological choices with the ethical impacts of these choices?
3. What individuals, groups, professions, and/or organizations are impacted by the ethical issues associated with technological choices?
4. Who has the primary social responsibility for ensuring continuous dialogue about the ethical implications of technology in society?

Technology's mass assimilation into education has created the need to examine the ethical impact of technology on students, teachers, parents, and the public. Let's look at some of the educational, social, and economic/cultural issues that have arisen as a result of this technological revolution.

Technoethic Issues in Education

Equitable access to technology

The modern marvels of the Web and the Internet invite the fundamental question, "How do we ensure equitable access to technology and access regardless of socioeconomic status, ethnicity, disability, and location?" (Snyder 1994). There continues to be a growing gap between the technology haves and have-nots. This becomes a central issue for colleges and universities, because access to courses is based upon the premise that all potential students not only have access to technology, but also the skills to use technology (primarily computers) in their learning process. Equitable access to technology and the skills to use that technology will be a continuing issue for the educational enterprise at all levels.

Information access and cyberspace monitoring

In 1996, passage of the Telecommunications Act included a separate provision entitled the Communications Decency Act (CDA). In effect, this provision was an altruistic attempt to legislate morality on the World Wide Web and the Internet regarding what was deemed "indecent" for minors. The act focused primarily on access to pornographic materials (U.S. Congress, 1996) and presumed that the construct of what defined "indecent" was universally accepted.

After considerable public and legal debate, the CDA was found in violation of the First Amendment. Once again, the preservation of free speech was challenged and ultimately upheld by the courts. And while the CDA's intent focused attention on an increasing ethical problem in the Knowledge Age, in retrospect it attempted to solve the issue by challenging our most cherished constitutional right.

It is important to understand that the issue around the CDA was about controlling who has access to certain kinds of information, not whether the information or materials in themselves were appropriate. And yet the legislation focused on punishing those responsible for making the information available. For institutions of higher education, this ruling indirectly supports academic freedom; but it also suggests that institutions must monitor who and what is made available via technology to students and the public.

Perhaps a similar analogy would be the motion picture rating system that physically restricts (in theory) access by minors to certain films due to violence, sexual content, nudity, adult themes, and other objectionable content. In short, access is restricted based on content. Do we attempt to restrict or punish the producers, directors, writers, and actors of these films? Of course not. But that is because access can be physically controlled. Even for the most controversial film, we have yet to see the police or FBI staking out a movie theater, regardless of the film's content.

The Web and the Internet, conversely, cannot restrict access by physical boundaries, although security access can be restricted electronically. Access is electronic, unrestricted by time and space. Without some form of monitoring, children and minor teenagers can access everything from pornography and paramilitary organizations to racial hate groups and religious fanatics. The potential of knowledge that is infinitely more accessible creating greater opportunity for new forms of societal violence is growing.

The dichotomy in this environment is that access to diverse and multiple sources of information is good and educationally sound. Access to inappropriate forms of information (a value judgment) creates ethical dilemmas. The lesson, of course, is that given that content cannot be controlled, our focus must be on monitoring access.

Monitoring access has implications for higher education. First, colleges of education must educate prospective teachers about the importance of monitoring children's access to the Web. Second, practicing teachers must engage parents in a dialogue about monitoring their children's use of the Web at home. And finally, university-level Web courses that present sensitive or potentially objectionable content must alert students about what to expect in certain courses.

The delusion of technology = classroom quality

There is a common perception that, since university students are being taught with and are learning to use technology in the classroom, the quality of the educational experience rises proportionally. Many educators would like to embrace this premise, particularly if it were true. However, the assumptions behind this premise are questionable.

The presumption of quality related to the use of learning technologies in classrooms has several deficiencies. First, it assumes that all teachers are technologically literate and have mastered the art of facilitating learning via technology. Second, it presumes that student computer simulations capture the essence of real-life experiences and yet fails to recognize that, for all computers can do (and it's a lot), they cannot do everything (Turkle 1997). Finally, the use of technology in distance learning presumes that everyone is suited for learning at a distance, which they are not. It presumes that all distance learners are highly motivated, independent, autonomous learners who don't need human interaction in the teaching learning process (Reed and Sork 1990).

Social issues

The "technology as progress" axiom is often contradictory when one examines its social consequences. Consider the following recent newspaper headlines: "Alleged Gang Members Charged over Web Site," or "Internet Use Leads to Loneliness and Depression," as well as the dramatic increases in school-based violence. Again, technology affords us all unique opportunities and yet creates impending social consequences.

Olcott (1997) identifies the term *techapathy*, referring to societal frustrations over technology taking control of our lives. We have become a technologically dependent society that survives on cellular phones, televisions, video games, portable CD players, VCRs, computers, the Internet, and even electronically warmed car seats.

This technological dependency manifests itself in a youth generation that is becoming not only technologically literate, but technologically cultured (Olcott 1997); many of today's youth accept that technology is universally good and without impending social consequences.

Technology also brings with it issues around personal privacy and protection against unauthorized access to information. And finally, the consolidation of technological resources in unprecedented corporate mergers and individual companies creates a monopoly of sorts that converts into political and economic power with the potential to impact all of society (Olcott 1997).

Economic and cultural issues

While technology affords many opportunities, it must first be affordable. Certainly the costs of computers and software have begun to decrease, but the fact remains that not everyone has the resources to invest in home computers and related technologies.

We must also be equally sensitive to cultural differences among students and how these differences influence perceptions of how technology enhances their learning. As Janet Poley observes in chapter 10, differences in attitudes toward technology across gender, ethnicity, and income levels are critical public policy and ethical issues. The Information Age will require almost everyone in education and the employment sectors to be computer aware and even literate. In this new environment, universities must prepare traditional eighteen- to twenty-two-year-olds to address ethical issues related to technology, and enable the growing population of returning adults to operate and act ethically in this new environment.

A Decision-making Framework for Technoethic Issues

Figure 9.1 presents a decision-making framework for addressing technoethic issues. This framework builds upon the theoretical work of Rhodes (1986), Bebeau, Rest, and Yamoor (1985), and Rest (1982) discussed earlier in this chapter. It is adapted for analyzing ethical issues related to technology. Decision-making

Figure 9.1
Decision Making Framework for Technoethic Issues

Decision-making parameter	Technoethic issue (s)	Impacts	Decision alternatives
	Equitable access to technology	Underserved populations fall behind	Public policy of access for all
	Information access and Cyberspace monitoring of sensitive material	Children and minor teenagers have access to inappropriate materials	Monitoring by parents and teachers
	Perception of technology being synonymous with	Parents, students, public, teachers develop false expectations about technology in learning	Improve technology education for teachers and invite parents and students to work together
Education	Americans with Disabilities Act (ADA)	Persons with disabilities who need access	Design technology for students with disabilities
	Computer simulations can't teach it all	Prospective student learners rely on technology without doing the hands-on work	Challenge students with hands-on activities and reduce dependency on technology
	Assumptions about distance learners	Students don't receive accurate information about the skills needed to be successful	Provide distance learners with "real" information for successful distance learning
Social	Technology synonymous with progress	Pervasive belief that all technology is progress without negative consequences	Educate students about the unanticipated consequences of technology
	Techopathy	Societal frustrations with increasing technological intrusion	Engage students, parents, and public about "when is technology too much technology"

Figure 9.1
Decision Making Framework for Technoethic Issues

Decision-making parameter	Technoethic issue(s)	Impacts	Decision alternatives
Social	Technological dependency	Reliance on technology to solve all our problems	Demonstrate problem-solving strategies that are not technology based
	Privacy issues	Societal concerns about who has access to private information via technology	Ensure security in the design of and access to personal information
	Political and economic power of technology	Society becomes subservient to technology control that converts into political-economic power	Appropriate controls by government, industry, and education organizations
Economic/ Cultural	Affordable technology	Expanding gap between the technology haves and have-nots (low-income families)	Community and economic development must ensure technology access for all
	Male-female participation	Female exclusion from some employment fields reinforces gender biases	Education and the private sector must create technology careers and recruit women into them
	Ethnicity issues	Inequitable access to technology tools for ethnically disadvantaged populations	Focused incentives programs to ensure access to technology tools for all
	Designing culturally sensitive content	Retention and participation of ethnically diverse students in technology courses will decrease	Require Web-based courses that include culturally- sensitive design and content

parameters are defined in the education, social, and economic cultural domains, and they examine the technoethic issues, impacts, and decision alternatives in each arena.

The figure is designed to help educators identify key technoethic domains and issues (educational, social, and economic cultural), analyze their potential impacts, and provide some decision-making alternatives. This framework is not all-inclusive and does not purport to cover all issues or decision alternatives to technoethic issues in the education, social, and economic cultural domains. It is designed to assist educators in establishing their own frameworks from which to analyze the ethical issues surrounding technology.

A Case Study in Ethics and Technology

Presenting a case study on ethical issues related to technology is inherently problematic. One reason it is so difficult is that ethical issues typically are complex and related to many factors. Moreover, an ethical issue may exist separately in a vacuum for one situation and yet be one among multiple issues in another situation. And educators will have different values that affect which ethical issues should be addressed and resolved.

Notwithstanding these challenges for educators, the following case study is based upon real situations that were taken from individual events. Consequently, for the purpose of relating ethical issues to employing figure 9.1, they have been combined into one scenario to illustrate a variety of potential issues.

> A university department chair decides to convert a traditional, upper-division, on-campus course entitled "Current Topics in Government and Politics" for delivery via the World Wide Web. Because the development costs are high and the faculty member will be compensated with tuition revenue, the department decides to offer the course through the continuing education unit and charge twice the tuition costs of the on-campus course. The faculty member teaching the course has never taught via technology and has only re-

cently completed a training seminar on teaching via the Web.

Due to the expediency of getting the course up and running, there was not sufficient time for analyzing instructional design and assessment related to the course. In effect, the instructor transferred the classroom version of the course to the Web. Presently, the institution does not allow students to transfer Web-based courses into degree programs at the university, although this is not stated in the marketing materials.

Typically, this course would require a prerequisite course in American Government, but the department decides to waive the prerequisite course since at least twenty-four students are needed to offer the course and cover all associated costs. This prerequisite waiver is also not included in the marketing materials, and no enrollment limit is established. The faculty member's department chair assigns one teaching assistant. Regarding access to technologies required for the class, the marketing materials state only that students must have access to the World Wide Web, even though the instructor has already decided that e-mail would be a good addition to the course. One hundred twenty-six students enroll in the course.

The following is a summary of the potential ethical issues associated with the above scenario:

- *Teacher Competence:* The faculty member has minimal experience teaching via technology and has just completed a Web seminar. The course is basically a replica of the classroom course transferred to the Web. Should the course be offered?

- *Academic Quality:* Can this faculty member effectively teach a Web-based course to 126 students? In this scenario, economic factors were more important than academic quality issues. No instructional design or assessment components unique to Web-based teaching were employed.

- *Truth in Advertising:* The course will not transfer to the university if the student decides to apply for formal admission to a degree program at a subsequent date. The prerequisite has also been waived, which will set up many students for failure or substantial additional study. Students must have access to the World Wide Web, but the marketing materials do not state that students should also have an e-mail account. The marketing of this course violates just about every truth in advertising ethical standard.

- *Justifiable Costs:* The cost of the course compared with campus tuition has been doubled. Given all the other ethical issues associated with this scenario, expecting students to pay twice the tuition may also be questioned.

Aligning the Case Study Analysis with the Decision-making Framework

Before we employ the decision-making framework presented in figure 9.1, there are a number of prerequisite questions that must be answered by the continuing education unit during the identification stage of interpreting the situation (Rest 1982, 29):

- Does the continuing education unit have an "ethical sensitivity" that unit actions and policies may affect the welfare of others?

- Does the continuing education unit as well as its members have a clearly defined set of ethical values that guide their actions?

- Do the actions of the continuing education unit affect the welfare of others "by violating a general practice of a commonly held social standard"?

The importance of these questions is that they provide all organizations the opportunity to reassess their normative values related to standards of practice and the ethical standards associated with practice. Common sense suggests that organizations would aspire to have clearly defined ethical values, a broad awareness of ethical sensitivity, and standards of practice that do not adversely affect others (e.g., students in this particular scenario).

How do educators employ the Decision-making Framework for Technoethic Issues to examine the aforementioned case study on truth in advertising? First, one must identify the potential issues and determine which domain the issues fall within (e.g., education, social, and/or economic/social). Second, whom do the issues affect and what are the potential impacts? Third, what are the potential decision alternatives to resolve the issues?

Domains and technoethic issues

The truth in advertising issues fall within three major domains: education, social, and economic/cultural. First, because the course does not subsequently transfer to the institution and students were not informed of this, there is an ethical issue in the education domain. A second education-domain issue is that the prerequisite for the course was waived, which suggests that some students may not be academically prepared to be successful. The third education-domain issue is that students were not informed up front about the requirement of e-mail and access to the World Wide Web.

In the social domain, the unit offering the course has embraced the tenet of "technology equals progress," and yet it has not given the end-users (students) the appropriate information they need to be academically successful. Finally, the economic/cultural domain arises because students may take the course even though it doesn't transfer, as a result they may need to take additional credits if they pursue further study in the future. There are also potential economic impacts on the student who may need to gain access to additional technology, which was not clearly specified in the course marketing materials.

Impacts

Potential students comprise the group most directly impacted by these issues. The potential impacts for them include a course that will not transfer, economic costs associated with technology access, and the potential for failure for those lacking the course prerequisite. These are not, however, the only adverse impacts. The continuing education unit and the academic unit may have a credibility issue associated with truthful advertising and a commitment to student academic success. The academic unit may rely, without question, upon the benefits of technology, without systematically examining the needs of students to be successful in a mediated learning environment. It is worth remembering that ten students echoing their dismay about these issues reflects poorly upon the institution, the continuing education unit, and the academic unit.

Decision alternatives

What are some possible courses of action to address these issues? There are several possibilities, but let's look at some obvious solutions. First, while nearly all courses transfer to colleges and universities in some context (e.g., elective, general education, major), the crucial issue is how a course applies in a particular program or department. In this scenario, the academic unit and the continuing education unit need to clearly communicate in their marketing materials the policy issues related to the transferability of the course. Second, the prerequisite or a demonstrated knowledge of the topic should be required for registration in the course. Third, all technology requirements and associated costs should be clearly communicated to potential students in the initial marketing materials. Is the student required to own a computer? Does the department require a minimum level of computer competency? The continuing education unit and the academic unit should be available to advise students on all issues and questions associated with the course.

Given this abbreviated analysis, it is essential to recognize that the above issues are not exclusively about truth in advertising. They are also about institutional integrity and image, standards of professional and ethical practice, commitment to quality and student success, and the foremost premise: that employing technology to improve teaching and learning, rather than for economic or "cutting-edge" reasons, should drive the use of educational technology in higher education.

This analysis illustrates that interpreting ethical issues and their potential impacts and assessing decision-making solutions is a complex process that requires the systematic reflection of all educators.

Implications for Practice: Developing a Code of Ethics for Technology-based Education

Developing a Code of Ethics for technology-based education is a challenging and immense task. At the same time, however, the increasing use of technology in education demands that we begin this process. The following draft is an invitation for other educators to contribute their recommendations to developing a Code of Ethics for technology:

Code of Ethics for Technology Delivered Education

1. Institutions delivering technology-based education shall ensure that the content, design, and evaluation reflect the highest standards of academic quality commensurate with those standards employed in campus-based instruction.

2. Institutions that employ differentiated fee or tuition costs for technology-based education shall provide justification and explanation of these costs to all potential students. This shall include any hidden technology fees and additional costs to the student to enroll for a technology-based course.

3. Institutions shall be bound by truth in advertising and shall communicate clearly and in writing all information regarding student technology requirements, online access charges, expected previous experience with technology, course prerequisites, transfer policies applicable to the course, registration policies and deadlines, and course refund policies.

4. Institutions shall provide in their marketing materials general information pertaining to how to be successful in distance learning courses, attributes and skills associated with successful distance learners, and success tips for new distance learners.

5. Institutions shall establish minimum training requirements for faculty teaching via technology and ensure that instructional support services are a required part of course development. These include instructional design, assessment, asynchronous communications strategies, online testing, strategies for effective teaching, and pedagogical information for teaching adult learners. These expectations should apply for all faculty, whether they teach on campus or off campus.

6. Faculty shall ensure that distance students adhere to the same course requirements required of students in on-campus courses; that standards and policies governing testing and academic dishonesty are strictly enforced; and that distance learners have continuous access to the instructor for feedback, advising, and assignments.

Educators and other individuals who are interested in providing comments and recommendations to the above Code of Ethics draft can e-mail them to the author at the following address: dolcott@u.arizona.edu.

Recommendations for Higher Educators

Education, by its very nature, is always an endeavor with ethical implications (Cunningham 1987). If one accepts this premise, then institutions that offer technology-based instruction on campus or at a distance, will be faced with ethical issues in the process of designing, delivering, and evaluating educational programs (Reed and Sork 1990).

Olcott (1998) provides some general recommendations to help educators address ethical issues related to technology:

- Encourage technology training programs on and off campus to include a section on "Ethics and Technology." Encourage distance teaching faculty to devote one class section to this topic to engage students in discussions about the relative merits of technology.

- Expect educators to exert discretion in the classroom by monitoring the use of educational technology.

- Work with campus governance bodies that review and approve the curriculum (e.g., faculty senate, curriculum council) to develop a course on "Ethics and Technology" as part of the undergraduate core requirements, particularly in teacher preparation programs. Graduate programs in educational technology, distance learning, instructional design, and continuing education should include a similar program requirement.

Educators should also build their own frameworks drawing upon the parameters outlined in figure 9.1. All educators have some value differences, so certain ethical issues may be viewed differently. This process is not solely about being right or wrong. Rather, it is about engaging ourselves in a self-analysis of the ethical issues of our profession. This is a noble and essential endeavor.

Summary

This chapter began on the war-torn battlefields of Europe following World War II. Technology transformations had transcended the ethical and moral standards of humanity and had left us pondering just where technology fit in our future.

Today, as we enter the next millennium, technology once again has transformed society's major institutions. For many, this is seen as positive with the "technology as progress" axiom, leading us to the technological promised land. For others, the unprecedented change wrought by technology brings many consequences and a time for ethical and moral reflection. Indeed, both perspectives are critically important to integrate into our decision making. What is needed is a blending of these two perspectives that results in embracing many aspects of technology while at the same time questioning other aspects.

The questions are not easy, and the answers are not definitive. There will be alternative answers to these ethical questions related to technology, and more than one will be right. What is definite, however, is that if the questions are not being asked, and not being discussed, they will not be answered. From an ethical perspective, that would be the ultimate travesty for our children and their children.

REFERENCES

Bebeau, M. J., J. R. Rest, and C. M. Yamoor. 1985. Measuring dental students' ethical sensitivity. *Journal of Dental Education* 49(4): 225-235.

Cunningham, I. 1987. Openness and learning to learn. In *Beyond distance teaching — towards open learning*, edited by Vivien E. Hodgson, Sarah J. Mann and Robin S. Snell: Open University Press.

Goodchild, Peter. 1981. *J. Robert Oppenheimer: Shatterer of worlds*. Boston: Houghton-Mifflin Company.

Halberstam, David. 1993. *The fifties*. New York: Fawcett Columbine.

Olcott, Donald John, Jr. 1997. Where are you George Orwell? We got the year ... missed the message. *Open Praxis* 2: 22-24.

Olcott, Donald John Jr. 1998. An orwellian view of technology: Promise or peril? *Continuing Higher Education Review* 62(Fall): 75-81.

Reed, Diane, and Thomas J. Sork. 1990. Ethical considerations in distance education. *The American Journal of Distance Education* 4(2): 30-43.

Rest, J. R. 1982. A psychologist looks at the teaching of ethics. *The Hastings Center Report* 12(1): 29-36.

Rhodes, Margaret L. 1986. *Ethical dilemmas in social work practice*. Boston: Routledge and Kegan Paul.

Snyder, Tom. 1994. Blinded by science. *The Executive Educator* March: 1-5.

Stromberg, Ronald N. 1992. *Europe in the twentieth century*. 3rd edition. Englewood Cliffs, NJ: Prentice Hall.

Turkle, Sherry. 1997. See through computers: Education in a culture of simulation. *The American Prospect* (March-April): 76-82.

U.S. Congress. 1996. *Telecommunications Act of 1996*. Washington, DC.

Chapter 10

Global Access to Learning: Gender, Poverty, and Race

By Janet Poley

Indigenous Knowledge and the Do Fors

We stood there in amazement, my friend and I. The setting was the Global Knowledge Conference put on by the World Bank in Toronto. The date was January 1998, and our location was on the perimeter of the buffet food tables. Nearly twice as many people came as were expected, insisting that they be allowed a place at the table (a seat in the packed conference room). Bank officials found it difficult to say "no" to these influentials with whom they negotiate on world economic issues. The food was attacked by the multitudes; person reaching over person to get a morsel of fish, meat, and vegetables. Many of the developing-country representatives attending this meeting came to Canada not to eat jumbo shrimp, but rather to let the world know that they wanted more than the crumbs from the great promise of the Internet and World Wide Web. They wanted an opportunity to contribute to the information diet and to have the knowledge, culture, and language of their nations and villages included. Everybody knows the World Wide Web isn't really worldwide yet — in content or reach.

There were men and women in reasonably equal numbers and of all races. The gender breakdown seemed equal enough that no one had to comment on the underrepresentation of women at the meeting. North and South, rich and poor nations made it known that their countries could not afford to be left out of the Information Revolution.

At the conference, an entire day was devoted to the fact that women in developing countries, particularly rural women, have little or no access to new information and technologies. They struggle in poverty with issues related to water, food production, health, and time. These women are the source of much of the world's indigenous knowledge. They know what plants have been used for what medical purposes and with what effect. They have the history and experience of coping with harsh soils, difficult climates, and pests of all types. Everyone was interested in what these women know. Then two women speakers asked, "But who will really 'own' this information if it is taken to the Net, if it is captured on a CD-RO?. Will these rural women benefit? Do we, in information-wealthy countries, care only about the knowledge, not about the people themselves?"

We also talked about women in the cities and their work in the developing world. We learned that a lot of the tedious labor associated with microchip manufacturing has moved out of the developed nations and now replaces sewing as the new handwork of urban Asian women. There was talk that some of this work was just as debilitating to the eyes, hands, and wrists as the traditional stitching. Factories do not have to meet the safety and lighting standards expected in the United States.

As my friend and I looked at this collection of people of all complexions, heights, weights, and dress from places far and near, whose citizens were not yet connected, the potential became more clear. Half of the world's population *still* has never made a phone call. While there are Internet connections now in nearly every country in the world, the majority of the population that is networked is very small. Many countries cannot afford the infrastructure, especially into remote areas. Telephones do not work and wireless methods are not yet available or may not be trusted. Even the United States has made little progress in anything but pretty poor dial-up service in much of rural America. Also, open communication anytime, anywhere is a frightening concept to some national leaders who trade on keeping knowledge and power to themselves.

And then we saw the Do Fors. There were a number in attendance, those who came to "do for" the poor black, brown, beige, yellow, and white people from *other* places. They had plans for beaming down and sending out — just press a button or wind it up. Never mind that many folks in developing countries can barely afford school fees for their little ones, let alone expensive wind-up toys. The cost of computers is geared to the wealthy markets, which means little or no access for most of the world's population. Slow rollouts of new technology to milk the old for all it is worth, minimal competition in telephone service areas, and *more of the same* may be good for some. But it's a disaster for many. We might all benefit if we changed this picture.

Global Connectivity and Women's E-commerce

I returned home to Nebraska, fired up my e-mail, and saw that I had mail from my daughter, a Peace Corps volunteer in Ecuador. With a brand new master's degree from a major land-grant institution, she was working with a group of local women starting a handmade-paper project. The project was designed to help the women earn some of their money from the diverse plants and flowers nearby. This was a dual use idea: women protect the forest/women earn money. Additional payoffs expected were learning and more investment in children's welfare. The women planned to use the Internet to set up shop, which they eventually did with marginal success in terms of export earnings. It will take a lot more than technology to make electronic commerce work in these settings. Even if the economics could be managed for putting these small-scale enterprises on the Web in a way that generated income, most local groups, like these women, are not assured of longer-term access to technology and the opportunities to continue learning. If continuing education is essential to working in a knowledge marketplace, then the gap between rich and poor countries is certain to grow wider, with potentially destabilizing effects.

All Circuits Are Busy

Not long ago I received an e-mail message at work from a close Tanzanian friend employed in a bank in Dar es Salaam, telling me that a colleague of ours had passed away. I had worked regularly with this man while living in Tanzania for six years. I answered the message wishing *pole sana* to my friend and to the family of the deceased. *Pole sana* literally means, "I'm sorry," but also much more. There is no real English equivalent, as is so often the case with literal translations. I asked how I might be able to send a memorial, but based on past experience I expected it might be a long time before that e-mail message really reached my friend. I came home and decided to call. After an hour I gave up. All circuits were busy. To my surprise, the next morning I had mail. My friend would take care of the memorial. He wished me another *pole sana*.

It is nearly impossible for the individual who has never lived outside the United States in a developing country to understand what an incredible difference widespread, affordable connectivity to people, education, and commerce could make in daily lives and expectations. The pent-up demand is tremendous. It will take both more rapid technology deployment *and* the political will to make this one small planet. At the International Conference for Open and Distance Education in 1997, Nicholas Negroponte told the 1,000 attendees that it was ethically wrong that we did not yet have a computer that is inexpensive enough that it can connect people everywhere.

On the Domestic Front

On Wednesday, August 26, 1998, I was back in my e-mail, with smoke rising from the top of my head as I read a *Los Angeles Times* article on "Women in Computing" that was circulating among the faculty. The article documented the fact that women were leaving or avoiding careers in computing citing discrimination, family, unfriendly work environments, a lack of role models, and a general sense that the field is irrelevant to their interests. According to the *Times* article, some implications of the gender gap are subtle, as in the lack of computer products designed with women in mind. The most immediate effect is to worsen the nation's shortage of high-tech workers.

The article went on to note that some educators blame the narrow focus of training, which tends to emphasize technical expertise over practical applications. "A far higher percentage of men are concerned with the technical details, while a far higher percentage of women are concerned with putting the technology to use," said Allan Fisher, associate dean at the School of Computer Science at Carnegie Mellon (*Los Angeles Times* 1998).

Without the brainpower and involvement of women and minorities in the development of these technologies, the United States could be facing serious workforce, workplace, and consumer issues.

Consider that, in 1990, European Americans accounted for 78 percent of the U.S. civilian labor force, African Americans accounted for 11 percent, Latin Americans 8 percent, and Asian Americans 3 percent. By 2005, minorities will make up at least 5 percent more of the total; the applicant pool will be 85 percent minority, female, or immigrant (Oblinger and Verville 1998). The workforce will age, with the retirement age moving past seventy (Drucker 1998).

There are significant challenges and choices for higher education in this changing workforce: higher education must be affordable, accessible, and relevant for the women and minorities expected to contribute to the Knowledge-Age, high-tech economy that now characterizes the United States.

A recent poll released by the American Association of School Administrators and The Lightspan Partnership shows that the investment in technology for schools is improving student achievement and leveling the playing field for at-risk students. Unfortunately, while educators in the poorest schools said technology is a "very important" part of their plans for improvement, the poll showed that students in these schools are least likely to have access to technology at school or at home. Access to home computers has a strong correlation to student achievement (American Association of School Administrators 1999).

A Department of Commerce (1997) study, "Falling through the Net II," documents the growing digital divide. Although 50 percent more Americans owned computers in 1997 than in 1994, the digital divide has widened between the upper- and lower-income segments of society. People living in rural areas at the lowest income levels are the least likely to be connected to the Net, creating the probability of widening the already existing economic gap between rural and urban populations. The report found that white households are more than twice as likely as African American and Latino homes to own a computer, breaking the estimates down to 40.8 percent for white households, 19.4 percent for Latino homes, and 19.3 percent for black households. Computer ownership levels are lower for minorities living in rural areas. While this gap in ownership is significant at all income levels, it is especially important to note that among lower income households that the gap has increased by approximately a third from 1994-1997. As noted in table 10.1, the problem is growing dramatically.

Table 10.1
U.S. Household Computer Penetration Gap
By Income
1994 vs. 1997 Under $15,000

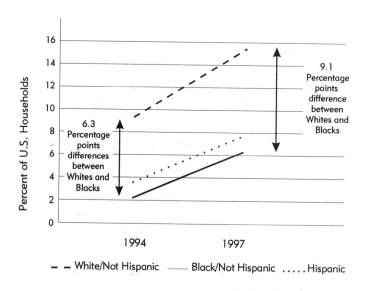

Single-parent, female households were also found to lag significantly behind the national average. They are also significantly less likely than dual-parent households to have a personal computer, 25 percent versus 57.2 percent (U.S. Department of Commerce 1997).

The American Association of University Women (AAUW) is studying the dramatic drop in the ratio of women to men involved in computing from high school to graduate school. "Girls have narrowed some significant gender gaps, but technology is now the new 'boys' club' in our nation's public schools," said AAUW Executive Director Janice Weinman. "While boys program and problem solve with computers, girls use computers for word processing, the 1990s version of typing." The report (American Association of University Women 1998) flagged trends that threaten to create or sustain gender gaps into the next decade, including:

- demographic changes that could lead to more pronounced gaps among girls, based on racial, ethnic, economic, and regional differences, even as the gaps between boys and girls on the whole diminish;

- emergence of twenty-first century industries such as computer science, biotechnology, and environmental science, for which girls may be unprepared;

- teacher preparation programs that do not sufficiently focus on gender equity issues;

- educational reform efforts, such as home schooling and charter schools, that could impact various groups of students differently.

Led by Maryland Representative Constance Morella, the U.S. Congress passed legislation to create an eleven-member commission on Women in Science, Engineering, and Technology Development to determine whether employers recruit, promote, pay, and retain women at the same rate as their male counterparts. Morella and other lawmakers want to know why more women are not filling top jobs that the high-tech industry claims it needs increasing numbers of highly skilled foreign workers to fill. The commission is charged with uncovering gaps in education and addressing what happens to women who enter the workforce; whether they are mentored and climb the ranks at the same level as men with equivalent experience (Macavinta 1998).

The digital divide does not seem to be limited to the computer and information technology areas. In late 1998, a study by the Women in Cable and Telecommunications Foundation (WICT) found that women in technical positions earn 12 percent less than do men with comparable jobs (Higgins 1998).

Still worse is the situation in network evening news. According to the "Who Speaks for America" study, sponsored by Freedom Forum's Free Press/Fair Press Project, 87 percent of TV experts are male and 92 percent are white, while women account for only 13 percent and minorities for just 6 percent. Andrew Tyndall, director of the study, concluded that the networks were more likely lazy than biased in their selection of experts (McClellan 1998).

Let's Take a Break for Some Good News

In the January 13, 1999, *Times of London*, it was reported that a sixteen-year-old Irish schoolgirl had devised a new code that will send e-mail ten times faster, and just as securely, than the current data protection code for e-mail. The report said that she was being deluged with job and scholarship offers (Edupage 1999).

A November 1998 survey released by the Pew Research Center for the People and the Press showed that Internet use almost doubled since 1996, with 41 percent of adults, about 74 million Americans, saying they use the Internet. While the study showed that usage was beginning to look more like mainstream America, the average online Net surfer remained younger, better educated, and more affluent than the population at large (Jones 1999).

Another bright spot is Mosser Elementary School in the Allentown, Pennsylvania, School District. Here, a group of fifth-grade girls have been nicknamed the "Cyber Sisters." Penn State Lehigh Valley runs the program as part of Youth Enrichment Partnership 2000, a program designed to encourage the development of reading, writing, and critical thinking skills in inner-city youth (Penn State Outreach 1999).

Travel to Texas and the Austin Learning Academy (Austin Learning Academy 1999) and you will meet the "Texas Buffalo Soldiers" or the "11th/12th Street Corridor Producers." You'll find the creative art and literature of the ESL and GED learners. The ALA is guided by "radical common sense" and works with individuals, families, and neighborhoods. The academy calls its work "street-level research and development," and it assures the work revolves around:

- a nurturing learning environment;
- Family Learning Centers;
- access to the right learning tools;
- quitable access to technology;
- development of human resources;
- ALA staff and families serving as partners;
- "learning as we are teaching";
- research and development.

And Who Has Access to the Resources?

U.S. foundations are currently awash in riches, yet there is little of consequence being funded in the critical areas that could reduce the digital divide (Spragins 1999). The Austin Learning Academy, with its "radical common sense" notion, states that to be the best you must have the best, and if you do not have the best — make it! The Virtual Institute for Technology Advancement in Education (VITAE) is a consortium including a dozen colleges and historically black institutions. Virginia Tech is also a member, in part because officials there want to help prepare potential

VT graduate students from these institutions. These are just two examples of worthy programs that could benefit from some additional resources from the foundation sector. Money isn't always the most limiting resource, generally programs can be improved by attracting and engaging quality people to organize appropriately to address the issues. However, funds that are somewhat more flexible could flow from this wealthy foundation sector to improve access for those who are left behind by the fast pace of technological change.

Many tribal colleges, Hispanic-serving institutions, and historically black colleges and universities are stepping up efforts to bring technology to their campuses and promote its use. The cost of computing technology is a challenge for these colleges, especially the smaller ones. In general, the amount of technology on these campuses lags far behind that of larger and wealthier colleges and universities. Unfortunately, these programs and their basic requirements do not seem to interest most foundations.

Back to the Incredibly Shrinking Pipeline

As we move from the halls of minority-serving institutions and the streets of Austin, let's focus on another major issue. While access to bandwidth *pipe* is a real issue, more important may be the incredibly shrinking *pipeline of women and minorities* entering technical fields (Camp 1997). Although women make up 50 percent of high school computer science classes (Walker and Rodger 1996), they do not earn many B.S., M.S., or Ph.D. degrees. In addition, for women who become faculty members, the pipeline shrinks through the academic ranks.

Walker and Rodger's study further shows that the percentage of degrees awarded to women is lower when the computer science department is within the engineering college than when it is not. It is important to note that some institutions, including Pennsylvania State University and the University of Washington, have moved their computer science departments from a non-engineering college to the engineering college, potentially negatively affecting their enrollment of women in the future. If this trend persists, we may continue to see a decrease in the percentage of bachelor's degrees awarded in computer science to women. Creating women- and minority-friendly climates, in part by considering different types of department homes, is something institutions of higher education can and must do if they want to expand the pipeline.

It is clear that business and industry care that higher education institutions award more degrees in the computer science field; the quicker the better. As John White, dean of engineering at Georgia Institute of Technology, said, "If we want a different outcome, we're going to have to do things differently. We're making too little progress doing more of the same thing. The time for evolution is passed: it's time for revolution" (White 1995, 41).

Attention: More Good News

Is the Internet a better equalizer when it comes to women in small business? It appears that working in the high-tech arena is a story of contrasts for women. While the number of women entering highly technical jobs lags, Internet businesses spotlight some of the most successful women in American business today (Hoffman 1998).

Women are responsible for 85 percent of purchase decisions in the U.S. Women who can tap markets are very valuable to new media ventures. Business is beginning to realize that women are (again) the most underutilized domestic resource, but women have to be careful that they are not undervalued and underpaid. The issues of labor shortages today are as much about workplaces, job structures, and benefits as they are about too few trained workers.

An IBM-commissioned study, "Embracing the Information Age: A Comparison of Women and Men Business Owners," uncovered the findings in table 10.2.

Women say that the most important reason for using new technology is to "explore new strategies for growth." Women business owners plan to increase their investment in hardware and software by 51 percent during the next year. Women answered the survey by saying that technology helps their busi-

Table 10.2
A Comparison of Technology Use between Male
and Female Business Owners

	Homepage	E-mail	Internet research	Contracts
Women-owned Businesses	23%	51%	22%	9%
Men-owned Businesses	16%	40%	14%	3%

Source: (Yudkowsky 1998)

nesses to respond to customers, speeds up product or service introductions, and improves marketing. Women business owners are generally younger than men are, and they like to make decisions after having more varied information sources.

Women tend to be less hierarchical than men in management style and are more apt to get input from peers and staff for all decisions. Thus, they are able to see the benefits of some technologies earlier than their male counterparts can.

Avon found (Yudkowsky 1998) that women do not see technology as the "new sports car in the driveway." Rather, they see it as important when it produces reliable results. Smart vendors will increasingly recognize that female customers are more apt to buy technology that produces results rather than focusing on the amount of RAM or the speed of the chip. Even the language used in this field needs a major overhaul, away from descriptions of the machine to how it is useful and friendly.

Things May Be Worse in Britain

Scientific American picked up on the "Incredible Shrinking Pipeline" story in August highlighting the fact that women are staying away from computer science as a profession (Grossman 1998). It noted that this pattern is not unique to the U.S. In Britain, the decline of women in computer science is even more marked. Rachel Burnett reports that, "The intake of women into university IT courses has declined. It used to be a third; it's now 5 percent."

The Association for Computing Machinery's Committee on Women in Computing has been trying to find out what is going on. Some of its hypotheses are (Camp 1997):

- Computer games tend to be more male-oriented; thus, boys get earlier computer experience. (Girls actually find these "boy's" games boring; girls are looking for characters with whom they can imagine having a relationship.)

- Women do not like the way computer jobs are structured in the workplace. Long, nonstop exploitation in terms of hours is not compatible with being a parent.

- Gender discrimination is rampant.

- Few role models exist within the profession. The antisocial image of the "hacker" turns women off.

- Sexual harassment is perceived to be higher in the computer industry than in other fields.

- Women do not want to be labeled as "babes" who can code.

Proposed Solutions

Camp (1997) argues that the "shrinking pipeline" does matter. Unless leaders in business and industry believe that their chances of getting a cheaper, qualified labor force rest with underpaying immigrants, the most likely solution to the labor force issue is to raise the percentage of women entering the profession. This requires making female role models more visible, improving mentoring, and encouraging equal access to computers from kindergarten through the twelfth grade.

Anita Borg (1996), director of the Institute for Women and Technology at the Xerox Palo Alto Research Center, notes that there are a number of issues resulting from having too few women in this growing segment of the economy and labor force.

She points out that early speech recognition software could not understand the female voice, and that we are currently experiencing a male bias toward isolating the individual, resulting in products that may not be attractive to women. Examples include personal digital assistants and interactive kiosks. Women, she says, "would be more likely to design hand-held computers that keep track of an entire family, or cylindrical kiosks with a facility for group discussion." Her goal is 50/50 by 2010.

Nearly everyone agrees that getting to girls early, during the critical, vulnerable period of adolescence, is crucial. Girls can turn off quickly to math and science. Many institutions already have in place workshops, camps, and weekends that introduce high school girls to successful women role models in math, science, and technology. These experiences allow girls to develop skills mentoring relationships that are so important to keeping young women interested and in the field.

The goals and project areas for the Institute for Women and Technology provide a useful and important framework for higher education as well as industry. They focus on the development of information technologies and tools based on the perspectives, talents, and needs of women. They seek to catalyze industry, academia, government, and the nonprofit sector through workshops, design projects, improved Internet technology, communities of interest, publications, and conferences. Too few resources are systematically compiled on women's perspectives on information technologies and on innovations created by or serving women. There are wonderful opportunities to use the virtual environments to develop innovations and solutions more suited to women's lives. Large gaps exist, and opportunities abound for studies, research, and information collection. One only needs to do a Web search on "Internet and the Family" to recognize how little is really being done of value in the human development area. The "systers" community of interest, which includes 2,500 members in twenty-five countries at over one hundred companies and one hundred universities, is one example of a professional women's community supporting connections to bring about change and development.

In addition, it must be recognized that these problems are a reflection of an "out of kilter" workplace. It is possible that, with the tremendous consolidation and resulting lack of real competitive environments, those who are making money want to make more money by continuing to bring in immigrants. Employers may count on this workforce to tolerate more abuse in the workplace and demand less money.

You've Got Mail, Sister

Patricia Wirth is the first woman fellow at AT&T Laboratories. She and her colleagues were recently honored by the president of the United States for their work in bringing women and minorities successfully into the technology workplace. She also happens to be my real younger "sister," and I thank her for allowing me to share this private communication to me via e-mail.

Letter from Dr. Patricia Wirth, AT&T Labs

Hi Jan,

Yes, this is a critical problem that is getting worse with time. There are numerous initiatives that I am aware of that are aimed at trying to turn things around. The problem is multifaceted, and I cannot think of any silver bullets. Here's a quick cut at my preliminary thinking on some possible intervention points:

K-12: More/better instruction in computer science/engineering. Less emphasis on hacking and action-packed games, more on the discipline and broad range of applications. More exposure to practicing professionals. More familiarity with successful programs for girls. Look at successful programs that have excellent records in science and math education for girls. Learn from these successes.

College: Provide more mentors who can help guide students through these difficult years and the choices they make. Provide training to faculty on how to encourage, support, and promote their female students, and hold them accountable for doing so. The University of Washington and the Stevens Institute of Technology have done this well.

Graduate School: Make graduate school family friendly, including [providing] day care. Have more mentors and role models in addition to financial support. Successful programs include the AT&T Labs Fellowship Program (AT&T 1998). It is important to study the turning points in successful professionals' lives. Why did they stay? What do we need to institutionalize in order to support women and minorities through these crisis points? Studies in this area are available from MIT and the University of Maryland.

World of Work: Much of the computer science world of work is driven by a "Wild West" culture. It can feel very foreign and threatening to women. We may need more training for women (and men) in how to cope with and/or subvert such an environment. Again, enlightened companies can do a lot of things to create a supportive environment for women, but they have to want to. This may currently be missing from much of the software industry businesses.

Professional Organizations: Premier organizations need to break out of current molds and actively nurture and mentor professional women to the point where they can become full academy members. Professional organizations need to put this issue on their agenda and actively work to resolve it. It's an issue for all, not just for women trying to promote women.

Government: The National Science Foundation (NSF) is very concerned about this issue. Their studies can be found on their Web page < http://www.nsf.gov/sbe/srs/databrf/db96331.htm >.

I'm thinking of working on the following:

- developing an engineering/technology program/curriculum aimed at high school girls;
- documenting the "choice points" of successful professional women and trying to generalize a support structure from that;
- etc.

More later,

Pat

Summary and Conclusions

While some may think that all we have to do is give unlimited online access to underserved communities and the world will be better, the problem is cultural, political, and social in nature. Access is a necessary, but certainly not sufficient, condition for broad-based change in human, social, political, and economic life throughout the world. Rather amazing progress has been made in the last century, and there are tremendous opportunities for improvement. However, the possibility exists that we will have more of the same, further widening existing gaps, and some peoples' greed may spell disaster for many others. Higher education has a wonderful opportunity to take leadership in this area, joining with partners in industry and foundations.

Conclusions Found At the Bottom of the Usenet FAQ

Those who have never tried electronic communication may not be aware of what a 'social skill' really is. One social skill that must be learned, is that other people have points of view that are not only different, but 'threatening' to your own. In turn, your opinions may be threatening to others. There is nothing wrong with this. Your beliefs need not be hidden behind a facade, as happens with face-to-face conversation. Not everybody in the world is a bosom buddy, but you can still have a meaningful conversation with them. The person who cannot do this lacks in social skills (Szabo 1999).

REFERENCES

American Association of School Administrators. 1999. Keeping pace or not keeping pace [Website]. *Converge*. Available from <http://www.aasa.org/>.

American Association of University Women. 1998. Gender gaps: Where schools still fail our children [Website]. Available from <http://www.aauw.org/2000/gg.html>.

AT&T. 1998. Fellowship program [Website]. AT&T. Available from <http://www.research.att.com/academic/>.

Austin Learning Academy. 1999. Austin Learning Academy, a research and development [Website]. Austin Learning Academy. Available from <http://www.alaweb.org/>.

Borg, Anita. 1996. Women's science contributions [Website]. *Computing Research News Online*. Available from <http://www.cra.org/CRN/html/9603/expanding/ab.ahmji.3_1_t.shtml>.

Camp, Tracy. 1997. The incredible shrinking pipeline [Website]. *Communications of the AMC*. Available from <http://www.mines.edu/fs_home/tcamp/cacm/paper.html>.

Drucker, Peter. 1998. The future that has already happened. *The Futurist* 32(8): 16-18.

Edupage. 1999. Irish girl creates code to improve e-mail speed by factor of ten [Website]. *Educause*. Available from <http://www.educause.edu>.

Grossman, Wendy. 1998. Access denied [Website]. *Scientific American*. 8 August. Available from <http://www.sciam.com/1998/0898issue/0898cyber.html>.

Higgins, J. 1998. *Technical pay gap* [World Wide Web]. Women in Cable and Telecommunications. Available from <http://www.wict.org/foundation/salary/part3.html>.

Hoffman, Karen Epper. 1998. Internet as gender-equalizer? [Website]. *Internet Week*. 9 November. Available from <http://www.internetworld. Com/print/1998/11/09/intcareers/19981109-internet.html>.

Jones, T. 1999. Internet world gaining women, less-affluent users as it grows. *Chicago Tribune*, 15 January.

Los Angeles Times. 1998. Women in computing. 25 August.

Macavinta, Courtney. 1998. Congress OK's tech gender gap study [Website]. *CNET.* Available from < http://www.news.com/News/Item/0,4,27105,00.html >.

McClellan, S. 1998. < http://www.freedomforum.or/newstand/reports/wmm/printwnn.asp >.

Oblinger, Diana, and Anne-Lee Verville. 1998. *What business wants from higher education.* American Council on Education/Oryx Press series on higher education. Phoenix, AZ: Oryx Press.

Penn State Outreach. 1999. *Fifth grade girls learn about World Wide Web* [Website]. Penn State University. 20 March. Available from < http://www.outreach.psu.edu/News/Magazine/Vol_2/41_ReachOut.html >.

Spragins, Ellyn E. 1999. What a nice problem : The bull causes some overendowment. *Newsweek,* 22 March.

Szabo, Nick. [Usenet FAQ]. 1999. Available from < http://faqs.org/faqs/usenet/what-is/part1/index.html >.

U.S. Department of Commerce. 1997. *Falling through the net II* [Website]. Available from < http://www.ntia.doc.gov/ntiahome/net2/falling.html >.

Walker, E., and S. Rodger. 1996. PipeLINK: Connecting women and girls in the computer science pipeline. Paper presented at the National Education Computing Conference. June. Minneapolis MN.

White, J. 1995. Women in engineering and science: Does anyone care? Paper presented at Bridging the Gender Gap in Engineering and Science: The Challenge of Institutional Transformation, Carnegie Mellon University, Pittsburg PA.

Yudkowsky, Chaim. 1999. Women who love the 'net [Website]. *Baltimore Business Journal,* 18 May. Available from < http://www.Amcity.com/baltimore/stories/1998/05/18/smallb2.html?h=Yudkowsky >.

Chapter 11

Redefining Faculty Policies and Practices for the Knowledge Age

By Donald Olcott, Jr. and Kathy Schmidt

Universities and their faculties are at a crossroads. The technology revolution has redefined the global community and has transformed every societal institution, from education, business, and government to entertainment, banking, and leisure (Oblinger and Rush 1997; Olcott 1997b). The latest infusion of technology into education has once again raised our hopes of improved learning and increased academic productivity. Today, calls for increased accountability by the public, legislatures, and new student "consumers" has served as a catalyst for academic leaders and policymakers to reexamine the traditional mission, structures, and functions of the university and its faculty.

The challenges of the technology revolution and of increased accountability are further confounded by reduced financing for higher education at the same time student enrollments are increasing (Breneman, Finney, and Roherty 1997). Moreover, private sector immersion (and its infusion of resources) into higher education markets accentuates the fact that the Knowledge Age gives more students more choice for meeting their educational needs (Dolence and Norris 1995).

Many academic leaders are, however, redefining their institution's future around technology, restructuring, selective streamlining, outsourcing services, and positioning the outreach curriculum to respond to "new" educational consumers, increased competition, and the utilitarian application of knowledge by society (Duderstadt 1999; Guskin 1996). Conversely, others believe they are immune to the winds of change and are staking their futures on the traditions of the past and business as usual (Hooker 1997; Olcott 1996). And while "business as usual" may suffice in the next three to five years, the long-term consequences for institutions may be catastrophic (Duderstadt 1999; Guskin 1994a).

The new currency in the Knowledge Age is information (Dolence and Norris 1995). More precisely, it is the creation, analysis, preservation, and distribution of information in efficient, easily accessible venues that give users the immediate capacity to apply information and knowledge (Duderstadt 1999). This knowledge monopoly was once the exclusive domain of higher education and its faculty. But with rapid advances in communications technologies, the monopoly has disappeared (Blustain, Goldstein, and Lozier 1999). Moreover, the unprecedented proliferation of knowledge has made it impossible for colleges and universities to be the sole gatekeepers of information. As a result of these forces, higher education has lost its once exclusive knowledge base.

The capacity of future universities to re-create themselves successfully will be dependent on how well the next generation of faculty adapt their practices and philosophies to the needs of society (Guskin 1994a). How we redefine what our faculty do, the policies and practices that empower them to respond, and the incentives that reward their work are essential success factors for the twenty-first century university (Duderstadt 1999; Wolcott 1997).

The challenge facing academic leaders and policymakers to restructure the role of faculty is immense. Guskin (1994a) reminds us of the ultimate paradox in this process. The decision processes and mechanisms for restructuring the role of faculty are controlled by the faculty through traditional governance and policymaking structures. Faculty resistance to change to protect the status quo is pervasive.

This chapter will examine a number of critical issues affecting the next generation of faculty and their role(s) in the Knowledge Age. How do we balance academic traditions with technological innovations? What characteristics will define the next generation of faculty? How will new student consumers and new market demands affect faculty roles and responsibilities? What incentives and rewards must be developed for faculty? What training will faculty need for technology-based instruction? What do instructional design and assessment mean in the new environment?

Finally, the authors will offer recommendations for faculty restructuring and how these suggestions ultimately can move the modern university toward a successful future.

Balancing Academic Traditions with Technological Innovations

Given the challenges of restructuring the role of university faculty, we must first understand the traditional cultural norms of the academy. These norms have defined the role of faculty for decades and have become embedded in the mainstream academic culture. Moreover, this culture inherently creates faculty resistance to change, technological or otherwise. These norms are summarized below (Duderstadt 1999; Guskin 1994a; Guskin 1996; Hanna 1998; Hooker 1997; Olcott 1997a):

Academic Freedom. Autonomous and free expression of ideas, beliefs, and content by faculty.

Self-Regulated Governance. Faculty control of structures, curricula, policies, and deliberative processes essential to faculty change (e.g., faculty senate, committees, promotion and tenure review, teaching load, productivity issues). At the institutional level, board of trustee governance strives to be independent from the political or business environment.

University Change. Deliberation, consensus, and incrementalism controlled by faculty, administrators, and policymakers. This process is labor and time intensive and ineffective for responding to major institutional and societal change.

Institutional Policy. Focus on preserving the campus as the primary locale of teaching and learning. This is reinforced by strict residency requirements, consecutive-semester enrollment, inflexible academic calendars, restrictions on credit outreach initiatives, and defined institutional service regions. Autonomous faculty governance and deliberative, consensus-driven policymaking control this policy arena.

Faculty Advancement. Based on promotion and tenure requirements typically defined as teaching, research, and service, not necessarily in that order. Few incentives for creative and innovative work outside these parameters.

Teaching Philosophy. Faculty member is expert and source of knowledge. Students are passive and lecture is characteristic teaching mode. Instruction is measured by student seat-time.

Learning Technology. Generally used to supplement or enhance lecture format. Pervasive belief by faculty that technology will diminish their academic autonomy and that technology-based instruction is inferior to face-to-face teaching. Belief by faculty that there will be no support services available and that the rapid pace of technological change will make investments in technology obsolete before faculty get their feet wet with the new systems. In some institutions, there also is a pervasive belief that faculty jobs are going to be replaced by the adoption of technology.

Funding. Measured by dollars expended per full-time student equivalent (FTE). Institutional, college, and departmental funding are based on how many students are served, not how well they are served.

Productivity and Quality. Measured in student credit-hours and degrees. These are elusive outcome measures that assume quality and student learning. Research productivity and external service imply increased instructional quality. Selective admissions suggest higher-quality programs, with a focus on inputs rather than outputs measured in student learning. In many institutions the research emphasis separates out faculty. Those good at research do research. The rest teach and, by implication, teaching is devalued in the process.

Libraries. More volumes with greater depth of disciplinary holdings imply greater quality. Increased access to electronic sources is beginning to challenge traditional assumptions of this relationship to quality.

Credentialism. Primarily the awarding of degrees and certificates authorized by state boards and regional and discipline-based accrediting agencies. Once the exclusive domain of college and university campuses, this monopoly is being challenged by private institutions, corporate educational providers, and virtual universities.

These norms of the academic enterprise remained, with a few intervening exceptions, relatively immune to public, government, and corporate scrutiny until the early 1990s. They have changed somewhat over the last decade due to advanced technology, increased accountability, shifts in market demands, more selective consumers, and, perhaps most important, the perception that traditional colleges and universities are unable to keep pace in responding to the rapid changes transforming society (Duderstadt 1999; Oblinger and Rush 1997).

In this new environment with information as the premium currency, the traditional norms of the academy clearly are being challenged. No longer are faculties the sole guardians of knowledge. And technology is not the only threat to these norms. Innovations can come in many forms: modified policies, changing roles for faculty, new approaches to teaching and learning, increased productivity measures, new governance structures, and changes in promotion and tenure criteria (Rogers 1983).

The problem, however, is that many faculty members and administrators, who generally come from the faculty ranks, do not want to embrace any fundamental changes that challenge the status quo. It is an either/or proposition for most faculty because they control the mechanisms of change. The roots of resistance among faculty, however, are more complex. The academic subculture, known as the department, is the first level of peer acceptance for most faculty members. If a faculty member deviates from departmental norms or engages in activities that require new resources or release time, or that challenge the status quo of past practices, he or she faces peer scrutiny rather than acceptance.

Interestingly, senior tenured faculty can venture out and be innovative, while junior non-tenured faculty must adhere to the traditional norms. Translated, this means strict adherence to promotion and tenure criteria. In sum, for many junior faculty members there are not only few incentives but, in fact, underlying disincentives operating in this subculture. Consequently, if some innovations are adopted, an entire restructuring of the system will occur.

Blending the best of traditional norms with needed innovations for the Knowledge Age is viewed as a challenge to the status quo. Future institutions must find an optimum balance between tradition and innovation in all arenas.

Let's examine what the next generation of faculty might look like in the Knowledge Age.

The Next Generation of Faculty

The future role of a university faculty member might be analogous to that of a symphony conductor. On the one hand faculty will be motivating, directing, and empowering players (students). At the same time, they will be challenging, facilitating, and creating a whole that is greater than the sum of individual students. This role will include a diverse array of responsibilities that can enrich the composite role of each faculty member and create a dynamic teaching, learning, and mentoring environment for both students and faculty alike.

The following provides a summary of how the traditional norms of the academy listed above may evolve to enable these new roles for faculty:

Academic Freedom. Autonomous and free expression will actually be strengthened rather than diminished. The change, however, will be that the knowledge explosion will provide students and faculty with unlimited access to the ideas, knowledge, and creativity of other experts, thus enriching themselves. The knowledge resources will create a greater depth of knowledge for students, who will bring that knowledge to the classroom (or to the computer). The result: deeper intellectual interaction between instructor and student as well as among students. This depth will also result in more students challenging the viewpoints and beliefs of faculty (Guskin 1994a).

Governance. The embedded governance processes of deliberation, consensus, and incremental change will not disappear, but they will of necessity become faster and more efficient (Blustain, Goldstein, and Lozier 1999). These changes will be influenced by external competition and pressure for increased responsiveness, but decision making will also accelerate because of internal demands for greater efficiency and use of resources. As this occurs, faculty will become empowered to assume greater leadership roles in the long-term direction and purpose of the institution. And since faculty control these many institutional decision-making processes, systemic change in this area will demand strong administrative leadership and great courage on the part of senior faculty (Duderstadt 1999). Faculty governance will need to be flexible to new ideas, and continuous review of policies and processes will become the "norm." Static governance is simply incompatible with the demands of the Knowledge Age.

University Change. The next generation of faculty will be critical to an institution's capacity to organize and implement change. And because faculty will be responsible for restructuring the governance processes, they will be equal partners with academic leaders in moving the institution in new directions. In the academy, revolutionary ideas typically are transformed into evolutionary change (Guskin 1994b). Faculty must align the expediency of deliberation, consensus, and incrementalism to respond to changing needs and priorities.

Faculty Advancement. Research, teaching, and service will become more integrated, and definitions of each will expand to include a vast array of activities that reflect the best of everything faculty do (Boyer 1990; Krahenbuhl 1998). The next generation of faculty will play an important role in redefining the criteria for promotion and tenure, a process that will become more flexible in determining "legitimate activities" (Miles 1998). These legitimate activities also will be more clearly defined across the institution and will elevate distance teaching, Web-designed courses, and other activities related to educational technology to equal status with traditional research, teaching, and service activities for promotion and tenure review.

Teaching Philosophy. From autonomous expert to classroom, Web, and TV maestro — the faculty member of tomorrow will be the creative force for moving away from faculty-centered approaches to student-centered, collaborative, and action-oriented approaches to teaching and learning. However, faculty will need to analyze their beliefs about instruction and learn how to connect their beliefs with actions in the classroom. As Hanna noted in chapter 2, faculty members will spend less time in formal lecture and more time in dispersed activities (e,g., designing new learning environments, engaging students with online resources, building collaborative learning experiences, evaluating hands-on learning competencies, supervising independent learning, and developing students' capacity for performing new mentoring roles) (Guskin 1994a; Olcott 1997a).

Learning Technology. Institutions will give faculty richer and more in-depth training on using educational technologies. The challenge is to look creatively at pedagogical implications for instructional technology. Faculty will use technology for teaching, research, and service in ways that will allow them to restructure their time more efficiently. Faculty will direct students to the vast array of online resources and will integrate asynchronous teaching and learning strategies into their courses. This will occur for both campus and distance learners. Faculty members will spend less time in the classroom and students will spend less time on campus. Faculty will create more mediated instructional resources, which will require new intellectual and royalty structures (Katz 1999; Mayadas 1997; Olcott 1997b).

Funding. The next generation of faculty will not become mainstream businesspersons. They will, however, be involved in more for-profit work that generates resources for their departments and colleges. They will also be courted by private-sector companies, publishing firms, and government to develop technology-based content and instructional packages. Faculty salaries will tend to become more differentiated rather than standardized. Different faculty members will spend their time in different roles that align with their strengths. Institutional and unit budgets will be more dependent on hybrid sources of funding rather than strictly FTE, state-funded allocations.

Productivity and Quality. Faculty productivity for teaching, research, and service will be more tied to student learning outcomes and contributions to the public (Krahenbuhl 1998). Quality will increasingly be measured by student mastery or competencies rather than seat-time. Faculty will play the major role in establishing outcome measures that truly assess learning. For some faculty members in some disciplines, defining outcome measures and learning competencies will be a collaborative process with private-sector businesses and employers.

Libraries. Digital libraries and online resources will give faculty members and students access to an unprecedented repository of rich learning resources. Faculty members will guide students to these resources, help them assess alternative online resources, and define new approaches to research via technology. These activities will strengthen the role of faculty members as facilitators rather than the sole sources of knowledge.

Credentialism. Faculty will play an increasing role in developing nondegree-based certificate and modularized learning packages, credit and noncredit, for meeting specific educational and skill needs of students and employees. Credit may constitute some form of professional credit by professional organizations, industry, or government, and not necessarily academic credit. In general, the range of institutional credentials will increase, and departmental faculty will assume major leadership and networking roles with the private sector in the development of these credentials. Faculty will also play a major role in helping the accrediting agencies understand the quality measures of these new credentials, how these credentials relate to institutional mission, and how educational technology creates "value-added" substance to these new credentials. Assessment of the quality of these credentials will be more dependent on content and skill mastery and less dependent upon formal seat-time or computer time.

The next generation of faculty will have many challenges but will also have more opportunities than ever before. Moreover, the expanding roles of faculty for recreating academic governance are critical responsibilities that, if embraced by our new faculty, will create a higher education environment in which quality education can occur anytime, anywhere, using a variety of media and knowledge resources.

This empowered role of faculty will occur for several reasons. First, gradual acceptance of technology will alter the norms of the academic culture and create new norms. For example, Internet use will become as normative as the telephone, simply because academe and society have embraced them in everyday life. Second, institutional leaders (and their faculty) recognize that for all the things colleges and universities do, the academic mission will remain front and center. And faculty leadership, not presidential leadership, is where change in this arena will emerge.

The changing roles of faculty will not affect university faculty alone. Community college faculty, whose traditional focus has been on teaching, will be affected by the mass access to information, and they will similarly become facilitators of information resources. Even K-12 teachers, while perhaps affected less than higher education faculty, will be confronted with how to redefine their teaching roles in ways that use information resources to expose and educate children in new ways.

In sum, the art of teaching will itself undergo a significant transformation as a result of unlimited knowledge resources that are readily accessible to most of society.

Transformational Markets and the New Student Consumer

The next generation of faculty will be faced with two major shifts affecting higher education. The first is the increasing number of competitive providers in the higher education market (Hanna 1998; Marchese 1998; Oblinger and Rush 1997; Olcott 1997a). The second is a new generation of students who are more demanding, selective, and vocal about their educational choices. What are the implications of these shifts for faculty?

The competitive marketplace may affect faculty only indirectly in the short term. Faculty will be less concerned about these new providers due to their belief in the quality and rigor of their own programs, or they will criticize the new providers without examining them closely. They will ardently defend the traditional status quo of the resident campus, because doing so protects their position status. And yet, ask five business colleges to collaborate and they say "yes." Ask them who has the best program and each will tell you it is theirs. Collaborative intent turns to competitive elitism. The point is that universities are highly competitive with their own sister institutions, which often blinds them to new market realities and competition.

The next generation of faculty must take a more active role in assessing viable markets for their programs. And this does not mean trading in their academic gowns for business suits. It will require faculty to be active participants in differentiating their programs from those of their competitors, whether by quality, responsiveness, cost, or all three.

In this new era of "transformational markets," in which the definitions of the market and consumers are constantly changing, only those organizations that can respond effectively will be successful. Olcott (1998) accentuates how the internal perceptions of what's important diverge from the perceptions outside the academy. We in higher education may argue that our traditions, policies, traditional service regions, and philosophical foundations are essential even in the Information Age. And yet the fact is that no one fifty yards from campus cares about these. The public, the legislature, and consumers care about quality, competence, cost-effectiveness, and producing graduates who are employable and who have abilities needed to enter the workforce.

The Knowledge Age will mean more students with more choices for meeting their educational goals (Dolence and Norris 1995). Faculty-centered teaching environments may be transformed into student-centered learning environments. Students will be more demanding, more selective, and more likely to question the sole expertise of the instructor. And the teacher or professor will be analogous to the conductor of a symphony.

This will be a major transition for faculty, but one that must occur to create these highly engaging, student-centered learning environments. And student-centered learning environments will not emerge because of more demanding students or idealistic rhetoric. They may emerge simply as a result of the unlimited information resources available that will require faculty to direct students to these resources and mentor students in how to select, disaggregate, and apply the most useful information. Changing faculty roles may be the primary impetus for the emergence of a more student-centered learning environment.

Many faculty and administrators adamantly oppose the term "consumers" being applied to students (Lust 1998; Swenson 1998). In fact, many dislike any business jargon applied to higher education. Lust (1998) argues that using the term "consumers" devalues students. She argues that the term makes students a business entity and discards their active role as students. And while she makes a valid point that education is much more than teaching pragmatic skills or delivering knowledge, and tells us to not lose sight of the heart and soul of education, she has missed an essential fact: we in higher education never have had and do not presently have consensus on what the heart and soul of education is.

Lust goes on to imply that increasing consumerism in higher education could be related to a decline in academic standards. Yes, this could be the case. But it's highly unlikely, since accountability issues have been intensifying for over a decade, well before the emergence of business rhetoric in higher education circles.

If a decline in academic standards has occurred, the reasons are much more complex than a change in rhetoric. This is analogous to arguing that university focus on research, or higher costs, or technology, is solely responsible for the "perceived" decline in academic standards — a premise few would support. It seems that a more plausible reason is that what our institutions do, even if done well, does not align well with the needs of society and what students need to function successfully in society. Simply put, the new student consumers care about getting what they need, at a time and place convenient to them, at a fair price, and through a variety of delivery venues (Olcott 1998). Students care about quality, but accessibility is also an increasingly important value.

New Relationships between Faculty and Institutions

The Knowledge Age will usher in new relationships between faculty members and their institutions. Many of these new relationships will have policy and legal ramifications. Here are just a select few:

Intellectual Property. As Tallman notes in chapter 8, faculty participation in the development of mediated instructional packages, some with high market-revenue potential, will require institutions to renegotiate new agreements governing who owns what and why. Institutional royalty agreements are already under serious revision, largely due to the impact of educational technology to create instructional resources with significant revenue potential (Duderstadt 1999; Hooker 1997; Katz 1999).

Institutional Loyalty. Faculty are loyal to their disciplines. In the Knowledge Age, external providers and distributors in the private sector will go directly to faculty for content development and instructional packaging. Some faculty members will serve multiple masters. Developing, packaging, and distributing content will be a premium revenue source in the information market. Publishing companies, private businesses, and for-profit universities will court talented faculty in this enterprise (Katz 1999; Olcott 1997a).

Advancement Criteria. The knowledge environment and asynchronous technologies make students and faculty mobile. Faculty teaching roles will change dramatically and will include a broader range of activities, such as mentoring and resource facilitation, in concert with redefined teaching, service, and research roles (Krahenbuhl 1998; Wolcott 1997). Faculty will teach and conduct research from home, from abroad, and from a multitude of locales away from campus. Institutions will define these new roles and expectations in faculty contracts, and faculty will not only be encouraged, but expected to engage in outreach initiatives.

Expedient Governance. A rapidly changing market will drive institutional leaders to empower faculty to play an even greater role in academic governance and making it more efficient, flexible, and responsive to societal and market needs (Guskin 1994a; Guskin 1994b).

Curriculum Control. Faculty will retain primary control over curricula, although current trends suggest that state boards, the private sector, and even students will play increasing roles in the curricular design process. This will be a difficult transition for faculty members. But it is a natural consequence of responding more effectively to the needs of society.

Faculty Training, Rewards, and Incentives

Distance and distributed learning in the Knowledge Age will require nothing less than a complete restructuring of the current reward and incentive structures for faculty. Research and practice over the past decade have clearly documented that, without equitable rewards for faculty to use technology (campus or distance), faculty members will not participate (Hanna 1998; Olcott 1997b; Olcott and Wright 1995; Wolcott 1997). Without active participation by faculty, responsive and quality programs may not be developed.

Given the ubiquitous use of educational technology in our society, our new faculty will have to be highly competent using technology for instruction, research, and service. There are still many faculty members who either do not have or do not use computers on a regular basis, probably due to fear or lack of resources. Today's students are computer literate and familiar with a range of technologies in their everyday lives.

Institutions must make technology literacy an absolute prerequisite for new faculty. Moreover, they must provide continuous training for upgrading skills as technology changes. This training must concentrate equally on behaviors, not just skills accomplishment. It must also engage faculty in the "when" and "why" of using technology for teaching. Technology is not going away, and it will be essential for faculty to be productive and creative in the Knowledge Age.

Another important training issue for tomorrow's faculty is that they must be given training in instructional theory and teaching methodologies. The unchallenged formula that disciplined degrees equal quality teaching in the university is often a misleading assumption. More important, faculty may be unable to harness the pedagogical potential of technology to improve teaching unless they understand the basics of designing, delivering, and evaluating instruction.

Finally, policy changes will be important in the technology environment. Promotion and tenure criteria must provide equal weight for all technology teaching, content design, innovative packaging, and related activities, whether for campus or distributed instruction. Departments must rethink incentives such as training, release time, and course development resources to enable faculty to take advantage of technology in the classroom. This will mean shifting traditional budget priorities to support these activities. And yes, higher education must provide attractive salaries for new faculty. If it doesn't, the private sector will.

A summary of these issues is provided below.

- Faculty must have highly developed technology skills. This should be an institutional prerequisite. Faculty must also have training in teaching methodologies, new assessment approaches for classroom and technology teaching, adult learning theories, asynchronous learning strategies, and the formal design of instruction. Computer literacy should be a required skill for all new faculty as well as existing faculty.

- Promotion and tenure criteria must give equal weight to technology teaching, content design, and innovative uses of educational technology (Olcott and Wright 1995).

- Academic units must give faculty release time, unit resources, and continuous training in the uses of technologies and related teaching and assessment approaches.

- Departments must develop more flexible policies governing faculty consulting and external service so that they can take advantage of private-sector opportunities. Faculty capitalize on these opportunities, and it would be prudent for departments to begin thinking about how these actions can be supported with equitable return to the department and without restricting faculty participation.

- Policies defining faculty productivity must become all-inclusive. All activities in which faculty engage must be included in measures of productivity. In the Knowledge Age, there will be instances when designing a Web-based course will be more important that teaching a five-hundred student 101 course or writing an article for publication. Productivity goes hand in hand with promotion and tenure criteria and should be revised concurrently.

Effective Instructional Design and Assessment

College faculty must begin to *design* instruction and not just *deliver* instruction. Empowered by the communications revolution and new emerging technologies, students in higher education will demand flexible learning environments that are enriched with today's technological tools. Many faculty members have avoided technology-enhanced teaching because of a historical attachment to the physical classroom and the reality that classrooms have traditionally been the last institution in our society to embrace new innovations such as calculators, VCRs, or computers (Soloway 1991).

While these obstacles and restraints, based on habit, tradition, and culture, have so far kept faculty from addressing pedagogical practice and instructional innovations, this will no longer suffice. For faculty to explore technology-enabled learning, they must first look at current instructional practices through a critical lens, and they must be given genuine institutional support to promote their efforts.

It is a common assumption that conventional university-level instruction is not an intensive and demanding instructional design endeavor. While some posit that all teachers design instruction (Briggs 1977), it doesn't appear that many faculty are well versed in the science of instructional design, which is based upon psychological principles, cognitive-science research, and instructional models.

Furthermore, instructional designers study and apply "all the events that may have a direct effect on learning of a human being, not just those set in motion by an individual who is a teacher. Instruction may include events that are generated by a page of print, by a picture, by a television program, or by a combination of physical objects, among other things" (Gagne, Briggs, and Wager 1992). Attempts have been made to disseminate instructional systems design models to teachers, but there is a paucity of literature on efforts to relate instructional design theory and methods to teaching practice (Martin 1990; Martin and Clement 1990).

Lessons from Traditional Pedagogy

A great deal of college teaching is lecture based. It is a fairly low-cost way to distribute education, and it produces large numbers of student credit-hours. Typically, college students taught in lectures are able to retain only about 5 percent of what is said at least a day after the lecture (Klein 1995). A lecture-based, textbook-oriented model is often the norm. And yet this model restricts the transfer of information from publishers to individuals and thus precludes a more learner-centered model in which students are empowered to acquire, correlate, and reflect on their own and others' thoughts.

We cannot conclude, however, that all traditional classroom teaching is ineffective. Many students have learned and will continue to learn from lectures and discussions and textbook readings. The limitation of the traditional model, however, is that far too often students are uninvolved, passive learners. New variations of lectures that employ instructional technologies offer better educational efficiency and prompt student involvement and discovery learning (Pence 1996-97). It is not enough to take a traditional lecture and merely "add-on" technology in a peripheral relationship.

How does the next generation of faculty foster these teaching/learning conditions that promote information and require learners to interact with it, comprehend it, and transfer it? The first step for faculty is to develop a deep understanding of what learners need to be able to do at the end of instruction. Far too often, the focus is placed on how and what to teach and which technological bells and whistles to ring. We must shift the focus to how students learn and how the material can best be conveyed. Then we must explore the faculty's role in facilitating student learning. In general, undergraduate education promotes three types of learning: accumulation of information and knowledge, skill development, and conceptual development (Guskin 1994a). We can encourage such learning through technology-based strategies that provide optimal learning environments.

Tomorrow's faculty must be able to participate in designing instruction that is fully delivered via technology and enhanced by the use of technology. Faculty who have been successful in face-to-face instruction, in which they can spontaneously adapt lessons to accommodate different audiences and their needs, may feel that they don't need to become steeped in instructional design processes.

When one views teaching as an "art" that relies heavily on intuition as a basis for action, it may be difficult to make the leap to teaching as a "science," for which research, systematic approaches, and principles serve as the basis for action. Many faculty members have not studied or were not taught instructional systems design (ISD), for which models and principles emanate from a variety of disciplines: general systems theory, learning theory, and instructional theory (Richey 1986).

Instructional Design Strategies

Instructional design is a concentrated process in which planning and delivery of instruction involves analysis, design, development, implementation, and evaluation. Various ISD models provide theoretical frameworks to enhance instruction by identifying what is and what should be, along with the subsequent activities and strategies to bridge the two (Moallem and Earle 1998).

"The fundamental principle of the ISD approach is that all aspects of learning and instruction should be defined behaviorally, so that what the student is expected to learn can be measured and teaching can concentrate on the student's observable performance" (Moore and Kearsley 1996, 102). At its most basic level, ISD begins by asking three basic questions: First, what do I expect a student to be able to do? Second, in what way should the student demonstrate learning? Third, what student performance is acceptable as evidence of learning?

The focus of the entire ISD process is on the learner. The more the instructor knows about the learner — such as his or her academic background, reading level, standardized test scores, study habits, background in the discipline, and motivation for studying the subject — the greater the likelihood of delivering effective instruction.

The key for using ISD is to incorporate the following instructional events: 1) motivating the learner; 2) specifying what is to be learned; 3) prompting the learner to recall and apply previous knowledge; 4) providing new information and relating it to the existing knowledge base; 5) offering guidance and feedback; 6) testing comprehension; and 7) supplying enrichment or remediation (Dick and Reiser 1989).

Successful design requires an understanding of the technology, the learner, and interactions between the two. Selecting the medium or media is done during the development phase of ISD. Consideration must first be given to selection of the most efficient and effective methods of instructional delivery. Before developing any new instructional materials, one must survey what is available and then adapt existing materials. Given the dynamic state of emerging technologies, it is possible to develop instructional materials and easily make ongoing revisions to improve instruction. Good teaching has always involved the ability to revise and to adapt to different students and context. With today's technology tools, evaluation and revision can be an integral part of college teaching.

Assessment for Distributed Education

Another challenge for the next generation of faculty is to ensure that technological convenience is not given precedence over pedagogy. If assessment is relegated to those measures that are most easily created and graded, then students will miss out on more meaningful projects, assignments, and collaborative studies. Often, tests are isolated events and fail to paint a more detailed picture of learning. Technology gives faculty the tools to automate testing, but we must remember that new assessment techniques are needed to measure the effectiveness of newly developed classrooms.

College faculty are faced with a challenging set of obstacles in creating assessments to demonstrate the complexity of learning in the academy. Accountability is seldom measured in high skills, standardized exams, or state-mandated end-of-course exams. Student learning is generally assessed by an individual faculty member, and standards for assessment are created on an individual course basis. It would appear that such intellectual freedom would result in more creative classroom environments, but some critics claim that higher education offers a one-size-fits-all approach to teaching (Twigg 1994).

Can current and emerging informational technologies give us the power to create authentic assessments that encourage self-directed learning? There are always ways that technology can be used to create optimal learning environments and to measure deeper and broader learning objectives. Assessment can mean much more than only tests; it can also include projects, assignments, and case studies. High-tech resources such as animation, video, and hyperlinks can be used to create in-depth student products and to develop information-rich testing environments.

Student discourse and collaboration are readily facilitated by distributed learning environments, as are more individual and faculty-student interactions. The faculty's role in assessing student learning will become more expansive. Faculty will guide students to sources, coach students, and be an integral part of the students' ongoing learning.

Finally, while a simple concept, we must always remember to match instruction with assessment, as Gary Brown elaborates upon in chapter 13. If assessment is added as an afterthought or as a necessary evil, we do not move toward a better understanding of student learning. Today's technology is an enabling tool, but only when instruction and assessment are based upon sound instructional principles. These principles are not only the key to effective learning, they are also the key to successful teaching via technology by the faculty of tomorrow.

Recommendations for Practice: Empowering the New Faculty

Institutions are working to restructure the role of faculty (Guskin 1994a). Institutions should engage key faculty members and administrators in this process immediately and develop a "Faculty Futures Institute" on their campuses to define the new roles and support mechanisms to ensure systemic change. Restructuring the role of the faculty also means the institution must reallocate its budgets to support this process or find new and significant sources of funding for faculty development.

Technology and computer literacy, training in teaching methodologies for technology, and new assessment models should be required for all faculty (Olcott and Wright 1995). And faculty need to be encouraged to be creative and innovative in their teaching. There are no "silver-bullet," simple solutions. Some of the best innovations in teaching and learning come through trial and error. Faculty should be rewarded for experimenting, not chastised for failure.

Promotion and tenure requirements need to be expanded. They also must be inclusive of all faculty work and productivity, particularly with respect to those activities that support educational technology applications and use (Krahenbuhl 1998; Olcott 1997a; Wolcott 1997).

Institutions will be required to develop new policies governing intellectual property, royalty structures, and consulting for faculty. The rules have changed, and institutions will need to recognize the role of faculty in this new environment (Duderstadt 1999).

The traditional concepts of teaching, research, and service must be realigned with faculty talents and expertise (Krahenbuhl 1998; Olcott 1999b). It makes little sense to establish the same requirements for all faculty members if we want to develop valid measures of productivity that build on faculty strengths. Good researchers should be more involved in research. Good teachers should be engaged in teaching assignments.

Institutions also need to create a balance between tradition and the innovations and demands of the Knowledge Age (Olcott 1998; Olcott 1999a). It is, despite the rhetoric of our critics, not an either/or proposition. However, it is clear that higher education must change and become more competitive and responsive in selective markets to the demands of employers, students, and the public.

Creativity and innovation must be embraced as a norm for faculty in the academic enterprise. This means embracing change. Innovation by faculty members has historically been considered a challenge to the status quo and resisted vigorously by other faculty and administrators (Guskin 1994a).

Both to empower the faculty and to be responsive to changing external needs, academic governance will need to become more efficient, flexible, and responsive. And for many who have spent years in the academy, converting this rhetoric to reality is a continuing challenge. Academic governance in this century has meant deliberation, consensus, and incrementalism. It worked for most of the century. Today, however, in a dynamic and turbulent external environment, decision-making structures and institutional governance must be streamlined and rebuilt.

Summary

The next generation of faculty has the opportunity to create exciting and challenging educational environments for students. Successful and innovative learning environments will become an increasingly important factor in influencing student choice of institutions. As a result, faculty who are most adept at transforming the classroom will be in demand, and institutions able to develop a significant cadre of such faculty members will prosper. The learning environment in the future will look and function much differently than the system that has taken us this far.

Restructuring the role of faculty will require exhaustive energy and dedicated commitment and courage on the part of the faculty and the institution. Institutions will require collective leadership from the faculty and the administration to implement systemic and successful change across the academy. Perhaps Machiavelli (1950, 21) best sums up this test of courage, commitment, and leadership:

> There is no more delicate matter to take in hand, nor more dangerous to conduct, nor more doubtful of success, than to step up as a leader in the introduction of change. For he who innovates will have for his enemies all those who are well off under the existing order of things, and only lukewarm support in those who might be better off under the new.

The question is, are our faculties up to the challenge?

REFERENCES

Blustain, Harvey, Philip Goldstein, and Gregory Lozier. 1999. Assessing the new competitive landscape. In *Dancing with the Devil: Information Technology and the New Competition in Higher Education*, edited by Richard N. Katz et al. San Francisco: Jossey-Bass, Publishers.

Boyer, Ernest L. 1990. *Scholarship reconsidered: Priorities of the professoriate*. Menlo Park, CA: Carnegie Foundation for the Advancement of Teaching.

Breneman, David W., Joni E. Finney, and Brian M. Roherty. 1997. *Shaping the future: Higher education finance in the 1990s*. San Jose, CA: California Higher Education Policy Center.

Briggs, Leslie J. 1977. Designing the strategy of instruction. In *Instructional Design*, edited by Leslie J. Briggs. Englewood Cliffs, NJ: Educational Technology Publications.

Dick, Walter, and Robert A. Reiser. 1989. *Planning effective instruction*. Englewood Cliffs, NJ: Prentice-Hall.

Dolence, Michael G., and Donald M. Norris. 1995. *Transforming higher education: A vision for learning in the 21st century*. Society for College and University Planning.

Duderstadt, James J. 1999. Can colleges and universities survive in the information age? In *Dancing with the Devil: Information Technology and the New Competition in Higher Education*, edited by Richard N. Katz et al. San Francisco: Jossey-Bass, Publishers.

Gagne, Robert M. , Leslie J. Briggs, and Walter W. Wager. 1992. *Principles of instructional design*. 4th ed. Fort Worth, TX: Harcourt Brace Jovanovich College Publishers.

Guskin, Alan E. 1994a. Restructuring the role of faculty: Part II of reducing student costs and enhancing student learning. *Change* (Sept/Oct): 16-25.

Guskin, Alan E. 1994b. Restructuring the administration: Part I of reducing student costs and enhancing student learning. *Change* (July/Aug): 23-29.

Guskin, Alan E. 1996. Facing the future: The change process in restructuring universities. *Change* (July/Aug): 27-37.

Hanna, Donald E. 1998. Higher education in an era of digital competition: Emerging organizational models. *Journal of Asynchronous Learning* 2(1).

Hooker, Michael. 1997. The transformation of higher education. In *The Learning Revolution: The Challenge of Information in the Technology*, edited by Diana G. Oblinger and Sean C. Rush. Bolton, MA: Anker Publishing Company, Inc.

Katz, Richard N. 1999. Competitive strategies for higher education in the information age. In *Dancing with the devil: Information technology and the new competition in higher education*, edited by Richard N. Katz et al. San Francisco: Jossey-Bass, Publishers.

Klein, Thomas. 1995. Electronic revolution at the educational crossroads: Foot-dragging on campus. *College Teaching* 43(4): 151-155.

Krahenbuhl, Gary S. 1998. Faculty work: Integrating responsibilities and institutional needs. *Change* 30(6): 18-25.

Lust, Patricia. 1998. Students as customers: The devaluation of learning. *The Journal of Continuing Higher Education* 46(2): 38-41.

Machiavelli, Niccolo. 1950. *The prince and the discourses, modern library of the world's best books.* New York: The Modern Library.

Marchese, Theodore. 1998. Not-so-distant competitors: How new providers are remaking the postsecondary marketplace. *AAHE Bulletin* 50(9): 3-7.

Martin, Barbara L. 1990. Teachers' planning processes: Does ISD make a difference? *Performance Improvement Quarterly* 3(4): 53-73.

Martin, Barbara L. , and Rebecca Clement. 1990. Instructional systems design and public schools. *Educational Technology Research and Development* 39(2): 61-75.

Mayadas, A. Frank. 1997. Asynchronous learning networks: New possibilities. In *The Learning Revolution: The Challenge of Information Technology in the Academy*, edited by Diana G. Oblinger and Sean C. Rush. Bolton, MA: Anker Publishing Company, Inc.

Miles, William F. S. 1998. Tenure, promotion, and pig-killing. *Change* 30(5): 30-32.

Moallem, Mahnaz , and Rodney Earle. 1998. Instructional design models and teacher thinking: Toward a new conceptual model for research and development. *Educational Technology* 38(2): 5-22.

Moore, Michael, and Greg Kearsley. 1996. *Distance education: A system's view.* Belmont, CA: Wadsworth.

Oblinger, Diana G., and Sean C. Rush. 1997. The learning revolution. In *The Learning Revolution: The Challenge of Information Technology in the Academy*, edited by Diana G. Oblinger and Sean C. Rush. Bolton, MA: Anker Publishing Company, Inc.

Olcott, Donald John Jr. 1996. Destination 2000: Strategies for managing successful distance education programs. *Journal of Distance Education* XI(2): 103-115.

Olcott, Donald John Jr. 1997a. Renewing the vision: Past perspectives and future implications for distance education. *The Journal of Continuing Higher Education* 45(3): 2-13.

Olcott, Donald John Jr. 1997b. Transforming university outreach: integrated technology systems design for the twenty-first century. *Journal of Public Service and Outreach* 2(3): 55-69.

Olcott, Donald John Jr. 1998. Transformational markets and the new student: The enigmatic response of continuing and distance education. *Distance Education Report* 2(14): 1-4.

Olcott, Donald John Jr. 1999a. Balancing academic tradition and technological innovation in R1 institutions. *Syllabus* 12(8): 22-26.

Olcott, Donald John Jr. 1999b. Distance learning in R1 institutions: Recommendations and strategies. *Syllabus* 12(9): 28-30.

Olcott, Donald John Jr., and Stephen J. Wright. 1995. An institutional support framework for increasing faculty participation in postsecondary distance education. *The American Journal of Distance Education* 9(3): 5-17.

Pence, Harry E. 1996-97. What is the role of lecture in high-tech education? *Journal of Educational Technology Systems* 25(2): 91-96.

Richey, Rita C. 1986. The theoretical and conceptual bases of instructional design. London: Kogan Page Ltd.

Rogers, Everett M. 1983. *Diffusions of innovations*. New York: Free Press.

Soloway, Elliott. 1991. How the nintendo generation learns. *Communications of the ACM* 34(9): 23-26.

Swenson, Craig. 1998. Customers and markets: The cuss words of academe. *Change* 30(5): 34-39.

Twigg, Carol. 1994. The changing definition of learning. *Educom Review* 29(4): 23-25.

Wolcott, Linda L. 1997. Tenure, promotion, and distance education: Examining the culture of faculty rewards. *The American Journal of Distance Education* 11(2): 3-18.

Chapter 12

Integrated Technology Systems Design: A Model for Aligning Pedagogical Quality with Learning Technology

By Kathy Schmidt and Donald Olcott, Jr.

During the last decade, the expanding range of learning technologies has created more choices for colleges and universities to deliver instructional programs. Today, this arsenal ranges from interactive television, audiographics, and audio teleconferencing to computer-based training, Web and Internet applications, and print materials supplemented by audio, video, fax, and computer (Duning, Van Kekerix, and Zaborowski 1993; Olcott 1997a). From what was once an educational environment dominated by live-interactive video as the premium technology delivery system, we have moved to a variety of integrated, asynchronous technologies and approaches (Hanna 1998; Mayadas 1997; Moore and Kearsley 1996; Olcott 1997b).

The impetus for this changing environment has been the global utilization of the World Wide Web and the Internet and an increasing, consistent body of research documenting the pedagogical and economic effectiveness of lower-end technologies (e.g., audio, Web, print, computer-based training) (Hardy and

Olcott 1995; Moore and Kearsley 1996; Moore and Thompson 1998; Oblinger and Rush 1997).

Despite the unprecedented range of technologies available to colleges and universities, questions related to the most effective pedagogical, economic, and logistical integration of technologies at the course level remain uncharted empirical territory. Moreover, the development of integrated technology approaches has been problematic due to institutional reliance on one technology and the tendency to embrace the technology of choice at the outset rather than systematically examining instructional objectives, pedagogical strategies, student learning styles, and assessment outcomes before making technological choices (Moore and Kearsley 1996; Olcott 1997b).

And for most institutions, technology investments have often been choices about taking advantage of available resources either internally or externally, without the luxury of systematically selecting technologies that best meet program and instructional needs (Duning, Van Kekerix, and Zaborowski 1993; Hardy and Olcott 1995).

Consequently, most institutions build their distance and distributed learning budgets and programs on a hybrid of resources ranging from state funding, federal grants, and corporate partnerships to cost-recovery tuition, inload teaching assignments, and technology fees for students. The result, of course, is that pedagogical and instructional design considerations have been fitted to particular technologies rather than matching technologies to meet specific, well-defined teaching and learning objectives.

This chapter will present an Integrated Technology Systems Design (ITSD) model for integrating learning technologies into individual courses based upon learning objectives, learner characteristics, and assessment outcomes. Building upon the ITSD framework (Olcott 1997b), the authors will examine the pedagogical, economic, and quality benefits of integrating various technologies into effective course design. The chapter will conclude with the authors' recommendations for implementing the ITSD model.

A Framework for Integrated Technology Systems Design (ITSD)

Given the range of available technologies today, it is useful to view ITSD from its macro applications to the present emphasis on micro applications at the course level. Olcott (1991) presented a model for delivering extended degree programs that combined traditional and distance delivery systems. Institutions design their extended degree programs by delivering blocks of courses via technology, correspondence study, off-campus face-to-face instruction, and campus-based instruction.

Olcott (1992) expanded this framework to an interinstitutional design in which multiple institutions integrate traditional and distance learning systems to deliver an extended degree program. There are several advantages to this approach to developing extended degree programs. First, it decreases dependency on a single system to deliver an extended degree program and allows institutions to maximize the use of available delivery systems. Second, it provides institutions with an expanded range of delivery options to address design, cost, and logistical factors. Finally, in the interinstitutional framework, institutions can share fiscal and human resources in designing program curriculum blocks, thereby relieving individual institutions from absorbing the total cost of program delivery.

In sum, the effectiveness of these ITSD approaches is predicated on institutions examining the pedagogical attributes of various delivery systems to meet instructional objectives and learning outcomes. Blending traditional and distance learning systems in an arbitrary manner is not synonymous with maintaining instructional quality. Systematic design and technology selection must consider pedagogical attributes for ITSD to be successful. Institutions that arbitrarily assign popular or preferential delivery systems, traditional and distance, will only create an instructional mosaic devoid of pedagogical considerations.

The micro application of ITSD involves integrating multiple delivery systems at the course level by considering instructional objectives, learning outcomes, and technological attributes that are pedagogically proven to enhance teaching and improve learning. Before we examine the pedagogical factors, costs, and logistical attributes of educational technologies, we must review what we know about effective teaching and learning.

Prerequisites to ITSD: Effective Principles of Teaching and Learning

Following each successive technology wave in this century, educators have asked themselves whether today's informational technologies would be able to surpass previous technological teaching tools in promoting learning. Back in 1984, the claim was, "Each new technological development for storing and delivering information rekindles the hope that we will increase the learning outcomes more than the 'older' media" (Clark 1984). Now, in the years since, with the advent of the Internet and digital technologies, advocates of educational technology are echoing that a new promised land of technology-infused education is at hand.

Today's information technologies are becoming ubiquitous in the marketplace and in higher education. Can these technologies really reshape how we teach and learn? And perhaps more important, how will we be able to measure how they impact teaching and learning? The place to start in examining these questions is to look at what we already know about effective teaching and learning.

Good Practice in Higher Education

Social, political, and economic factors institute change in higher education. However, recent changes in higher education are being enabled more by technological developments than by political or social forces. The very nature of this recent progression of change may be fundamentally different from previous changes in higher education. "What's different this time, however, is that the focus of change efforts is less on building new institutional structures, redefining the curriculum, or expanding access, and more on the heart of higher education — the teaching/learning process" (Angelo 1996). Such a focus on improved teaching and learning has not always been the case when change is involved in higher education. University teaching that is synonymous with traditional teaching rarely reflects a learning-centered approach. And while traditional pedagogical approaches can be cost- and time-efficient, the day has come for faculty to stop viewing teaching as "covering the content" and to instead approach teaching as "helping students learn" (Svinicki 1990).

Learning by its very nature is a complex process, and good instruction is deliberate. Although it is not easy to predict or understand human behavior, many useful psychological principles and theories exist that help us better approach teaching and learning. "In its simplest sense, to teach is to impart skills, knowledge, attitudes, and values. It involves bringing about, or at least facilitating, changes in learners" (Lefrancois 1988, 7).

The propositions that "good teachers are born, not made" and that "teachers can teach because they used to be students" are erroneous. Providing for enhanced student learning requires faculty to rejuvenate their commitment to lifelong learning and to challenge themselves as learners. Faculty face many obstacles, as Palmer (1997, 15) points out: "No matter how we devote ourselves to reading and research, teaching requires a command of content that always eludes our grasp."

Furthermore, most college faculty receive little preparation for teaching. They come to their courses armed with content knowledge but little exposure to an understanding of how learning occurs and the variables that affect learning. While content may be "king" to the professor, university-level students are there for more than just subject matter expertise. According to Chickering and Reisser (1993), college students work on seven developmental tasks: achieving intellectual, physical, and social competence; managing emotions; becoming autonomous; establishing identity; managing interpersonal relationships; clarifying purpose; and developing integrity.

Searching for a panacea on the best way to teach these diverse students is futile. There isn't one approach or methodology that exists that will teach all subjects to everyone. And reaching a consensus on good practice is highly unlikely. Someone who can really teach weaves a complex web of connections among themselves, their subject area, and their students, enabling students to weave a world for themselves (Palmer 1997). Good teachers use a variety of techniques to implement their instructional goals, teaching methods, and assessment practices.

Theoretical Contributions to Instruction

There is a body of knowledge that contains descriptive theories on how learning occurs as well as prescriptive theories that outline the steps to take to obtain certain types and amounts of learning (Ausubel 1968; Brunner 1966; Pavlov and Anrep 1927; Piaget and Inhelder 1969; Skinner 1954; Thorndike 1931; Watson 1957; Case 1985; Gagne and Briggs 1974; Vygotsky 1978). It is a common assumption that research on cognition and learning has many practical instructional implications.

The two major learning theory groups are behaviorism (theorists who are concerned with the explanation, prediction, and control of behavior) and cognitivism (theorists who are concerned with the organization of memory, information processing, and decision-making behavior). A behaviorist teacher is the information giver and stresses content presentation. Students are viewed as information receivers. From a cognitive psychologist's perspective, a teacher helps to foster student discovery of knowledge. Students are viewed as active processors of information.

Given that a typical university-based teaching experience has been conducted in a traditional face-to-face format, teaching often has leaned toward a behaviorist approach. The faculty member's role is to offer information, wisdom, and, hopefully, guidance, while the student diligently takes notes and writes papers and exams. At question is: does such teaching "... enable the student to move from a lower to higher level of understanding or abandon less efficient skills for more efficient ones?" (Demetriou 1996, 33).

However, educational research provides ample evidence that certain practices and settings foster learning. According to the psychologist Donald Norman (1993), optimal learning occurs when the instruction:

- provides a high intensity of interaction and feedback;

- has specific goals and established procedures;

- is able to motivate, promoting a continual feeling of challenge that is neither too taxing nor too easy;

- provides a sense of direct engagement, producing a feeling of directly experiencing the environment;

- provides a set of appropriate tools that fit the user and task so well that they enhance, and do not distract learning;

- avoids distractions and disruptions that intervene and destroy a subjective experience.

Additional research on the characteristics of consumate professors reflects these three themes: 1) outstanding teachers love the subjects they teach; 2) they respect and like their students; and 3) they are committed to and skilled at connecting the two things they care deeply about—their subject matter and their students (Carson 1996). The challenge is to take these findings and put them into instructional practice.

Creating effective learning that is based on empirical evidence requires time and the willingness to experiment. Additionally, the notion that summative evaluation — in the form of decision making with respect to reappointment, promotion, tenure, and compensation — is the means by which instructional improvement occurs (Keig and Waggoner 1999) has often kept faculty members from seeking new methods to improve their teaching.

Pedagogy in the New Teaching Environment

Few incentives have existed for faculty to explore ways to vary instructional delivery. The assumption is made that if you are tenured, then you can teach. Time to critique and collaborate with others about teaching activities is seldom created. Add informational technologies to the instructional palette and faculty may feel very perplexed in justifying how they and their students can benefit from learning to use new technology. "The proposal to a successful professional educator that he or she needs to learn new media for teaching and scholarship implies that the old way was somehow inadequate, insufficient, or not optimal: a potential threat to self-concept" (Cravener 1998).

But staying with the "old way" may preclude a faculty member from achieving the recommended research-based practices in college teaching. According to Chickering and Reisser (1993), the best practices in undergraduate education include:

- encouraging student/faculty contact;
- encouraging cooperation among students;
- encouraging active learning; giving prompt feedback;
- emphasizing time on task;
- communicating high expectations;
- respecting diverse talents and ways of learning.

Thus, we want to create learning that promotes students learning by themselves, learning from others, spending less time overall with faculty, but spending more creative, focused time with faculty. Students engaged with powerful interactive technologies can readily experience the type of education that best promotes thinking. Their ability to do so rests in a faculty member's ability to create student-centered learning environments.

Faculty who have an interest in pedagogy over technology will be the ones leading the way in technology-enhanced learning. Both faculty and students will need to invest time to learn how to use new technologies, just as they have in the past. But we must remember as we move forward into the new millennium that the focus should be on the learner and ways to foster active, constructive student participation. The learning should be designed to promote information integration and transfer and interactions. It should also help students see connections between what is taught and the world beyond the classroom.

An awareness of the profound changes these new learning technologies can make on teaching and learning is beginning. No longer can educators shut the door and teach. Because of the sheer amount of information available in today's world and the societal explosion of information technologies, educators are forced to examine the assumption that technology is the choice of the teacher, a luxury for a student and not a necessity (Welsh 1997).

Some universities experimenting with distance delivery and new learning technologies are touting distance learning as a tool for faculty development (Filipczak 1995). Educators are sharing tales from the instructional technological frontier, and it is not uncommon to find stories of their realizations that the new learning environments are causing them to question conventional instructional methods and course design.

One seasoned professor describing his first encounter with distance learning delivery writes: "The traditional style of presentation of sequential lectures stumbled over the nonlinear communications, relational concept structures, and real-time interactivity that are encouraged by new technologies" (Alley 1996, 51). Alley goes on to list (1996, 52) the eight primary areas in which he found that expertise is needed to redesign courses. Professors need to:

- understand the role of motivation in learning;
- assess and use students' prior learning;
- inventory students' learning styles;
- understand the nature of learning processes and how to best fit learning styles;
- use collaborative/cooperative learning;
- use problem-based learning;
- assess course and student outcomes;
- know how to use instructional technologies.

Careful consideration must be given to the above tasks before one ever selects the technology. Given that people have a natural capacity to learn, we need to develop instruction that goes beyond measuring learning by seat-time and by how the learning is delivered. Technology should not be selected just because it is new and available. How can we best employ alternative teaching styles, integrate knowledge of the students and their learning needs, and assess learning for deeper understanding if we start first with media selection?

Technology does not make the instruction. Rather, it enables the instructor to teach based on the needs of students and to engage and motivate them with relevant content and course objectives. However, advances in technology are providing the means for education to be more constructive and collaborative by promoting multi-modal representations of knowledge, interface designs that encourage interactivity and ease of use, and tools that readily enable communication.

The general principles of effective teaching and learning outlined in the previous section provide the demarcation point from which to assess the technology landscape and develop ITSD at the course level. Figure 12.1, ITSD Implementation and Selection Factors, summarizes the pedagogical, cost, logistical, and design and assessment attributes of video, computer, and audio delivery systems.

The factors outlined in figure 12.1 demonstrate the complexity of designing individual courses by selecting and integrating multiple technologies (Olcott 1995; Olcott 1997b). The number of factors to consider is immense, and there is no "silver-bullet" formula to simplify the process. Yet the optimum design strategy must be selected to balance quality, access, and costs (Western Cooperative for Educational Telecommunications 1995).

While a great deal of college teaching is information giving, good instruction requires refined teaching skills that motivate, question, and evaluate — skills that often must be planned and then arranged in instructional sequencing. Using a systematic approach to teaching helps an instructor to understand and evaluate the various components of instructional delivery and highlights where an instructor can most effectively use his or her scholarly expertise.

By using a rational course development approach, faculty can select instructional methods that release them from merely

Table 12.1
ITSD Implementation and Selection Factors

Delivery Systems	Pedagogical Attributes	Costs and Support Services	Instructional Design and Assessment
Video	• Replicates traditional classroom • Connects audio and video interaction • Visual components are normative for most students, but immediate feedback is restricted • Learning objectives can be demonstrated, and students can observe what they have to do and at what proficiency level • Selected use of video allows for integration of other media, such as audio, Internet, Web, print, and fax. • Video systems cannot serve unlimited numbers of students, particularly for multiple sites. There is a limit on the number of students.	• Video systems are costly and often require additional expenditures for upgrading and maintenance • Multiple sites require extensive coordination of instructional and student support services • Downlink or receive sites require fiscal and physical resources for delivery • Students are placebound; video systems are not mobile nor asynchronous • Video systems require numerous personnel on campus and at sites. • Live video cannot be delivered anytime or anywhere. It is time and location restricted. • High cost of video systems often means institutions must charge fees/increase tuition	• Typical lecture format is transferred to video teaching. Instructional design is often given minimal consideration, and assessment relies on traditional pencil-and-paper tests • Video requires extensive training for faculty, technicians, and site coordinator • Tendency for assessment to be arbitrary rather than tied directly to instructional goals and objectives • Live, observable assessment is cost prohibitive • Many faculty are not comfortable with being on television. • Reliance on video sessions limits innovative integration of supplemental media in design
Computer	• Anytime/anywhere access by students • Asynchronous interaction between student-instructor and student- student • Internet, Web, print, audiotapes and videotapes, can be easily integrated into instructional package • Can serve greater numbers of students, but not unlimited numbers of students	• Hardware and software costs are moderate and can simultaneously be used for on-campus instruction. • Online student service models are still in their infancy and yet can provide "one-stop shopping" for students • Minimum restrictions due to time, place, and space. Computer costs are declining.	• Instructional design and assessment are labor intensive • Online assessment is relatively new and requires close alignment of objectives to outcomes • Assumes both student and faculty literacy with computers and software applications

Table 12.1

ITSD Implementation and Selection Factors

Delivery Systems	Pedagogical Attributes	Costs and Support Services	Instructional Design and Assessment
Computer (cont'd.)	• Worldwide geographical scope • Web creates unlimited access to learning resources • Instructional quality of online courses is suspect in the eyes of many faculty and administrators • Immediate feedback to students	• Faculty must spend more time directing students to resources than preparing for didactic delivery of content • Security issues for access and testing • Asynchronous delivery allows faculty to spend time on other activities, such as research.	• Extensive training for faculty and orientation for students • Similar to most distributed learning systems; students must be highly motivated and self-directed learners • Competency-based assessment can provide valid and reliable feedback to students
Audio	• Effective for communicating basic information and knowledge in synchronous and asynchronous venues. • Easy to use by faculty and students • Can serve many students • Repetition and feedback for students can be immediate • Can be supplemented by print, Web, chat rooms, and videotapes • Lacks visual learning component	• Low cost • Mobile and not restricted by time or space • Coordination of student services requires systematic planning and development • Faculty can teach from home, hotel room, even their car • Minimal training for faculty and students • Faculty must develop picture boards of students to facilitate interaction and give direct feedback to specific students at all sites	• Lack of visual component requires creative instructional design • Observable assessment is difficult, resulting in reliance on traditional paper-and-pencil tests for all students • Alternative assessment approaches can be used to compensate for lack of visual venue • Faculty must be animated and creative to retain student attention and interest

being information givers so that they can become facilitators of student learning who are capable of altering instructional practice based on student outcomes and needs. Faculty members who engage in thinking about all aspects of the teaching/learning cycle are able to move beyond the self-absorption that focuses on their purposes and activities and can instead begin to think about the learners.

Effective Course Design

With the current prevalence of learning technologies and the realization that it is fruitless to use these technologies simply to replicate traditional instruction, a linking of pedagogical practice with technological capabilities is part of instructional planning. "At the least, substantial affinity exists between newer pedagogical emphases and the capabilities of learning technologies; it is likely that the sum of the two will be greater than either aspect alone" (Batson and Bass 1996, 43).

Any good course design begins with selecting student objectives: why is this material being taught, and what should students be expected to know and do at the end of instruction? Some professors object to rigorously examining their courses by narrowly defining student behaviors into measurable, observable behavior. They contend that intellectual growth is intangible and that it may take years to measure what students have learned. However, course objectives perform three important functions by (Kemp, Morrison, and Ross 1994):

- guiding the instructional process;
- providing a framework for evaluation and assessment;
- guiding the learner.

Most of us can remember courses in which we were not sure what the course was about — and then the instructor further compounded our frustrations by lecturing on one thing and testing on another. The best way to avoid such pitfalls is to begin by delineating curricular outcomes and planning accordingly for instructional sequences and assessment. When the focus is on the learner, developing clear, unambiguous goals and objectives that help students understand precisely what is expected is the way to begin course design.

In addition to focusing on the learner and learning outcomes, course design involves instructional analysis and developing an instructional strategy. Empirically derived criteria and checklists of good practice in undergraduate education are available (Chickering and Gamson 1991). Good teaching includes the use of highly interactive instructional methodologies. A decision has to be made to select an appropriate medium of instruction. Begin by examining the instructional situation and then decide which characteristics of the medium make it most appropriate for the instructional requirements. Teachers of today have access to powerful instructional tools to provide varied learning experiences.

Pedagogical, Cost, and Logistical Characteristics of Learning Technologies: An ITSD Case Study

One way to incorporate these technological wonders that can enhance teaching and learning is to employ the ITSD framework (Olcott 1997b). By using the ITSD as a guide, it is possible to design courses that integrate sound pedagogical practice enhanced by today's informational technology tools.

In the ITSD matrix below (figure 12.2) is an example of a graduate level instructional systems design course based on a fifteen-week semester timeline. In the matrix, only a single objective for each week is included. The intention here isn't to provide explicit detail for a particular course, but rather to illustrate the ITSD process.

These are the overall course objectives:

- Students will be able to describe and demonstrate knowledge of the different components of a systematic design process, their rationales, and their uses.

- Students will be able to design instructional modules using a systematic design process.

- Students will be able to identify, compare, and contrast design modules applied in a variety of settings.

Recommendations for Practice

ITSD provides institutions and faculty members with a responsive strategy for blending educational technologies into cost-effective, pedagogically effective course delivery packages. The following recommendations (Olcott 1997b, 67) are designed to assist institutions in implementing this process:

- Conduct an inventory of existing technology systems. Are they cost-effective? Do they demonstrate high instructional quality?

- Assess whether resource (human and fiscal) allocations could be expanded to include a range of other technologies for institutional outreach. It is important to underscore that demonstrating cost-effectiveness and instructional quality is good rhetoric and yet difficult to achieve in practice.

- Apply hypothetical applications of ITSD to existing outreach programs to assess pedagogical, economical, logistical, and practical delivery factors. How can other technologies be integrated into these programs effectively without diminishing program quality?

- Assess and modify institutional policies that are barriers to asynchronous delivery modes. Many institutions require seat-time or clock hours, which are difficult to assess when students are using the Internet, the World Wide Web, or independent study.

- Develop a comprehensive ITSD faculty training program that provides faculty with the knowledge and skills to design instruction utilizing multiple technologies. Instructional designers, continuing education specialists, and technical personnel who comprise the faculty member's design team also should receive this training.

Figure 12.2
ITSD Course Design Matrix

Week	Objectives	Student Performance	Pedagogy/Learning Theory	Technology	Cost
1	Examine how learning theory perspectives have influenced instructors own philosophy of education	Baseline knowledge paper	Assessing student's prior knowledge	Presentation software to present content on principles of teaching and learning	Low/Moderate
2	Identify the phases of ITSD	Quiz	Monitoring student understanding and progress	Paper/pen	Low
3	Create a matrix for needs assessment data collection	Matrix or checklist	Providing an opportunity for active student practice	Computer software or paper	Low/Moderate
4	Conduct a learner analysis and write a description of the learners	Team exercise	Creating a spontaneous discussion for student problem solving and reasoning	Videoconference with a classroom site	High
5	Label the component elements for the given behavioral objectives	Exercise	Assessing discipline-specific learning	Paper/pen	Low
6	Compare and contrast the ITSD process in an educational setting with one in an industrial setting	Participation in electronic chat with practitioners in the field and classmates	Encouraging student to participate actively with classmates and with professionals; increases the feeling of community within the class	Electronic chat room	Low/Moderate
7	Record in a journal perceptions/insights on class content	Journal to instructor	Providing student reflections upon his or her own learning processes	E-mail	Low
8	Describe the instructional events found in a typical lesson	Descriptive write-up and response to a classmate's write up	Reminding student of previous learned materials and providing an opportunity for curriculum content to develop as a group resource	Electronic bulletin board for a threaded discussion response	Low/Moderate

Figure 12.2
ITSD Course Design Matrix

Week	Objectives	Student Performance	Pedagogy/Learning Theory	Technology	Cost
9	Analyze the factors in a given learning environment	Participation in discussion and paper response	Encouraging student to acquire meaning on the basis of experience	Videotape of various learning environments	Moderate
10	In groups, select and research instructional design as applied to a particular setting	Outline of topic/presentation	Promoting collaborative learning for which meaning is derived from multiple perspectives	Application-sharing environment (sharing more than text messages)	Low/Moderate
11	In groups, present/teach instructional design topic	Presentation by small groups to whole class	Providing instructional feedback through peer and instructor review	Presentation software and Internet connection	Low/Moderate
12	Compare formative and summative evaluation purposes and procedures	Written assignment	Assessing disciplinessspecific learning	Word processing	Low
13	Locate and evaluate three Web sites on ITSD	Review of information provided at these Web sites	Improving student analytical skills	World Wide Web	Low
14	With a peer, critique each other's individual modules/assignments	Oral and written critique	Recognizing the student who self-questions and self-explains often performs more competently and show greater understanding	Paper/pen	Low
15	Present individual module/unit assignment	Individual instructional module	Fostering student sharing of class learning experience	Presentation software, Internet connection, handouts	Low/Moderate

- Invite campus faculty who have expertise in the field of human learning and instruction to assist in the development of the training program. ITSD is about teaching and learning rather than about technology.

This chapter has provided the essential building blocks one needs to design a comprehensive ITSD training program for faculty. Here is a summary of key elements that should be included in this program:

- General principles of effective teaching and learning in concert with the pedagogical advantages and limitations of video, audio, computer, and print delivery systems.

- Review of cost and support service factors for selecting and integrating various technologies to meet specified learning objectives.

- Differentiated assessment models that are directly aligned with sound instructional design strategies to achieve learning objectives. If we support the premise that students have different learning styles and preferences, then similarly they would probably have different testing preferences. The implication is that even at the course level, students would have alternative assessment choices that they could select consistent with their preferred learning style.

- Hands-on experimentation with different technologies, learning objectives, and outcomes to allow faculty to design integrative models of multiple technologies that demonstrate pedagogical, economic, and logistical effectiveness.

Implications for Future Research

Integrated Technology Systems Design (ITSD) is still very much in its infancy. The increasing range of available technologies suggests that empirical investigations will be critical for its success.

Here are a few of the important research questions that will need further study:

- What are the optimum technology integration models that demonstrate improvements in teaching and learning? Which models maintain instructional quality, are easily accessible to students, and are cost-effective?

- How do we measure the composite effects of using multiple technologies for teaching and learning? What are the implications of ITSD on instructional design approaches for integrating multiple technologies?

- What instruments must be developed to assess combined uses of synchronous and asynchronous delivery systems? What new assessment frameworks must be developed to measure student learning using ITSD?

- What disciplines and content lend themselves to ITSD applications? Why?

Summary

Integrated Technology Systems Design (ITSD) provides institutions with an outreach and campus strategy for harnessing a wide range of available technologies to design and deliver instruction. At the same time, ITSD is a viable approach to systematically assessing pedagogical, economic, and logistical factors to develop an optimum balance between access, cost, and quality.

There are several prerequisites faculty need to meet to effectively employ ITSD approaches. First, faculty must be given comprehensive training in 1) effective teaching strategies; 2) instructional design and assessment; 3) pedagogical attributes of video, audio, computer, and print media; and 4) the economic and logistical (support service) attributes of integrating various technologies. Moreover, faculty must be encouraged to be innovative, to experiment, to subsequently gather data on integrating media for instruction, and to identify effective attributes for specific learning and outcome objectives.

Olcott (1997b, 67-68) summarizes the potential advantages of ITSD:

> The strength of ITSD is that it creates the catalyst for faculty and support personnel in the distance-learning enterprise to critically examine how the synergistic blending of technologies operates in pedagogically effective ways. Empirical research using ITSD is still in its infancy, partially because the Internet and World Wide Web did not exist until recently, and partially because the field had not evolved to the point where lower-end technologies had reached a level of acceptance as viable teaching systems.
>
> Today, the technology landscape has undergone major transformations, and what has emerged is a range of technological options inconceivable even five years ago. The question is whether we take advantage of these tools before our competitors do.

Our competitors are, in fact, already exploring how to build instructional programs using multiple technologies. The ubiquitous use of learning technologies means that there will be more students with more choices in the future. Institutions will have unprecedented competition from existing and new providers who are expanding their technology-based programs.

Moreover, all providers will reexamine their academic calendar structures, student support services, and faculty incentives to create responsive delivery models for serving students anytime, anywhere, in accelerated time frames, and through both asynchronous and synchronous modalities.

Competition, however, is not a sound enough reason to adopt integrative approaches to technology if it means diminishing the overall quality and richness of the teaching and learning process. ITSD has the potential to create models that build on the best attributes of effective teaching, new technologies, instructional design and assessment, and efficient costing approaches. These challenges will be worth the effort for creating optimum uses of technology for students, by faculty, in the university of the new millenium.

REFERENCES

Alley, Lee R. 1996. An instructional epiphany. *Change*: 49-54.

Angelo, Thomas A. 1996. *Seven shifts and seven levers: Developing more productive learning communities.* [Website]. The National Teaching and Learning Forum. Available from http://www.ntlf.com/html/pi/9612/sev_lev.htm.

Ausubel, David P. 1968. *Educational psychology: A cognitive view.* New York: Holt Rinehart and Winston.

Batson, Trent, and Randy Bass. 1996. Teaching and learning in the computer age. *Change*: 42-47.

Brunner, Jerome S. 1966. *Toward a theory of instruction.* Cambridge: Harvard University Press.

Carson, Barbara Harrell. 1996. Thirty years of stories: The professor's place in student memories. *Change* 28(6): 11-17.

Case, Robbie. 1985. *Intellectual development: Birth to adulthood.* Orlando, FL: Academic Press.

Chickering, Arthur W., and Zelda Gamson. 1991. *Seven principles for good practice in undergraduate education.* San Francisco, CA: Jossey-Bass, Publishers.

Chickering, Arthur W., and Linda Reisser. 1993. *Education and identity.* 2nd ed. San Francisco, CA: Jossey-Bass, Publishers.

Clark, Richard E. 1984. Learning from computers: Theoretical problems. Paper presented at the Annual Meeting of the American Educational Research Association, New Orleans, 23-27 April, 1984.

Cravener, Patricia. 1998. *Faculty development programs: Teaching professional educators to drink from the fire hose* [Website]. Paper published in the proceedings of the NAU/Web.98 Conference: In the Footsteps of Web Pioneers, May. Available from http://www.cravener.net/articles/pioneers.htm.

Demetriou, A. 1996. Outline for a development theory of cognitive change: General principles and educational implications. *The School Field* 7:7-41.

Duning, Becky S., Marvin J. Van Kekerix, and Leon M. Zaborowski. 1993. *Reaching learners through telecommunications: Management and leadership strategies for higher education.* San Francisco: Jossey-Bass, Publishers.

Filipczak, Bob. 1995. Putting the learning into distance learning. *Training*: 111-117.

Gagne, Robert Mills, and Leslie J. Briggs. 1974. *Principles of instructional design*. New York: Holt Rinehart and Winston.

Hanna, Donald E. 1998. Higher education in an era of digital competition: Emerging organizational models. *JALN* 2 (1):

Hardy, Darcy Walsh, and Donald John Olcott, Jr. 1995. Audioconferencing and the adult learner: Strategies for effective practice. The American Journal of Distance Education 9(1): 44-59.

Keig, Larry, and Michael D. Waggoner. 1999. *Collaborative peer review: The role of faculty in improving college*. [Website]. Available from http://www.ntlf.com/html/lib/bib/94-2dig.htm.

Kemp, Jerrold E., Gary R. Morrison, and Steven M. Ross. 1994. *Designing effective instruction*. New York: Merrill.

Lefrancois, Guy R. 1988. *Psychology for teaching*. 6th ed. Belmont, CA: Wadsworth.

Mayadas, A. Frank. 1997. Asynchronous learning networks: New possibilities. In *The Learning Revolution: The Challenge of Information Technology in the Academy*, edited by Diana G. Oblinger and Sean C. Rush. Bolton, MA: Anker Publishing Company, Inc.

Moore, Michael G., and Greg Kearsley. 1996. *Distance education: A system's view*. Belmont, CA: Wadsworth.

Moore, Michael G., and Melody M. Thompson. 1998. *The effects of distance learning: A summary of the literature; ACSDE Research Monograph*. University Park, PA: The American Center for the Study of Distance Education.

Norman, Donald. 1993. *Things that make us smart: Defending human attributes in the age of the machine*. Reading, MA: Addison-Wesley.

Oblinger, Diana G., and Sean C. Rush. 1997. The learning revolution. In *The Learning Revolution: The Challenge of Information Technology in the Academy*, edited by Diana G. Oblinger and Sean C. Rush. Bolton, MA: Anker Publishing Company, Inc.

Olcott, Donald John, Jr. 1991. Bridging the gap: Distance learning and academic policy. *Continuing Higher Education Review* 55(1&2): 49-60.

Olcott, Donald John, Jr. 1992. Policy issues in statewide delivery of university programs by telecommunications. *The American Journal of Distance Education* 6(1): 14-26.

Olcott, Donald John, Jr. 1995. Building and managing the distance education capabilities of your organization. In *AT&T Training Manual*. University Park, PA: Department of Continuing and Distance Education, Pennsylvania State University.

Olcott, Donald John, Jr. 1997a. Renewing the vision: Past perspectives and future implications for distance education. *The Journal of Continuing Higher Education* 45(3): 2-13.

Olcott, Donald John, Jr. 1997b. Transforming university outreach: Integrated technology systems design for the twenty-first century. *Journal of Public Service and Outreach* 2(3): 55-69.

Palmer, Parker J. 1997. The heart of a teacher: Identity and integrity in teaching. *Change* 29:15-21.

Pavlov, Ivan Petrovich, and Gleb Vasil evich Anrep. 1927. *Conditioned reflexes: an investigation of the physiological activity of the cerebral cortex.* London: Oxford University Press: Humphrey Milford.

Piaget, Jean, and Barbel Inhelder. 1969. *The psychology of the child.* New York: Basic Books.

Skinner, B.F. 1954. The science of learning and the art of teaching. *Harvard Educational Review* 24: 86-97.

Svinicki, Marilla D. 1990. *The changing face of college teaching.* San Francisco, CA: Jossey-Bass, Publishers.

Thorndike, Edward L. 1931. *Human learning.* New York, London: Century Co.

Vygotsky, Lev S. 1978. *Mind and society: Development of higher psychological processes.* Cambridge, MA: Harvard University Press.

Watson, John B. 1957. *Behaviorism.* Revised ed. Chicago: University of Chicago Press.

Welsh, Thomas. 1997. From multimedia to multiple-media: Designing computer-based course materials for the computer age. *TechTrends* 42(1): 17-21.

Western Cooperative for Educational Telecommunications. 1995. *Balancing access, quality, and costs.* Boulder, CO: Western Interstate Commission for Higher Education (WICHE) Project, funded by the Fund for the Improvement of Postsecondary Education (FIPSE).

Chapter 13

Learning and the Web:
Reflections on Assessment

By Gary Brown

Science is built up of facts, as a house is with stones. But a collection of facts is no more a science than a heap of stones is a house. — *Jules Henri Poincare (1854-1912)*

Nuts and Bolts and Assessing Technology

Halio's (1990) article reporting that students who wrote with Macintosh computers wrote better than students who wrote with IBMs reflected our assessment efforts at the outset of the decade the way a fun house mirror reflects our mocking faces. She provided a case study on the pitfalls of research on learning with technology, particularly the pitfalls associated with research that embraces the spirit of the comparative methodology but neglects the critical substance and rigorous methods essential for such comparisons. Halio was taken to task by several composition scholars who rightly pointed out that Halio's methodology failed to identify the different word processing software, obvious differences in instruction, clear differences in population samples, and, most important, reasonable criteria for writing quality (Slatin et al. 1990). For example, the differences in software interfaces, these critics argued, is certainly more telling than the name brand of the computer. For a comparison to be meaningful, we need to have a clear understanding of the salient features that shape the comparison. Identifying meaningful variables is a considerable challenge, however. After all, had Halio identified the particular features of the different interfaces used in her study, those interfaces would no doubt have been obsolete by the time the study made it to press.

This is not to say research focusing on the technology and interface design is impossible or unimportant. And consumer-oriented evaluations (Scriven 1974) can be adapted to examine these and other product features. Yet assessment of new technologies, even technical assessment, requires more than a superficial conceptualization that accommodates the transitory nature of technologies that are changing more often than most of us change our car's oil.

Among the more technically oriented approaches to assessment, information processing research, largely neglected by educators, may be the most viable avenue for informing Web design. Information processing research bypasses the issue of changing technologies because the research focuses on the predictable functions of our eyes, ears, and brains — the interstices between human and media interaction.

For instance, one avenue of information processing research examines the valence of an image (Bradley et al. 1992). Valence refers to the emotional response a picture elicits. A smiling infant, for example, has a positive valence. A gun barrel pointed at the viewer has a negative valence. Information processing researchers measure, in turn, the ways those images influence what subjects notice and what they learn. For example, Bradley et al. (1992) found that a particularly gruesome, provocative image, though it would be remembered by subjects later, may also wash out students' recall of the preceding material or mask the information that follows. Equally fascinating and useful for instructional designers, Bradley et al. found that highly arousing pictures tend to be retained longer. Faster pacing of a message may correlate with a viewer's increased attention to the message, but often at the expense of recall of complex material (Reeves and et al. 1985). The body of information processing research suggests that there is much we can do with the images and animations that will help students recall messages[1], but learning is, *or at least should be*, more than just information retrieval.

From Recall to the Content Frenzy

The focus of most information processing research on the way the brain *automatically* responds to discrete message features, necessarily relies on cued or free recall. The assessment challenge for those who examine the integration of the Web and learning, however, calls for a different focus. Assessment of the instructional use of the Web should have less to do with how subjects automatically respond to content features and more to do with students' *considered* use of that content. The educational challenge is not to assess the way students respond to stimuli, but to assess learning — the conscious cultivation of habits and enthusiasm for ongoing skill development, and the changes in behavior associated with an expanded perspective and comprehension resulting from the acquisition, synthesis, and generation of new information or knowledge. Though there is certainly room to quibble with the complexity of the preceding definition of learning, educators need to agree that learning, however defined, is substantially more complex than recall.

Dissemination of the complexity of the educational enterprise is further challenged as higher education becomes more visible to the public, who call, understandably, for accountability. The message of accountability, however, is invariably reduced to test scores and other measures that do not adequately represent the intricacies of teaching and learning (House 1993). Both visibility and calls for accountability increase with growing competition in the education *market* (Blumenstyk 1999; Marchese 1998) made possible by new technologies and the World Wide Web.

With the rush to the market, however, there has emerged an additional complication. Now even educators scrambling to find a niche as "content providers" talk of the "quality" of Web materials, as if the quality of Web content and design were synony-

---

1   For an accessible summary of much of this work, see *The Media Equation* by Byron Reeves and Clifford Naas (1996).

mous with the quality of instruction and learning. For example, Brahler (1999) and her colleagues argue that for Web-based, computer-assisted instruction, "development time increases as the learning goals for the materials ascend Bloom's learning taxonomy..." The assertion implies that learning happens in the complexity of the material rather than in the mind of the learner. A book, it must follow, since it is not a complex technology, can be associated only with the most simplistic, lower levels of learning.

Similar assumptions often lurk in calls for peer-reviewed Websites, under the supposition that a good instructor's mediation and fostering of critical thinking requires content that has the blessings of an editorial board (which is not to suggest that peer-reviewed Websites for other purposes are necessarily a bad idea).

The most insidious example of the migration of learning from the minds of students to mechanisms of delivery is observable in the factory model approach to course *conversion.* The common approach for *converting* a course from the classroom and books to the Web is often accompanied by the assumption that such transformation makes an online course complete. And most Web-based courses look like they've been punched out of a similar mold: they present text, a few images, perhaps an interactive graph or two and the audio track from part of a lecture, and then a test that is more and more often automated. The Web is increasingly populated with volumes of such *stuff.* The beauty of the *spill, drill, and grill* approach to instruction is that it is purportedly cost-effective, in part because it can be teacher-proofed — with faculty relegated to the role of *content experts.*

The complexity of the notion that an online course may also require students to interact with that stuff, other students, and faculty who skillfully mediate the interaction is oddly left out of the equation. The general notion that we can build "sound tools" to deliver quality "content" and provide quality education drastically reduces the notion of teaching, perpetuates simplistic measures of accountability, and ignores the lessons we should have learned from identical assertions that go back at least as far as the early 1960s, when pundits asserted that educational television would transform education by providing "near perfect content every time" (Hill 1961, 41).

The growing number of education providers, unlike the largely commercial television explosion of the '60s, when educational television was consigned to the remote, fuzzy end of the bandwidth, has important implications for assessment. Education now confronts significant commercial competition. Students have been designated *consumers*. The corporate tax base from property tax revenues that support education has dropped by about 30 percent over the last forty years, and the trend shows no signs of reversing (Berliner 1996). Consequently, the challenge of illuminating the public's perception of the complexity of teaching and learning and responding to reasonable requests for accountability falls more heavily than ever on the shoulders of the assessment community and the communication of that assessment to its numerous constituencies (House 1993).

To understand the implications of the reduction of learning to outcomes of measurable recall, and to thereby grapple with the multifaceted challenges and opportunities for evaluation and assessment, it is necessary to examine the manifestations of those implications in our traditional classrooms.

Stifled Students

An extensive observational study of twenty classes by Nunn (1996) found that typically, students participate less than 2.28 percent of the time in traditional classes. Class sizes or formats, including formats designated as discussion based, did not significantly alter the findings. In conclusion, the author asks, "Why is a sizable group of students unwilling to describe participation taking place as worthwhile?" And "What reasons do students give for participating in discussion or for remaining silent?" (Nunn 1996, 262).

A study at Grinnell College (Trosset 1998) answers these questions. Most of the two hundred students in the Grinnell study reported feeling silenced. They did not value discussion as a mode of intellectual exploration. They would be unlikely to listen to someone with whom they disagreed. They have a right "to think or say whatever they like without challenge" (Trosset

1998, 48). They believe that knowledge comes exclusively from personal experience. Their responses reflect a clear belief that what students think is more important than how they have come to think it. Finally, further refuting the contentions of developmental theorists, the Grinnell study found no evidence that students changed their views over the course of their education.

That students do not value exploring ideas from multiple perspectives, learning from outside experience, or refining their own capacity to weigh evidence and reason is a complex and problematic outgrowth of education and the relationship of education to the culture. It is not reasonable to attribute students' disengagement to any particular aspect of educational practice. Nonetheless, it is hard to ignore the striking parallel between Trosset's findings that students have reduced the value of academic interaction with the public's conterminous notions of educational accountability. And it is, therefore, irresponsible to ignore the contribution of current evaluation practice to these phenomena and to fail to recognize the potential in evaluation practice for addressing it.

From Evaluation Practice to Disengagement

Last fall, I asked twelve students in my graduate Program Evaluation course what grades they hoped to earn in the course and on what criteria they expected their grades to be based. It was not a surprise to find that all of the students expected to earn A's. It *was* a surprise to see their grading criteria. Only one student noted that demonstration of creativity would provide evidence to support his grade. The rest of the class identified criteria that reflected nothing more than the logistics of class management — attendance, completion of assignments, participation in discussions. No one identified quality of work produced or the quality of their participation. When I pointed out to the class the lack of any criteria referencing quality, none of the students was surprised. One student observed, "You asked us how we should be graded, not what we expected to learn."

The student made a clear point. In the contemporary academic climate, even in the heart of the enterprise — graduate courses in educational evaluation — grades are not equated with the quality of student performance or learning.

This is not news. There is persuasive evidence that traditional tests and grades are neither valid nor reliable (Milton, Pollio, and Eison 1986; Pascarella and Terenzini 1991). The extent to which grades fail to reflect learning represents one of the primary challenges to researchers who hope to establish direct connections from an instructional innovation to increases in student learning. Yet the problem is even deeper.

A recent study by Wright and colleagues (1998) illustrates the point (and an innovative approach to addressing the challenge as well). A number of faculty were asked to interview students who had recently completed one of two distinct approaches to instruction in chemistry — the traditional lecture-based course or an active, collaborative-learning-based course. The faculty who interviewed the students developed their own criteria. Further, they did not know which of the two courses the students had taken. Even those conducting the ratings, who maintain excellent reputations as lecturers, identified the students from the active and collaborative course as significantly better prepared than students who had attended the lectures. More to the point, on the traditional tests used by the faculty in the study, there was no significant difference between the two groups. The traditional exam failed to capture qualities that faculty who designed and used those exams (and the interviews) clearly valued.

Though tests and grades do not necessarily reflect what faculty most value, what instructors choose to evaluate and how they go about evaluating it nonetheless says otherwise. As Cross (1996) observes, "If you want more of something, measure it." What our measurements get, illustrated by my students' empty evaluation criteria, is the perception of the academic primacy of inert content and, in graduate courses, academic manners rather than substance — the advanced stages of the virulent disengagement evidenced at Grinnell.

The Grinnell study reveals that students' disengagement has its roots in student identities that are derived from *what* they think rather than *how* they think. It is also reasonable to conclude that evaluation and assessment practice that focuses on what students think and ignores the processes yielding that thinking contributes to their disengagement. Evaluation and assessment practice, therefore, needs to include strategies that value *how* students think as well as *what* they think.

Ironically, to the extent that traditional education practice has already succumbed to academic somnambulism, then the concern that new technologies and online learning spell doom to the quality of education (Noble 1999) rings rather hollow. In fact, the enthusiasm the Web has precipitated coincides with increased calls for scrutiny. That attention to assessment has opened a window of opportunity for substantively and philosophically reinvigorating the role of assessment in shaping learning. To understand the possibilities, consider what we can learn from what the World Wide Web has already done.

The World Wide Web and Expanding Opportunities

Paul Dourish, a senior research scientist at Apple Research Labs, has observed that "people are most definitely not doing the things which the Internet was originally designed to do, moving large volumes of data around, getting remote access to supercomputer facilities, or whatever ... They're not connecting to other computers, but to other people" (Crow, Parsowith, and Bowden Wise 1999). Bill Condon's (Condon 1998) observation converges with Dourish's when he says: "The age of information is over. It's the age of interaction." With this new emphasis on communication and interaction, as Dourish says: "New media spaces provide more than just a reflection of the workplace, creating a new and different channel for other sorts of interactions, increasing both the opportunities and the range of interactive possibilities."

Unfortunately, as Glaser and Silver (1994, 394) observe: "Testing and assessment, as they have been institutionalized in contemporary educational systems, represent the product of earnest attempts of prior generations to meet the conditions of earlier times." But for evaluators who recognize the paradigm shifting, this combination of failing conventions and new, technology-enabled opportunities reflects a kind of möbius confluence. The very heart of the objections to new technologies that critics have held — based on a perceived lack of human interaction — is precisely what the World Wide Web and the Internet may best bring to instruction. The current paucity of that interaction and student engagement with faculty, with the content, and with each other in traditional classes, regardless of the configuration, again suggests that new approaches to education present opportunities to reinvigorate the active, engaged aspects of education that educators value.

Expanding Assessment

To establish an assessment agenda for the Web that optimizes its potential, it is important to articulate the distinction between *evaluation* and *assessment*. Usage has blurred the formal distinction between the terms, but for the purposes of this discussion, *evaluation* refers to the way faculty judge or grade students. *Assessment*, by contrast, refers to systematic efforts to determine the impact of the teaching and learning effort, which includes evaluation strategies. The general synonymous usage of the terms reflects more than semantic quibbling. It reflects a perceptual muddying. Educators' often rigorous reliance on *evaluation* measures is often at the expense of assessment that might better inform and ultimately improve the outcomes of the instruction. Faculty evaluation of student performance in courses, in other words, tends to be used summatively. Assessment, properly conducted, includes formative strategies.

To illustrate how assessment can improve instruction, consider Angelo and Cross's (1993) work with the Teaching Goals Inventory, which confirms that most faculty want their students to do more than recall inert facts. Angelo and Cross have assessed the goals of more than two thousand faculty and demonstrated that, in spite of interesting disciplinary distinctions among goal distribution and secondary goals, most faculty in higher education consistently identify higher-order thinking as one of the most important of their goals.

However, there is evidence that those goals are rarely reflected in faculty syllabi or in their exams. In a recent formative analysis of twenty-three general education syllabi from courses representing a variety of sizes, disciplines, and instructional approaches (some of which were partially Web based), Henschied (1999) found only one course that identified for students what the instructor hoped they would learn from the course.

In fact, the organization of most Web courses is consolidated so that the application of such a congruency analysis can be done in a relatively straightforward manner. Extending and complementing Henscheid's work with the Teaching Goals Inventory, Henderson and Brown (1999) assessed three online business courses and found few of the course assignments matched faculty goals. There was also little evidence that faculty's evaluation methods — traditional exams — called for more than recall. One of the three courses included activities designed to encourage student/student and student/faculty interaction. The other assignments in all three courses, though they might be construed to require higher-order thinking skills to understand the course content, had no accompanying assignments or activities that exercised the higher-order thinking necessary to comprehend the material or apply it beyond the requisite memory skills called for by quizzes and exams. If student engagement and higher-order thinking are valuable to instructors, then the articulation of those values needs to be clearly presented to students, and those values need to be reinforced through the sequence of activities and evaluation.

An assessment strategy that examines the alignment or congruence of a course has powerful formative implications. As faculty members improve their articulation of the goals they want to achieve and match them with activities eliciting those goals, they should in turn begin to develop more and more meaningful instructional activities than those requiring no more than recall. Moreover, these activities, especially as they are increasingly conducted on the Web, can be used to provide an ongoing archive or portfolio of student work that will focus less on what students think while increasingly providing assessment opportunities to explore *how* students think.

Many educators, however, do not generally appreciate process outcomes. When otherwise intelligent scholars say things like, "We do not have hard, consistent evidence documenting that [technology] enhances academic achievement and learning outcomes" (Green 1999, 13), they illustrate unreasonable expectations of both technology and evidence. Usually, such expectations are based upon a linear, hierarchical notion of learning divorced from the educational context shaping that learning and those outcomes. As Ehrmann (1999, 26) observes:

> Technologies such as computers (or pencils) don't have predetermined impacts; it's their uses that influence outcomes. This statement seems obvious, but many institutions act as though the mere presence of technology will improve learning. They use computers to teach the same things in the same ways as before, yet they expect learning outcomes to be better. It's an easy mistake to make... .

Assessment of Web learning, in other words, has to move beyond the "does it work" question and focus instead on the many ways we might *make it work*, and how those many ways change the interaction between faculty and students, students and students, and students and subject content. The variables reflect a complex set of issues that require multiple methods. "What is worth testing," Cohen (1987, 16) argued in his classic report on instructional alignment, is education's "most awesome challenge." The same might be said for assessment.

Once it is clear that straight measures of content outcomes evaluation *alone* do not provide adequate measures of learning or improving instruction, great possibilities of learning about learning (and subsequently improving that learning) open up.

One very useful assessment for shedding light on Web-based learning is to examine the ways students use tools for different tasks within the same class. Garnsey and Kennedy (1999) used the Flashlight Current Student Inventory[2] to survey students about their experiences using three technologies. They queried students using the same set of questions about video technology,

2   The Flashlight Current Student Inventory is available through the Teaching, Learning, and Technology Group, c/o The American Association for Higher Education, One Dupont Circle N.W., Suite 360, Washington, DC or contact: Amanda Antic Antico@tltgroup.org.

e-mail, and Web-based, threaded discussions. The survey was customized to examine students' previous technology experiences, their use of the technologies provided in the technical writing course, and their perceptions of the value and learning they gained using each of the technologies. The findings helped the instructors understand that, in their approach to the technical writing course, students rarely used the video, used and enjoyed e-mail, but were more frequently inclined to explore material and revise their work using a threaded discussion forum on the Web. Do these findings generalize to other Web-based courses? Perhaps not. But formative assessments of new technologies need not apply to all learners in all contexts at all times, just those necessary for improving a single course or program. The technology assessment grail, though it suggests a noble quest, will certainly remain elusive in times of protean technology change and perpetually shifting contexts.

In a strictly Web-based context, a similar *within* design might examine a threaded discussion, a chat, an interactive module, or a Web-based research project to determine which uses of the Web increase interaction with faculty, peers, and content. Which approach might students perceive to be most useful for helping them visualize complex concepts and comprehend subject matter? Which approach encourages students to seek out and consult with other content experts? And using a faculty survey, which of these findings correspond to faculty goals?

One of the most important spinoffs of this approach to assessing technology is that reports from such assessments and the adjustments that follow should help wean educators and the audiences of assessment research from the *does it work* mindset. First, *within* designs control for sample bias. Even more important, since *within* designs examine the different *uses* of a technology within a single class or program and yield distinct results for each different use of that technology, a single study illustrates that technology-based learning means many different things, depending upon the use.

The other advantage of a *within* design approach to assessment illustrates the value of student perceptions as they reflect the different ways instructional materials are used. The general lack of appreciation for student perceptions, and survey research in general, stems from another blurring of assessment measures in which faculty, in particular, frequently confuse student satisfaction, or attitudinal research, with the other aspects or discrete data an interview or survey can tease out.

It might be useful to consider that even multiple-choice tests, the harbor of "hard evidence," elicit a student's *response* based upon his or her *perception* of the question and the list of possible answers as often as they plumb a student's comprehension of the subject. Those questions and possible responses, after all, also reflect an instructor's or a committee's selection of the important material based upon their *perception* of what is important in a discipline. In other words, responsible assessment recognizes that the range of questions on a survey and on a test of learning reflects a continuum of perceptions — ranging from students' course satisfaction to an instructor's informed selection of questions and answers (with all of the attendant and necessary assumptions of objectivity and generalizability). With that recognition, it should be clear that survey and focus-group questions come in many hues and stripes, and that they can be grouped to examine any number of course or program attributes. Equally important, survey questions can also be honed to examine more subtle intricacies of learning processes, and, to a certain (albeit qualified) extent, learning outcomes. What matters most, finally, may not be the quantity of correct answers or the number of students who reported appreciation for various instructional activities, but rather the quality of those surveys and tests in fathoming what matters most in the *particular* educational transaction.

Hard evidence of learning outcomes also matters. None of the previous discussion is intended to suggest otherwise. But the question remains: what are the best ways to engage students in ways that foster desired outcomes? After all, the mindset that holds that what someone learns is more important than the habits or activities producing that learning, or that knowledge of a critical thought is more important than the ability to think critically, subjugates the learner to the learned, which is the recipe for short-term, mindless learning and disengagement. Assessment that asks learners to explore what they learn as inextricable from what they value provides the most powerful tool for improving learning — a peek into how learners represent the learning task. As Flower and Hayes (1988, 93) note, "People only solve the problem they give themselves to solve."

When exams require little more than recall, they trivialize the learning task, and we should not be surprised to find that content is the least valued learning students report after they have completed college (Pascarella and Terenzini 1991). Complicating the matter, however, increasing class sizes reduces possible alternatives in the minds of most instructors. And as most instructors know from experience, writing multiple-choice questions that encourage higher-order, conceptual thinking is very difficult (Haladyna 1989).

Ascertaining the extent to which any test or even an activity might encourage higher-order thinking takes more than conventional tests and assessing faculty and student goals, syllabi, and learning processes. Further complicating the issue, Henscheid's (1999) study revealed that higher-order-thinking instructional goals mean very different things to different people within and between disciplines, not to mention different things to faculty and students.

Certainly students' higher-order thinking skills will benefit more if they also are aware of and are given an opportunity to work with the criteria that will be used to evaluate their learning and to see if that evaluation tool actually reflects the higher-order thinking that faculty hope to encourage. Analyzing evaluation strategies, therefore, is an integral aspect of assessing instruction, and the Web's archiving of evaluation strategies makes such assessment accessible.

Just as it is possible, if unlikely, that a multiple-choice exam reflects more than a fact-based focus, it is important to recognize that the majority of essay exams — on the Web or on paper — are usually representative of learning tasks that require students to do little more than retrieve information. The emergence of automated tools designed to assess writing with superior reliability are so far principally based on keyword-search or pattern-matching algorithms (McCollum 1998). In effect, they transform the writing process into an exercise in "infofetch" or free recall (compared to multiple-choice exams, which are based on cued recall).

Even more problematic, the message communicated by automated writing assessment programs counters the notion of writing as communication with other minds and other people. Assessment programs perpetuate students' disengagement from learning by systematically discounting individual expression. As Eisner (1969) has argued, assessment specialists should not discount "expressive objectives," or the unique ways students gain from contact with faculty and peers. As Eisner suggested, our interests in reliability should not supplant our concerns for the quality of the "opportunity to learn."

In other words, when we resort to automatic grading, we send the wrong message about writing and the wrong message about learning. To envision writing and learning as thoughtful communication, we need to have a reader of at least one. Now, with technology, we have an *opportunity* to expand on that so that one learning can communicate with many, or even, as Condon (Condon 1998) observes, "many can communicate with many" — a rich context for engaging community in the enterprise of teaching and learning.

To both encourage and evaluate higher-order thinking and to capitalize on the potential community of learners the Web makes possible, more sophisticated evaluation strategies are necessary. Portfolios and rubrics are good methods (Wiggens 1998) in that they can be integrated into collaborative projects and customized to reflect what faculty value. But the criteria on which they are based still must articulate reliably and with validity precisely what higher-order thinking in any particular discipline might mean. The process unquestionably requires considerable investments of time and effort.

Brown et al. (1999) implemented a critical thinking rubric (see appendix 13.1) designed to assess the evidence of critical thinking in students' exchanges in online forums. Holding students to the criteria was an instructional challenge for faculty in the study. Assessment that integrates process and outcomes, in effect holding both students and faculty to a higher standard, is neither easy nor well received by students. Nonetheless, the results in three large classes demonstrated significant gains in higher-order thinking that were not apparent in the work of students who were not taught and evaluated with the critical thinking rubric but who received, in the traditional class, the same final grades.

Toward Responsible Assessment

Almost ten years since Halio's research debacle, a report on distance learning in higher education from the Institute for Higher Education Policy (Phipps and Merisotis 1999) emerges like déjà vu. The report reminds us how little progress we've made in our understanding of new technologies and learning as well as in conducting and disseminating useful research. The title of the report, "What's the Difference?," recalls another work that came out about the same time as Halio's: Pascarella's and Terenzini's (1991) *How College Affects Students: Findings and Insights from Twenty Years of Research*. In the preface of that work, the authors ask: "*Does* college make a difference?" (xvi). They respond to their own question with some irony, noting, after their extensive culling and confirming of an extensive body of research, that "the appeal of its straightforwardness notwithstanding, the question is really a naïve one" (xvi). They explain that it took more than four decades of research to inform the first significant *program-wide* synthesis of findings from more than 1,500 studies in *The Impact of College on Students* (Feldman and Newcomb 1969), the precursor to their own compendium. In that work, Feldman was the first to put forward a comprehensive synthesis surfacing the complexity of teaching, learning, and student cognitive growth. Though there are important points in Phipps' and Merisotis' (1999) aspersions on the current research in distance education, there is also something disingenuous about the form and tone of their report. They criticize the small culling of only ten years of research of different and changing technologies for failing to measure "the effectiveness of total academic programs" (5). Like Halio, they forget the dizzying rate of technological change. They argue, among a litany of the shortcomings on research in distance education, that "the validity and reliability of the instruments used to measure student outcomes and attitudes are questionable" (4). They ask, "Do the instruments — such as final examinations, quizzes, questionnaires, or attitude scales — measure what they are supposed to measure?" (4). These concerns, however, like others that point at methodology, are appropriate questions to ask of our face-to-face, traditional courses as well.

The point is that distance education and the Web as a medium for education are not likely to disappear. If the issue, as Gold and Maitland (in Phipps and Merisotis 1999) observe in the forward of the Institute for Higher Education Policy's report, is to assess how well higher education "prepares students for a lifetime as knowledge workers" (paragraph 2), then framing assessment in summative terms is irresponsible. The culture now and in the foreseeable future will call upon learners to find, synthesize, generate, and share information with the same technologies as those students in distance education programs. Learning and technologies in changing contexts are moving targets, so assessment of learning and technologies must remain nimble. More damaging, a report that creates the expectation of broad, generalizable, summative research fuels, again, a reductive public perception of assessment and the efforts of educators.

As we take up the challenge to assess the best ways to teach and learn with the Web and the Internet, we must do so with attention to imperatives like equity and access. We will be well advised to remember the lessons from conventional education as we do.

First, we should recall what evaluators had come to recognize before the technology explosion: There is as much difference between two teachers doing, purportedly, the same thing in conventional classes as there is between two teachers doing different things (Worthen, Sanders, and Fitzpatrick 1997). In that sense, the persistent efforts of some to divide assessment (for purposes of comparison) into distance and conventional education are more than a little dubious, especially as courses and programs increasingly integrate distance and campus programs and populations.

Second, the pitting of face-to-face, conventional instruction against technology-enhanced and distance strategies distracts us from assessment's most pressing and persistent challenge. The lament from evaluators is not that we don't have a grasp of ways to assess and enhance learning, which, as even Phipps and Merisotis discovered, are largely independent from technology issues. Rather educational research has, for all but a few, failed to inform practice (Richardson 1994; Robinson 1998). The problem is so widespread that many professional evaluators have come to identify the discounting or suppressing of research findings as an ethical transgression (Morris and Cohn 1993).

We need more and better assessment of learning with new technologies. But even more, we need to find ways to get what we already know about teaching and learning to be heard.

Appendix 13.1

Reader's Guide to Rating Student Critical Thinking

1) Identifies and summarizes the *problem/question* at issue (and/or the author's or source's position).

Scant	Substantially Developed
Does not identify and summarize the problem, is confused about the question at issue, or identifies a different problem or issue from the focus of the assignment.	Identifies not only the main problem, but also subsidiary, embedded, or implicit problems and identifies them clearly, distinguishing them from one another and stating their relationships with each other.
Does not identify the issue, is confused about the issue, or represents the issue inaccurately.	Identifies not only the basics of the issue, but recognizes nuances of the issue.

2) Identifies and presents the student's own *perspective and position* in relationship to the issue.

Scant	Substantially Developed
Deals only with a single source or view of the argument and fails to clarify the established or presented position relative to the student's own — either neglecting to state and develop the student's position or failing to establish other critical distinctions.	Identifies own position on the issue and clarifies distinctions at many levels. Students may forward a personal position drawing support from personal experience and from information not available from *assigned* sources.

3) Identifies and considers other salient *perspectives and positions* that are important to the analysis of the issue.

Scant	Substantially Developed
Deals only with a single perspective and fails to discuss other possible perspectives, especially those salient to the issue.	Deals with the perspectives alluded to or referred to previously, and includes additional perspectives that the student has identified by drawing on outside information.

4) Identifies and considers the influence of *context* on the issue.

Scant	Substantially Developed
Discusses the problem only in egocentric or sociocentric terms. Does not present the problem as having connections to other contexts—cultural, educational, technological, etc.	Analyzes the issue with a clear sense of scope and contexts, including a general *assessment of the audience* of the analysis. Students may also analyze the passage within other pertinent contexts.

5) Identifies and assesses the *quality of supporting data/evidence* or provides own supporting data/evidence about the issue.

Scant	Substantially Developed
Merely repeats information previously provided, taking it as absolute truth, or denies the information in the passage but does not engage the supporting data or evidence critically in any way.	Examines the information provided previously, questioning its accuracy, precision, relevance, and completeness. Questions differences between theory and application and evaluates the information sources.
Does not demonstrate distinctions between fact, opinion, and value judgments.	Clearly distinguishes between fact, opinion, and value judgments.

6) Identifies and assesses the key *assumptions* underlying the author's position.

Scant	Substantially Developed
Does not surface the assumptions and ethical issues that underlie the issue, or does so superficially.	Identifies the key assumptions and ethical issues that underlie the issue and assesses the assumptions to determine their validity.

7) Identifies and assesses conclusions, implications, and supporting logic.

Scant	Substantially Developed
Fails to identify conclusions or the implications of the issue, and/or fails to identify and assess the key logical relationships among the conclusions, implications, and key contextual factors, assumptions, data, and evidence previously presented.	Identifies and logically discusses conclusions and/or implications, contextual factors, assumptions, data, and evidence. Students may also turn a critical eye on conclusions and implications of their own assertions, and they may demonstrate a stylistically effective device of closure (a quote or metaphor).

Contexts for Consideration

Cultural/Social
(group/national, ethnic behavior/attitudes, costs)

Scientific
(conceptual, basic science, scientific method)

Educational Economic
(referring to schooling, formal training)

Economic
(systemic government of local)

Technological
(applied science, engineering, product related)

Personal experience
(personal observation, informal)

Ethical
(values, character)

REFERENCES

Angelo, Thomas, and K. Patricia Cross. 1993. *Classroom assessment techniques*. San Francisco: Jossey-Bass, Publishers.

Berliner, David C. 1996. Uninvited comments from an uninvited guest. *Educational Researcher* 25 (8): 47-50.

Blumenstyk, Goldie. 1999. The marketing intensifies in distance learning. *The Chronicle of Higher Education*, 9 April: A27-30.

Bradley, M. M., M.K. Greenwald, M. C. Petry, and P. J. Lang. 1992. Remembering pictures: Pleasure and arousal in memory. *Journal of Experimental Psychology: Learning, Memory and Cognition* 18 (2): 379-390.

Brahler, C. Jane, Nils S. Peterson, and Emily C. Johnson. 1999. *Developing on-line learning materials for higher eduation: An overview of current issues.* [Website]. Educational Technology and Learning. Available from < http://ifets.gmd.de/periodical/vol_2_99/jayne_brahler.html >.

Brown, Gary, Lori Baker-Eveleth, M. Glynn, Phil Scuderi, and D. Archibald. 1999. *Critical thinking, general education, and measuring growth in learning.* [Website]. The Center For Teaching & Learning. Available from < http://www.ctl.wsu.edu >.

Cohen, S. Alan. 1987. Instructional alignment: Searching for a magic bullet. *Educational Researcher* (November): 16-20.

Condon, W. 1998. The WSU online writing lab (OWL). In *NEH Crossroad Project*, edited by R. Bass. Pullman, WA.

Cross, K. Patricia. 1996. Classroom research: Implementing the scholarship of teaching. Paper read at Using Assessment to Improve Learning, at Washington State University, Pullman, WA.

Crow, David, Sara Parsowith, and G. Bowden Wise. 1999. *The evolution of computer supported cooperative work—past, present and future developments.* [Website]. SigChi, 29(2). Available from < http://www.acm .org/sigchi/bulletin/1997.2/students.html#HDR0 >.

Ehrmann, Stephan C. 1999. Asking the hard questions about technology use and education. *Change* 31(2): 24-29.

Eisner, E. W. 1969. Instructional and expressive educational objectives: Their formulation and use in curriculum. Edited by E. W. E. W. James Popham, Howard J. Sullivan, and Louise Tyler. Vol. Instructional Objectives, AERA Monograph Series on Curriculum Evaluation. Chicago: Rand McNally & Co.

Feldman, Kenneth A., and Theodore M. Newcomb. 1969. *The impact of college on students.* San Francisco: Jossey-Bass, Publishers.

Flower, L., and J. R. Hayes. 1988. The cognition of discovery: Defining a rhetorical problem. In *The Writing Teacher's Sourcebook,* edited by Gary Tate and Edward P. J. Corbett. New York and Oxford: Oxford University Press.

Garnsey, A., and G. Kennedy. 1999. *Question: What did you like best about your online course in technical and professional writing? Answer: Anonymity.* [Website]. Available from < http://www.aee.uidaho.edu/facultystaff/Ann/CV/MLApresshort/ >.

Glaser, Robert, and Edward Silver. 1994. Assessment, testing, and instruction: Retrospect and prospect. In *Review of Research in Education,* edited by Linda Darling-Hammond. Washington, DC: The American Educational Research Association.

Green, K. C. 1999. When wishes come true : Colleges and the convergence of access, lifelong learning, and technology. *Change* 31 (2):10-15.

Haladyna, Thomas M. 1989. A taxonomy of multiple-choice item-writing rules. *Applied Measurement in Education* 2(1): 37-50.

Halio, M. P. 1990. Student writing: Can the machine maim the message? *Academic Computing* 4: 16-19.

Henderson, Tom, and Gary Brown. 1999. *Assessment of three business courses.* Pullman, WA: Washington State University.

Henscheid, J. M. 1999. Doing versus thinking: The academic goals of freshmen and the faculty who teach them. *In Press.*

Hill, E. 1961. Education out of the blue. *The Saturday Evening Post.* 2 September: 16-17 & 40-45.

House, Ernest R. 1993. Professional evaluation: Social impact and political consequences. Newberry Park, CA: Sage.

Marchese, Theodore. 1998. Not-so-distant competitors: How new providers are making the postsecondary market. *AAHE Bulletin* 50(9): 3-7.

McCollum, Kelly. 1998. How a computer program learns to grade essays. *The Chronicle of Higher Education* XLV (2):37-38.

Milton, O., H. R. Pollio, and J. A. Eison. 1986. *Making sense of college grades.* San Francisco: Jossey-Bass, Publishers.

Morris, M., and R. Cohn. 1993. Program evaluators and ethical challenges: A national survey. *Evaluation Review* 17:621-642.

Noble, David. 1999. *Digital diploma mills: The automation of higher education.* [Website]. first monday. Available from < http://www.firstmonday.dk/issues/issue3_1/noble/index.html >.

Nunn, Claudia E. 1996. Discussion in the college classroom. *Journal of Higher Education* 67(3): 243-265.

Pascarella, Ernest T., and Patrick T. Terenzini. 1991. *How college affects students: Findings and insights from twenty years of research*. San Francisco: Jossey-Bass, Publishers.

Phipps, Ronald, and Janice Merisotis. 1999. *What's the difference? A review of contemporary research on the effectiveness of distance learning in higher education*. Washington, DC: The Institute for Higher Education Policy.

Reeves, Byron, and Clifford Nass. 1996. *The media equation*. Stanford: Center for the Study of Language and Information.

Reeves, B., E. Thorson, M.L. Rothschild, D. McDonald, R. Goldstein. 1985. Attention to television: Intrastimulus effects of movement and scene changes on alpha variation over time. *International Journal of Neuroscience* 25: 241-255.

Richardson, Virginia. 1994. Conducting research on practice. *Educational Researcher* 23(5): 5-10.

Robinson, Vivian M.J. 1998. Methodology and the research-practice gap. *Educational Researcher* 27(1): 17-26.

Scriven, Michael. 1974. Standards for the evaluation of educational programs and products. In *Evaluating Educational Programs and Products*, edited by G. D. Borich. Englewood Cliffs, NJ: Educational Technology Publications.

Slatin, J., T. Batson, R. Boston, M. E. Cohen, L. Crew, L. Faigley, L. Gerrard, G. Hawisher, E.M. Jennings, M. Joyce, N. Kaplan, S. Moulthrop, R. Norman, J. O'Connor, C. Selfe, G. Sir, M. Spitzer, P. Sullivan, R. Woodward, and A. Young. 1990. Computer teachers respond to Halio. *Computers and Composition* 7(3): 73-79.

Trosset, Carol. 1998. Obstacles to open discussion and critical thinking: The Grinnell College study. *Change* 30(5): 44-49.

Wiggins, Grant R. 1998. *Educative assessments*. San Francisco: Jossey-Bass, Publishers.

Worthen, Blaine R., James R. Sanders, and J. L. Fitzpatrick. 1997. *Program evaluation: Alternative approaches and practical guidelines*. New York: Longman.

Wright, John C., Susan B. Millar, Steve A. Koscuik, Debra L. Penberthy, and Bruce E. Wampold, Paul H. Williams. 1998. A novel strategy for assessing the effects of curriculum reform on student competence. *Journal of Chemical Education* 75(8): 986-991.

Chapter 14

A Vision for the Future: Choices and Challenges for Colleges and Universities

By Donald E. Hanna

Colleges and universities have faced a growing challenge of relevance in the last twenty years of this century. This challenge to the status quo has emanated from many quarters: students, organizations, businesses, government, and alumni/ae.

The transformation of our economy to a global network — which in the twenty-first century, will be organized around the value of knowledge and the capacity of people and organizations to use technological developments wisely, effectively, and efficiently — has placed universities squarely in the center of societal concern and focus. Recent developments of the World Wide Web, digital satellite technology, and new applications of virtual reality to build simulated learning environments have added substantially to the pressure for new levels of responsiveness and quality at all levels of higher education.

The Changing Face of Colleges and Universities

While at this point well short of a revolution, universities are:

- experimenting with improving accessibility to existing programs;

- using new learning technologies, especially the World Wide Web, to reduce barriers to accessing learning opportunities;

- responding to learner needs and desires such as convenience, timing, engagement, application of knowledge to the workplace, and learning by doing;

- being forced by the increasingly competitive and global marketplace for learning to develop new measures of institutional and program quality and responsiveness;

- beginning to think globally rather than regionally or nationally;

- designing new programs to take advantage of emerging technologies;

- marketing their programs to new audiences and in new ways;

- building new alliances with other campuses and corporations to take advantage of new learning technologies in extending access,

- reframing assumptions about characteristics of ideal learning environments;

- reconstructing their assumptions about the value of knowledge and its creation, and developing internal policies that promote or impede faculty members from innovation, experimentation, and creativity.

Rapidly developing for-profit corporations are engaged in experimentation and have formed both new organizations internal to the corporation and alliances with universities to promote learning using technology. And completely new models for universities are being developed to respond to the opportunities created by a growing worldwide market for learning and new technologies.

Strategic Choices for the Future

Among the choices that all colleges and universities face in this new digital environment are the following:

1. Who are the learners to be served? What are their needs? What are the intellectual and knowledge needs of learners today and in the future?

These questions may not be as simple as they appear given the competitive environment of the future. As Hanna notes in chapters 1 and 2, the job market is demanding new and more complex capabilities of individuals and requiring that they learn throughout their careers. This fact alone may change an institution's student mix and competitive position, and it will certainly affect the content and processes of instruction. Because students are more diverse, and because the skills demanded in many sectors of the job market are more diverse, institutions will need to personalize learning to each student's needs more so than in the past. Personalizing learning will require the development of new administrative and pedagogical processes, and learning technologies will play an important role in being able to accomplish this personalization effectively.

2. What is the broader context for the learning opportunities that universities provide? What are the most appropriate learning environments and contexts that can enable students to become lifetime learners?

As Hanna and Dede observed earlier, and Olcott and Schmidt reinforce in greater depth in chapter 12, the context of learning will, of necessity, gravitate away from large lecture halls beaming content orally and visually to students. Institutions already planning for and expediting this transition to greater interaction between teachers and students and among students, as described by Hanna in chapter 2, and to the overall personalization of learning, will develop comparative advantages over their competitors.

3. How can a university provide the maximum access possible for all students, including those who are not resident on the campus? How do new learning technologies support the development of effective learning environments?

The role of learning technologies is critical in achieving a vision of maximum access to higher education. Institutions will be tempted to implement technology in a linear way that enables them to do more of what they are already doing, and to do what they are already doing more efficiently. Instead, campuses should redesign instruction and learning from the ground up to incorporate the powerful new interactive capabilities of the World Wide Web and other advanced technologies so ably described by Dede in chapter 3.

4. What are the changes in culture, in mission, and in processes that need to be made in order to view a student as a lifetime client or customer, and to serve that student effectively?

Because institutions will need to be redesigned to accomplish the transformations noted above, major changes in mission, culture, and processes are to some extent both inevitable and necessary. This is organizational change in capital letters, meaning that such change will not come easily, it will not come without dissension and opposition, and it will not come primarily from the action of internal forces. The extent of change will vary by organizational type, history, and goals, and the overall competitive forces at play will vary by institution. What is most needed is what is most difficult to achieve: a culture that accepts and values risk taking, innovation, and creative collaboration across well-established internal and external boundaries. In one attempt to account for the lack of innovation in collegiate classrooms, a committee of the Midwest Higher Education Commission (Gifford 1999) concluded that:

- most innovative efforts were the product of individual faculty members working alone, with the use of innovative approaches and materials restricted to individual courses;

- concepts employed were largely disconnected from a coherent theory of instruction;

- computer-mediated instructional materials were simply attached to conventionally taught courses as an add-on.

Gifford also notes the absence of rewards for faculty members who are innovators in the classroom, but concludes that the overall sources of failure to integrate learning technologies into the classroom are complex and deeply rooted in both the organizational culture of higher education and also in the economic and business models of publishers and others producing products for the higher education market.

5. What are the elements of leadership and ethics that enable a university community to move forward strategically to address and implement needed changes?

Leaders of institutions that recognize both the inevitability and desirability of change will need to forge many linkages and partnerships with external organizations, and then use these partnerships to introduce and apply new approaches and ideas in the organization of learning environments, programs, and services. As Poley notes in chapter 7, the major challenge is how institutions can become more flexible, resilient, speedy, creative, just, and concerned, not how they can do what they are already doing more efficiently and effectively. In her discussion of leadership in higher education today, Poley finds an apparent absence of true passion and commitment to enabling and leading change within many institutions. Those who take risks in promoting change in higher education, where internal resistance is usually high, face the political admonition so forcefully articulated by Machiavelli and Gilbert (1963, 26), that:

> ...There is nothing more difficult to plan or more uncertain of success than an attempt to introduce new institutions[1], because the introducer has as his enemies all those who profit from the old institutions, and has as lukewarm defenders all those who will profit from the new institutions ... thus lukewarm subjects and innovating prince are both in danger.

---

1   Substitute "change" for "institution."

Leadership, passion, ethics, and choices about technologies in universities are intertwined, as both Poley and Olcott assert. One cannot address issues of change without also focusing upon the question of who will benefit from proposed changes, and without taking a passionate view of the important choices to be made and their consequences. If access increases as a result of investments in learning technologies, is the gap between rich and poor, majority and minority, male and female, increased or decreased as a result? Can competitive forces enable both improvements in access across the board, or must the digital divide continue and widen if competitive forces are not ameliorated by public investment on a large scale?

6. How are developing technologies changing the concept of knowledge and its intellectual origins, value, and ownership, and what policy options might be pursued by universities as a result? In what ways can the faculty exercise leadership for the changes that are needed, and how can its positive participation be enhanced?

Just as the printing press enabled ideas and knowledge to be fixed in time and place and attribution, the World Wide Web and other electronic technologies are enabling rapid dissemination and distribution of ideas and knowledge on a global scale. The rapid turnover, exchange, and adaptation of ideas are challenging individuals and organizations to be creative in how and ownership of content is asserted.

Many universities have reaped the financial rewards of patents received by individual faculty members. Few universities have been able to accomplish this with respect to publication of books, scholarly articles, or other creative works of faculty, including course syllabi and other teaching and learning materials. As Tallman noted in chapter 8, these educational products have generally been viewed as within the purview and ownership of the individual faculty member, not the employing organization, even when the authors or faculty members develop such works in conjunction with their university employment. The one clear and widely accepted exception is when such materials are the result of a specific contract calling for the faculty member to develop a course or course materials for which the university will clearly retain copyright ownership.

With the development of new courses and course materials offered on the Web, a new challenge regarding ownership is presented, both for institutions and faculty members. Recently, the business schools of the University of Chicago, Carnegie Mellon University, Stanford University, the London School of Economics, and several other leading universities signed lucrative contracts with UNEXT.com[2], a start-up company that trades on the Nasdaq stock market under the name Nextera. UNEXT.com was established in 1997 by a group of investors as a provider of online courses with an initial content focus in business. The original investors include a trustee of the University of Chicago, the university's dean of the law school, and Michael Milken, the one-time junk-bond king, who has invested in a number of educational online ventures and has also established the Milken Foundation[3] with a focus on introducing and supporting the use of learning technologies in K-12 schools. The contract for courses is between the university and UNEXT.com, not between faculty members and the company, and most of the money connected with the contract will be paid directly to the participating universities. This is what made the arrangement attractive to the participating universities, according to David Brady, associate dean at the Stanford Business School, quoted in *The Chronicle of Higher Education* (Blumenstyk 1999):

> Universities make money off patents, but "they missed out on textbooks," he says, describing the way universities traditionally claim rights to professors' inventions but not their books. Now, distance learning is opening up a whole avenue of opportunity to profit from intellectual property, and "universities want something out if it."

The American Association of University Professors[4] recently enacted a policy firmly stating that faculty members must play a crucial and essential role in decisions about distance learn-

---

[2] http://www.unext.com/

[3] http://www.milkenexchange.org/

[4] http://www.aaup.org/

ing. The policy also states that professors, rather than institutions, should generally retain the primary rights to materials prepared for online courses (Schneider 1999). Thus, the debate is forming on a national scale, and money is at the heart of the matter. Faculties are now tuned into the issue as one that is integral to the role definitions of both their institutions and the faculty in the future. Faculty members are currently in a strong position on this issue, but only if they lead positively and aggressively.

As Olcott and Schmidt suggest in chapter 9, faculties need to articulate policies and processes that ensure a commitment to greater access and attention to creative learning environments that incorporate advanced technologies, thereby creating the learning environments that will enable learners to develop the skills and perspectives they need to live and compete in a world that is very different from the world that existed only twenty or thirty years ago.

A stance from the faculty that communicates commitment only for the status quo will be met with ever more aggressive external pressures for change in traditional universities from legislators, public officials, alumni, and students. There will also be increasingly successful competition from new and emerging organizations from both the nonprofit and for-profit sectors.

7. What organizational models are being used to respond to an increasingly complex and dynamic environment for higher education? What are the strategic options available to a university in considering possible programs that could be offered internationally?

The emerging organizational models for higher education are fluid, and each model discussed in this book has borrowed features from every other model to some extent. Traditional universities are becoming more entrepreneurial in the face of competition from each other and from new for-profit universities. They are also adopting some of the processes developed by the distance-education, technology-based universities designed to serve students at a distance. For-profit universities are finding it difficult to meet student and public expectations of program quality without a qualified faculty. Distance-learning, technology-based institutions are faced with the challenge of incorporating new technologies at the same time that many students continue to rely on older print and mail technologies.

All universities have the potential in the future to become cross-national organizations. While traditional campus-based higher education is organized around a physical place, the evolution toward globally active, transnational universities will result in content and delivery mechanisms designed to minimize cultural and geographic barriers to attendance. It will also emphasize the combination of physical and virtual place and time. Many critics fear that this new global presence will have a very negative impact upon indigenous universities, especially those in countries not yet fully integrated into the global communications network. Universities of all types will have new opportunities to build upon diverse views of the world, of organizations, of opportunities, and of issues and problems, with the ultimate result possibly being the eventual reduction of barriers to cross-national study, just as international trade and competition are removing the barriers to the creation of a global economy.

Strategic Challenges for the Future

The choices for universities in the future carry with them numerous challenges, and these challenges suggest a path for strategic development and cultural adaptations for the future.

Among these strategic developments and cultural adaptations are the following:

Strategic Challenge 1: Ambiguous boundaries. Universities need to reduce the rigidity of boundaries between themselves and their external publics. What is within the university and what is external to it will be increasingly difficult to recognize. This blurring of boundaries is an inevitable outcome of greater communication and interaction made possible by increasingly powerful technologies. It is also a necessary element of both enabling and supporting substantive change within the academy. Over time, traditional universities will begin to look more like online universities, and they will be increasingly operated more like businesses. What is "on campus" and what is not will be less and less apparent. Such distinctions are already less and less an issue for students and faculty.

Strategic Challenge 2: Interdisciplinary programs. As individual learning becomes more connected with personal and professional experiences, learning and instruction will need to become increasingly interdisciplinary to mirror and deal with real problems and real issues. This always involves integrating the perspectives of many disciplines and approaches. University academic departments are being encouraged administratively and driven economically to reformat and reorganize courses, programs, and structures to respond to increasingly sophisticated and market-knowledgeable students.

Strategic Challenge 3: Supporting entrepreneurial efforts and technology. Technology support units that in universities have been concerned only with improvements in on-campus instruction are finding that their work intersects with continuing education units, whose role has been to extend access to programs through use of technology. The marriage of these units is inevitable and has already occurred in many universities.

Strategic Challenge 4: Redesigning and personalizing student support services. Student support services such as admissions, advising, registration, and career development need to focus on enabling and supporting university programs that reach out to serve students where they are, physically, economically, and academically, rather than centralizing all services in a single location. These direct and immediate personalized contacts with students are becoming increasingly central to organizational and educational quality, as perceived by the student.

Strategic Challenge 5: Connected and lifelong learning. Institutions are focusing more directly on helping students develop the skills necessary to be successful in today's economy, which values and rewards the ability to work in teams, to develop creative approaches to problem solving, and to learn constantly. In this sense, universities will become more and more concerned with ensuring that students know how to learn and to apply what they learn to real situations, and less concerned with measuring learning in abstract and relatively unconnected assessment processes such as class-by-class content examinations and multiple-choice tests.

Strategic Challenge 6: Technologically competent faculty. Universities will need to develop full-time faculty and staff dedicated to engaging a diversity of learners who will increasingly bring more complex learning needs to universities. In a world dependent on technology for its communications, its economy, and, increasingly, its day-to-day organization, universities that are serious about meeting the challenges of technology will invest in faculty members who are experienced with technology and who can both model and pass this experience on to students. Universities will also take seriously the need to bring other faculty members along in the use of learning technologies, and in experimenting with learning environments that are less oriented toward the activities and responsibilities of the instructor and more focused on those of the student. Universities where the students are leading the faculty in adopting technology are already at a significant competitive disadvantage. Without a systematic strategic planning effort, these institutions will become less and less attractive to students.

Strategic Challenge 7: Building strategic alliances with others. Over the past decade, universities of all types have built expanded alliances with each other and with the corporate sector. These alliances are essential business strategies, and all universities will seek to expand their web of alliances with others in the future. While demand for learning is growing and access to higher education is improving, competition is also increasing. This competition will cause universities and corporations alike to focus on their unique programmatic and delivery advantages. "Cooperate to compete" will be the name of the game and a critical strategy for universities in the future.

Corporate universities are beginning to broaden their missions to include certification and degree options for employees. While, in some cases, these corporations are developing and offering these programs internally, they are also forming new strategic alliances with universities. The corporation with hundreds of strategic alliances for learning is becoming commonplace, as is the university with many partnerships and alliances, both with other campuses and with business and industry.

Strategic Challenge 8: Incorporating learning technologies into the strategic thinking of universities. Universities are increasingly integrating the idea of learning technologies into their strategic planning and the setting of institutional priorities. Some universities are creating special executive-level positions to lead institutional efforts to integrate technologies into academic programs and enable the institution to respond more effectively to new program opportunities in distance learning. Academic strategies are being developed in many institutions to systematically utilize learning technologies to reduce the separation of students from each other, from their teachers, and from content relevant to their needs and interests.

The truly global nature of the educational marketplace is becoming increasingly clear, just as it has become apparent in this decade that the market for higher education is no longer singularly local. Universities need to build and integrate an understanding of the possibilities of using technology into every level of organization, including the executive level. The long-term impact of technology is not to create mass markets for learning, but to create options that are more and more customized and personalized for individual learners in organized patterns of inquiry.

Strategic Challenge 9: Measurement of program quality. Educational programs are being measured more and more on outcomes that matter to students and employers, rather than on inputs that matter to faculty and administrators. Criteria for accreditation and quality assessment are changing to reflect more specific measurements of learning. Some accrediting associations are already revamping their criteria and their processes used for accreditation. For example, the North Central Association of Schools and Colleges recently received a three-year, $1.5 million grant to design an innovative, more challenging alternative to traditional re-accreditation and to develop processes for concentrating on the academic enterprise — particularly teaching and learning (North Central Association 1999). Project goals also include involving faculty more directly in all academic improvement processes and responding to an institution's distinctive needs and aspirations.

A few institutions have begun to adopt and follow planning processes suggested by the Malcolm Baldrige National Quality Award, a process that emphasizes results-oriented goals and processes focusing on customers and markets, leadership, and strategic planning (Baldrige National Quality Program 1999).

Active engagement among learners, teachers, and content; between students and faculty, and between customers and institutions is increasingly an important element of measurement for accrediting associations. However, it is the performance of students in developing diverse perspectives and approaches to problem solving, critical thinking skills, working effectively in teams, and continuing learning in and out of the workplace that will define successful academic programs in the future.

Strategic Challenge 10: Achieving institutional advantage. For some universities, the new digital environment suggests focusing resources on just a few unique or particularly outstanding programs and delivering them globally. For others, it means organizing programs differently to take advantage of a combination of programmatic strengths. For still others, it means developing the right partnerships to shore up weaknesses in programs, delivery, service to students, or other areas important to offering high-quality programs. The abundance of opportunities demands greater focus and clarity about purposes and competitive strengths as organizations compete in a larger, more complex marketplace. No institution, even those that are currently positioned at the top of the higher education pyramid, can afford to ignore this larger environment.

Strategic Challenge 11: Bureaucracy, culture, and assumptions regarding change. In what is widely acknowledged as the most difficult challenge of all, traditional universities are being forced to transform decision-making processes and radically change past operating assumptions. Processes appropriate for a stable environment in which markets were clearly defined, program structures were relatively uniform, and competition was limited are no longer effective in a networked world. Universities are discovering that major changes are necessary in order to serve students effectively and to compete with aggressive for-profit institutions in an environment in which the concept of time to market for programs is becoming more critical.

Just One More Challenge

To end with just one challenge highlighted by this book, the most important and immediate task for universities facing an uncertain future is to build a culture that is friendly to and supportive of innovation and change at all levels of the organization. Leaders of universities cannot do this alone, yet it cannot be done without committed, passionate, and visionary leadership. New institutional strategies must be created, articulated, and adopted to enable institutions to survive and prosper in this new educational marketplace. And finally, all of us must make our way in a world that is changing much more rapidly than the one of a generation ago. To make our way successfully, we must ourselves become more effective lifelong learners and users of learning technologies.

References

Baldrige National Quality Program. 1999. *Criteria for performance excellence.* Washington, DC: National Institute of Standards and Technology.

Blumenstyk, Goldie. 1999. A company pays top universities to use their names and their professors. *Chronicle of Higher Education*, 18 June: A39.

Gifford, Bernard R. 1999. *Computer-mediated instruction and learning in higher education: Bridging the gap between promise and practice* [Website]. North Central Association. Available from http://www.ncacihe.org/conference/99material/gifford.pdf.

Machiavelli, Niccolo, and Allan H. Gilbert. 1963. *The prince.* Durham, NC: Duke University Press.

North Central Association. 1999. *Information about NCA's new academic quality improvement project* [Website]. North Central Association. Available from http://www.ncacihe.org/AQIP/index.cfm.

Schneider, Alison. 1999. AAUP seeks greater faculty role in distance-learning decisions. *Chronicle of Higher Education*, 25 June: A34.

About the Authors

Donald E. Hanna

Don Hanna is professor of Educational Communications, University of Wisconsin–Extension, with a concurrent appointment as Professor of Continuing and Vocational Education at University of Wisconsin–Madison. He has been an administrator and teacher at four land-grant universities, and has participated in and helped to lead major institutional change efforts at three of these universities. Each of these change efforts involved the development of academic programs offered at a distance using educational technologies. Don served as Chancellor of the University of Wisconsin-Extension from 1993-1997 and previously was Associate Vice-Provost for Extended University Services at Washington State University, where he served from 1983-1993. He also was Assistant Professor and head of the Division of Extramural Courses at the University of Illinois at Urbana-Champaign from 1979-1983. Don has received a number of awards for creative programming and leadership, including a Kellogg National Fellowship to pursue the study of telecommunications policy and applications of telecommunications that benefit developing countries and a fellowship with Northwestern University's Annenberg Communications Policy Program in Washington, D.C. He received his A.B. degree in anthropology and history from the University of Kansas, and his Ph.D. in Adult and Continuing Education from Michigan State University in 1978.

Gary Brown

Gary Brown is the Director at The Center For Teaching Learning and Technology (CTLT) at Washington State University, where he oversees the CTLT's assessment and technology efforts. Gary began his work in assessment in composition at San

Diego State in 1979 where he also developed programs that helped to assess hypertext curricula and interactive analysis. He has since directed and the development and assessed the impact of numerous software programs, ranging from interactive writing spaces to medical diagnostic simulations. He joined the team developing Washington State University's Writing Portfolio assessment program in 1991. Since that time, he has conducted studies investigating the impact of new technologies on student learning in food science, horticulture, engineering, composition, biology, zoology, math, and others. He teaches graduate courses in Program Evaluation and advanced Program Evaluation for the College of Education. He received his BA in English in 1975 and his Ph.D. in Interdisciplinary Studies from Washington State University in 1994.

Chris Dede

Chris Dede is a Full Professor at George Mason University in Fairfax, Virginia, where he has a joint appointment in the Schools of Information Technology and Engineering and of Education. His research interests span technology forecasting and assessment, emerging technologies for learning, and leadership in educational innovation. He currently has a major grant from the National Science Foundation to develop educational environments based on virtual reality technology. Chris was the Editor of the 1998 Association for Supervision and Curriculum Development (ASCD) Yearbook, Learning with Technology. He is a member of the National Academy of Sciences Committee on Foundations of Educational and Psychological Assessment and of the U.S. Department of Education's Expert Panel on Technology, and he is also on the International Steering Committee for the Second International Technology in Education Study spanning approximately thirty countries. Chris has recently completed a one-year term as Senior Program Director at the National Science Foundation, helping to guide the initial development of their new $25-30M funding program — Research on Education, Policy, and Practice. He has been a Visiting Scientist at the Computer Science Lab, Massachusetts Institute of Technology, and at NASA's Johnson Space Center. Chris received a double-major bachelor's degree in chemistry and English in 1969 from the California Institute of Technology and his doctorate in Education from the University of Massachusetts in 1972.

Donald Olcott

Don Olcott, Jr. is Associate Dean for Extended University and Summer Session at the University of Arizona. Previously Don was with the Western Cooperative for Educational Telecommunications where he served as Director of the Institute for the Management of Distance Education. Don has published extensively in the areas of institutional and faculty support systems for distance education and has served as a consultant to colleges and universities across the U.S. and Canada. Don has also received numerous national awards for leadership in the field of educational telecommunications and distance education, including the prestigious 1998 Charles Wedemeyer Outstanding Distance Education Practitioner in North America given by the University of Wisconsin–Madison and *The American Journal of Distance Education* in recognition of outstanding leadership and profession contributions to the field of continuing and distance education. He is a graduate of Harvard University's Institute for the Management of Lifelong Learning (MLE), and serves on the Editorial Staff of *The American Journal of Distance Education*. He earned both his bachelors and masters degrees from Western Washington University and his doctorate in 1994 from Oregon State University in higher educational administration and leadership.

Janet Poley

Janet Poley is President of the American Distance Education Consortium (ADEC), a consortium of 50 state and land-grant universities based at the University of Nebraska — Lincoln, where she also is a full professor. She has served as an advisor for Educom's Virtual University Think Tank, the National Association of State Universities and Land Grant College's Council of Information Technology, and Western Governors University and Penn State's Institute for Leadership in Distance Education. Prior to 1994, Janet served as Director for Communication and Information Technology for the U.S. Department of Agricul-

ture's Extension Service where she also served on the Federal
Networking Council of the National Science Foundation and
was named by Federal Computer Week as one of the Outstanding Leaders in Business, Government and Academia. She has
worked in more than 30 different countries focusing on international management, communication and gender issues. She has
received numerous awards, including the Excalibur Award from
the U.S. Congress and the U.S.D.A. International Honor Award
for her six years of work with the Training for Rural Development Project in Tanzania. She holds B.S. (Broadcast Journalism),
M.S. (Nutrition) and Ph.D. (Adult and Continuing Education)
degrees from the University of Nebraska–Lincoln.

Kathy Schmidt

Kathy Schmidt is Assistant Director for Instructional Design
and Distance Education Support at the Center for Instructional
Technologies at the University of Texas at Austin. Kathy has
over fifteen years experience in designing technology-based education in higher education, K-12, the military, and the private
sector. In her position at UT, she works in all aspects of distance
education including design and development, faculty training,
learner support, and evaluation. Kathy has teaching experience
in television production, teaching methodology, and instructional design at the university and community college level, has
published in the areas of instructional design and technology-based instruction, and has served as a consultant to a variety
of educational and private sector organizations. Kathy received a
bachelor's degree in radio-television-film from the University of
Texas at Austin in 1977, a master's degree in educational communications and technology from the University of Hawaii in 1982,
and a doctoral degree in curriculum and instruction from the
University of Texas at Austin in 1992.

John Tallman

John Tallman is an attorney who recently retired from his position as senior legal counsel for the University of Wisconsin System, where he served as a legal advisor for 30 years. A graduate of
the University of Wisconsin Law School, he has worked in nu-

merous areas of law in higher education, including copyright and intellectual property. His copyright work has included advising clients on a wide range of intellectual property and copyright issues as well as presenting workshops on the basics of copyright law, especially as they relate to a college or university. He continues to consult for the University on a variety of projects related to copyright and intellectual property matters.

Index

public domain and, 203-204
registration, 191
rights established by, 197-203, 211-212
symbol, 190
works covered by, 192
works posted on the internet and, 196-197
works-made-for-hire and, 193-194
course design, 295, 299-300. *See also* Integrated technology systems design
course conversion, for the web, 314
critical thinking, 325-236, 329-331 *See also* higher-order thinkingculture,
Culture,
    academic/collegial, 95-96, 171, 263-265
    developmental, 95, 171
    entreprenuerial, 96-97, 149
    managerial, 95, 171
    negotiating, 95, 171

D

Damrosch, David, 174
Daniel, Sir John, 124
Dede, Chris, 75-77, 168
developmental culture, 95, 171
DeVry, Inc. 148-149
Dewey, John, 9-10, 45-47, 55
Digital Millenium Copyright Act of 1998 (DMCA), 199-200, 208-209, 210, 212
Dillman, Don A. *See* Dillman et al.
Dillman et al., 24
distance education, 11, 36, 50, 117, 225
    in China, 125
    in France, 126
    preference for, 78
    in Thailand, 125
    types of providers of, 122-123
    in the U.S., 126
distributed learning, 72, 75-81
    communities, 88

for elementary school, 76-77
and science, 88-89
and university finances, 81
diversity education, 32-33
Dourish, Paul, 318
Drucker, Pter, 14, 16, 166-167

E

Education Management Corporation, 145-146
"Embracing the Information Age: A Comparison of Women and Men Business Owners," 251-252
emotional intelligence, 174
entreprenuerial culture, 96-97, 149
ethical sensitivity, 221-222
ethics, defined, 221-222
evaluation, 319
extened classroom, 127-128
extended traditional university, 93, 94
    characterizations of, 97
    compared to distance education/technology-based universities, 120-121
    compared to traditional universities, 97-98
    learner characteristics and, 99-100

F

faculty
    advancement of, 267-268, 273
    copyright of courses and, 195-196
    cost cutting and, 111-112
    in the future, 266-271
    goals for students, 319
    the growth in technology-based education and, 37-38, 108-264, 265-266, 276
    technology competency and, 345
    training of, 274-275
fair use, of copyrighted matetrials, 205-207
"Falling through the Net II," 246

engaged, 48, 51, 314-315
learning, 47, 291, 292, 321
  active, 48
  assessing, 10-11, 45, 280-281, 319, 346-347
  competition and, 54
  communities, 58
  environments, 51, 52, 56
  lifelong, 344-345
  optimal conditions for, 292-293, 294
  outcomes of, 47
  problem-based, 56-58
  process, 47-48
learning styles, 49-50. *See also*;
  collaboration, and learning;
  cooperation, and learning
    collaborative, 53-54, 55-56, 60
    cooperative, 53, 54, 55-56, 60
learning theory, 292
Lewin, Kurt, 55
Los Alamos, 220
Lust, Patricia, 272

M

managerial culture, 95
Manhattan Project, 220
Mason, Robin, 133-134
McLuhan, Marshall, 8
Magellan University, 132-133
mega-universities, 121, 134
metacognition, 47
Morella, Rep. Constance, 247-248
MUVE, 77
Myers, John, 54

N

National Science Foundation, 88-89, 256
National Technological University (NTU), 128-129
National Universities Degree Consortium (NUDC), 129-130
negotiating culture, 95, 171
Negroponte Nicholas, 9
niche programming, 102-103

Noble, David, 37-38

O

Olcott, Donald John, Jr., 219, 235-236
Old Dominion, 101-102, 103-104, 106
One-Minute Manager, the, 173
online university, 118, 131-133
Open University, 101, 121, 123
  in Canada, 124-125
Oppenheimer, J. Robert, 220
organizational change, 25
  universities and, 28, 30
organizational theory, 26-27
ownership, of faculty work, 340-341.
  See also copyright

P

Paintz and Paintz, 53
Palmer, Parker, 52
Penn State University
  World Campus of, 104-105
Peters, Tom, 173
printing press, 16
  and education, 14
problem-based learning, 56-58
  environments for, 56
program aggregation, 106
program and institutional
  replicating, 101
program diversification, 101-102
program duplication, 100-101
public domain, 203-204

Q

Quest, 146-147

R

Rest, J.R., 222, 231

S

Salant, Priscilla. *See* Dillman et al.